Praise for *Observability Engineering*

Finally, a principled alternative to the guess-and-test approach to answering operational questions like "Why is the system slow?" This book marks a watershed moment for how engineers will think about interrogating system behavior.

—Lorin Hochstein, senior software engineer and O'Reilly author

This book does not shirk away from shedding light on the challenges one might face when bootstrapping a culture of observability in an organization, and provides valuable guidance on how to go about it in a sustainable manner that should stand observability practitioners in good stead for long-term success.

—Cindy Sridharan, infrastructure engineer

As your systems get more complicated and distributed, monitoring doesn't really help you work out what has gone wrong. You need to be able to solve problems you haven't seen before, and that's where observability comes in. I've learned so much about observability from these authors over the last five years, and I'm delighted that they've now written this book that covers both the technical and cultural aspects of introducing and benefiting from observability of your production systems.

—Sarah Wells, former technical director at the Financial Times
and O'Reilly author

This excellent book is the perfect companion for any engineer or manager wanting to get the most out of their observability efforts. It strikes the perfect balance between being concise and comprehensive: It lays a solid foundation by defining observability, explains how to use it to debug and keep your services reliable, guides you on how to build a strong business case for it, and finally provides the means to assess your efforts to help with future improvements.

—Mads Hartmann, SRE at Gitpod

Observability Engineering
Achieving Production Excellence

Charity Majors, Liz Fong-Jones, and George Miranda

Beijing · Boston · Farnham · Sebastopol · Tokyo

Observability Engineering

by Charity Majors, Liz Fong-Jones, and George Miranda

Published by O'Reilly Media, Inc., 1005 Gravenstein Highway North, Sebastopol, CA 95472.

O'Reilly books may be purchased for educational, business, or sales promotional use. Online editions are also available for most titles (*http://oreilly.com*). For more information, contact our corporate/institutional sales department: 800-998-9938 or *corporate@oreilly.com*.

Acquisitions Editor: John Devins	**Indexer:** nSight, Inc.
Development Editor: Virginia Wilson	**Interior Designer:** David Futato
Production Editor: Kate Galloway	**Cover Designer:** Karen Montgomery
Copyeditor: Sharon Wilkey	**Illustrator:** Kate Dullea
Proofreader: Piper Editorial Consulting, LLC	

May 2022:   First Edition

Revision History for the First Edition
2022-05-06:   First Release

See *http://oreilly.com/catalog/errata.csp?isbn=9781492076445* for release details.

978-1-492-07644-5

[LSI]

Table of Contents

Part I. The Path to Observability

Part V.   Spreading Observability Culture

Foreword

Over the past couple of years, the term "observability" has moved from the niche fringes of the systems engineering community to the vernacular of the software engineering community. As this term gained prominence, it also suffered the (alas, inevitable) fate of being used interchangeably with another term with which it shares a certain adjacency: "monitoring."

What then followed was every bit as inevitable as it was unfortunate: monitoring tools and vendors started co-opting and using the same language and vocabulary used by those trying to differentiate the philosophical, technical, and sociotechnical underpinnings of observability from that of monitoring. This muddying of the waters wasn't particularly helpful, to say the least. It risked conflating "observability" and "monitoring" into a homogenous construct, thereby making it all the more difficult to have meaningful, nuanced conversations about the differences.

To treat the difference between monitoring and observability as a purely semantic one is a folly. Observability isn't purely a technical concept that can be achieved by buying an "observability tool" (no matter what any vendor might say) or adopting the open standard du jour. To the contrary, observability is more a *sociotechnical* concept. Successfully implementing observability depends just as much, if not more, on having the appropriate cultural scaffolding to support the way software is developed, deployed, debugged, and maintained, as it does on having the right tool at one's disposal.

In most (perhaps even all) scenarios, teams need to leverage both monitoring and observability to successfully build and operate their services. But any such successful implementation requires that practitioners first understand the philosophical differences between the two.

What separates monitoring from observability is the state space of system behavior, and moreover, how one might wish to explore the state space and at precisely what level of detail. By "state space," I'm referring to all the possible emergent behaviors a system might exhibit during various phases: starting from when the system is being designed, to when the system is being developed, to when the system is being tested, to when the system is being deployed, to when the system is being exposed to users, to when the system is being debugged over the course of its lifetime. The more complex the system, the ever expanding and protean the state space.

Observability allows for this state space to be painstakingly mapped out and explored in granular detail with a fine-tooth comb. Such meticulous exploration is often required to better understand unpredictable, long-tail, or multimodal distributions in system behavior. Monitoring, in contrast, provides an *approximation* of overall system health in broad brushstrokes.

It thus follows that everything from the data that's being collected to this end, to how this data is being stored, to how this data can be explored to better understand system behavior *varies* vis-à-vis the purposes of monitoring and observability.

Over the past couple of decades, the ethos of monitoring has influenced the development of myriad tools, systems, processes, and practices, many of which have become the de facto industry standard. Because these tools, systems, processes, and practices were designed for the explicit purpose of monitoring, they do a stellar job to this end. However, they cannot—and should not—be rebranded or marketed to unsuspecting customers as "observability" tools or processes. Doing so would provide little to no discernible benefit, in addition to running the risk of being an enormous time, effort, and money sink for the customer.

Furthermore, tools are only one part of the problem. Building or adopting observability tooling and practices that have proven to be successful at other companies won't necessarily solve all the problems faced by one's organization, inasmuch as a finished product doesn't tell the story behind how the tooling and concomitant processes evolved, what overarching problems it aimed to solve, what implicit assumptions were baked into the product, and more.

Building or buying the right observability tool won't be a panacea without first instituting a conducive cultural framework within the company that sets teams up for success. A mindset and culture rooted in the shibboleths of monitoring—dashboards, alerts, static thresholds—isn't helpful to unlock the full potential of observability. An observability tool might have access to a very large volume of very granular data, but successfully making sense of the mountain of data—which is the ultimate arbiter of the overall viability and utility of the tool, and arguably that of observability itself!—requires a hypothesis-driven, iterative debugging mindset.

Simply having access to state-of-the-art tools doesn't automatically cultivate this mindset in practitioners. Nor does waxing eloquent about nebulous philosophical distinctions between monitoring and observability without distilling these ideas into cross-cutting practical solutions. For instance, there are chapters in this book that take a dim view of holding up logs, metrics, and traces as the "three pillars of observability." While the criticisms aren't without merit, the truth is that logs, metrics, and traces have long been the only concrete examples of telemetry people running real systems in the real world have had at their disposal to debug their systems, and it was thus inevitable that the narrative of the "three pillars" cropped up around them.

What resonates best with practitioners building systems in the real world isn't abstract, airy-fairy ideas but an actionable blueprint that addresses and proposes solutions to pressing technical and cultural problems they are facing. This book manages to bridge the chasm that yawns between the philosophical tenets of observability and its praxis thereof, by providing a concrete (if opinionated) blueprint of what putting these ideas into practice might look like.

Instead of focusing on protocols or standards or even low-level representations of various telemetry signals, the book envisages the three pillars of observability as the triad of structured events (or traces without a context field, as I like to call them), iterative verification of hypothesis (or hypothesis-driven debugging, as I like to call it), and the "core analysis loop." This holistic reframing of the building blocks of observability from the first principles helps underscore that telemetry signals alone (or tools built to harness these signals) don't make system behavior maximally observable. The book does not shirk away from shedding light on the challenges one might face when bootstrapping a culture of observability in an organization, and provides valuable guidance on how to go about it in a sustainable manner that should stand observability practitioners in good stead for long-term success.

— *Cindy Sridharan*
Infrastructure Engineer
San Francisco
April 26, 2022

Preface

Thank you for picking up our book on observability engineering for modern software systems. Our goal is to help you develop a practice of observability within your engineering organization. This book is based on our experience as practitioners of observability, and as makers of observability tooling for users who want to improve their own observability practices.

As outspoken advocates for driving observability practices in software engineering, our hope is that this book can set a clear record of what observability means in the context of modern software systems. The term "observability" has seen quite a bit of recent uptake in the software development ecosystem. This book aims to help you separate facts from hype by providing a deep analysis of the following:

- What observability means in the context of software delivery and operations
- How to build the fundamental components that help you achieve observability
- The impact observability has on team dynamics
- Considerations for observability at scale
- Practical ways to build a culture of observability in your organization

Who This Book Is For

Observability predominantly focuses on achieving a better understanding of the way software operates in the real world. Therefore, this book is most useful for software engineers responsible for developing production applications. However, anyone who supports the operation of software in production will also greatly benefit from the content in this book.

Additionally, managers of software delivery and operations teams who are interested in understanding how the practice of observability can benefit their organization will find value in this book, particularly in the chapters that focus on team dynamics, culture, and scale.

Anyone who helps teams deliver and operate production software (for example, product managers, support engineers, and stakeholders) and is curious about this new thing called "observability" and why people are talking about it should also find this book useful.

Why We Wrote This Book

Observability has become a popular topic that has quickly garnered a lot of interest and attention. With its rise in popularity, "observability" has been unfortunately mischaracterized as a synonym for "monitoring" or "system telemetry." Observability is a characteristic of software systems. Further, it's a characteristic that can be effectively utilized only in production software systems when teams adopt new practices that support its ongoing development. Thus, introducing observability into your systems is both a technical challenge and a cultural challenge.

We are particularly passionate and outspoken about the topic of observability. We are so passionate about it that we started a company whose sole purpose is to bring the power of observability to all teams that manage production software. We spearheaded a new category of observability tools, and other vendors have followed suit.

While we all work for Honeycomb (*https://honeycomb.io*), our intention here is not to sell you on our tools. We have written this book to explain how and why we adapted the original concept of observability to manage modern software systems. You can achieve observability with different tools and in different ways. However, we believe that our dedication to advancing the practice of observability in the software industry makes us uniquely qualified to write a guide that describes—in great detail—the common challenges and effective solutions. You can apply the concepts in this book, regardless of your tool choices, to practice building production software systems with observability.

This book aims to give you a look at the various considerations, capabilities, and challenges associated with teams that practice using observability to manage their production software systems. At times, we may provide a look at what Honeycomb does as an example of how a common challenge has been addressed. These are not intended as endorsements of Honeycomb but rather as practical illustrations of abstract concepts. It is our goal to show you how to apply these same principles in other environments, regardless of the tools you use.

What You Will Learn

You will learn what observability is, how to identify an observable system, and why observability is best suited for managing modern software systems. You'll learn how observability differs from monitoring, as well as why and when a different approach is necessary. We will also cover why industry trends have helped popularize the need for observability and how that fits into emerging spaces, like the cloud native ecosystem.

Next, we'll cover the fundamentals of observability. We'll examine why structured events are the building blocks of observable systems and how to stitch those events together into traces. Events are generated by telemetry that is built into your software, and you will learn about open source initiatives, like OpenTelemetry, that help jumpstart the instrumentation process. You will learn about the data-based investigative process used to locate the source of issues in observable systems, and how it differs substantially from the intuition-based investigative process used in traditional monitoring. You will also learn how observability and monitoring can coexist.

After an introduction to these fundamental technical concepts, you will learn about the social and cultural elements that often accompany the adoption of observability. Managing software in production is a team sport, and you will learn how observability can be used to help better shape team dynamics. You will learn about how observability fits into business processes, affects the software supply chain, and reveals hidden risks. You will also learn how to put both these technical and social concepts into practice when we examine how to use service-level objectives for more effective alerting and dive into the technical details behind why they make alerts both actionable and debuggable when using observability data.

Then, you'll learn about inherent challenges when implementing observability solutions at scale. We'll start with the considerations you should take into account when deciding whether to buy or build an observability solution. An essential property of observability solutions is that they must provide fast answers during iterative investigations. Therefore, we will show you how to address the inherent challenges of efficient data storage and retrieval when managing extremely large data sets. You will also learn when to introduce solutions like event sampling and how to navigate its trade-offs to find the right approach to fit your needs. You will also learn how to manage extremely large quantities of data with telemetry pipelines.

Finally, we look at organizational approaches to adopting a culture of observability. Beyond introducing observability to your team, you will learn practical ways to scale observability practices across an entire organization. You will learn how to identify and work with key stakeholders, use technical approaches to win allies, and make a business case for adopting observability practices.

We started writing this book nearly three years ago. Part of the reason it has taken so long to produce is that the observability landscape has been changing rapidly and practices are advancing. We believe this book is the most up-to-date and comprehensive look at the state of the art in observability practices as of the time of its publication. We hope you find the journey as fascinating as we have.

Conventions Used in This Book

The following typographical conventions are used in this book:

Italic
> Indicates new terms, URLs, email addresses, filenames, and file extensions.

`Constant width`
> Used for program listings, as well as within paragraphs to refer to program elements such as variable or function names, databases, data types, environment variables, statements, and keywords.

 This element signifies a general note.

Using Code Examples

Supplemental material (code examples, exercises, etc.) is available for download at *https://oreil.ly/7IcWz*.

If you have a technical question or a problem using the code examples, please send an email to *bookquestions@oreilly.com*.

This book is here to help you get your job done. In general, if example code is offered with this book, you may use it in your programs and documentation. You do not need to contact us for permission unless you're reproducing a significant portion of the code. For example, writing a program that uses several chunks of code from this book does not require permission. Selling or distributing examples from O'Reilly books does require permission. Answering a question by citing this book and quoting example code does not require permission. Incorporating a significant amount of example code from this book into your product's documentation does require permission.

We appreciate, but generally do not require, attribution. An attribution usually includes the title, author, publisher, and ISBN. For example: "*Observability Engineering* by Charity Majors, Liz Fong-Jones, and George Miranda (O'Reilly). Copyright 2022 Hound Technology Inc., 978-1-492-07644-5."

If you feel your use of code examples falls outside fair use or the permission given above, feel free to contact us at *permissions@oreilly.com*.

O'Reilly Online Learning

 For more than 40 years, *O'Reilly Media* has provided technology and business training, knowledge, and insight to help companies succeed.

Our unique network of experts and innovators share their knowledge and expertise through books, articles, and our online learning platform. O'Reilly's online learning platform gives you on-demand access to live training courses, in-depth learning paths, interactive coding environments, and a vast collection of text and video from O'Reilly and 200+ other publishers. For more information, visit *https://oreilly.com*.

How to Contact Us

Please address comments and questions concerning this book to the publisher:

O'Reilly Media, Inc.
1005 Gravenstein Highway North
Sebastopol, CA 95472
800-998-9938 (in the United States or Canada)
707-829-0515 (international or local)
707-829-0104 (fax)

We have a web page for this book, where we list errata, examples, and any additional information. You can access this page at *https://oreil.ly/observability-engineering*.

Email *bookquestions@oreilly.com* to comment or ask technical questions about this book.

For news and information about our books and courses, visit *https://oreilly.com*.

Find us on LinkedIn: *https://linkedin.com/company/oreilly-media*

Follow us on Twitter: *https://twitter.com/oreillymedia*

Watch us on YouTube: *https://youtube.com/oreillymedia*

Acknowledgments

This book would not have been possible without the support of executive sponsors at Honeycomb: many thanks to Christine Yen, Deirdre Mahon, and Jo Ann Sanders. Nor would this book have been possible without the domestic sponsors who put up with many odd hours, lost weekends, sleepless weeknights, and cranky partners: many thanks to Rebekah Howard, Elly Fong-Jones, and Dino Miranda. Without all of them, we would probably still be trying to find the time to fully develop and tie together the many ideas expressed in this book.

We'd especially like to thank additional contributors who have made the content in this book much stronger by sharing their varied perspectives and expertise. Chapter 16, "Efficient Data Storage", was made possible by Ian Wilkes (author of Honeycomb's Retriever engine, the basis of the case study), and Joan Smith (reviewing for technical accuracy of references to external literature). Chapter 14, "Observability and the Software Supply Chain", was authored by Frank Chen, and Chapter 18, "Telemetry Management with Pipelines", was authored by Suman Karumuri, and Ryan Katkov—all of whom we thank for sharing their knowledge and the lessons they've learned from managing incredibly large-scale applications with observability at Slack. Many thanks to Rachel (pie) Perkins for contributions to several early chapters in this book. And thanks to the many bees at Honeycomb who, over the years, have helped us explore what's achievable with observability.

Finally, many thanks to our many external reviewers: Sarah Wells, Abby Bangser, Mads Hartmann, Jess Males, Robert Quinlivan, John Feminella, Cindy Sridharan, Ben Sigelman, and Daniel Spoonhower. We've revised our takes, incorporated broader viewpoints, and revisited concepts throughout the authoring process to ensure that we're reflecting an inclusive state of the art in the world of observability. Although we (the authors of this book) all work for Honeycomb, our goal has always been to write an objective and inclusive book detailing how observability works in practice, regardless of specific tool choices. We thank our reviewers for keeping us honest and helping us develop a stronger and all-encompassing narrative.

PART I

The Path to Observability

This section defines concepts that are referenced throughout the rest of this book. You will learn what observability is, how to identify an observable system, and why observability-based debugging techniques are better suited for managing modern software systems than monitoring-based debugging techniques.

Chapter 1 examines the roots of the term "observability," shows how that concept has been adapted for use in software systems, and provides concrete questions you can ask yourself to determine if you have an observable system.

Chapter 2 looks at the practices engineers use to triage and locate sources of issues using traditional monitoring methods. Those methods are then contrasted with methods used in observability-based systems. This chapter describes these methods at a high level, but the technical and workflow implementations will become more concrete in Part II.

Chapter 3 is a case study written by coauthor Charity Majors and told from her perspective. This chapter brings concepts from the first two chapters into a practical case study illustrating when and why the shift toward observability becomes absolutely necessary.

Chapter 4 illustrates how and why industry trends have helped popularize the need for observability and how that fits into emerging spaces, like the cloud native ecosystem.

CHAPTER 1

What Is Observability?

In the software development industry, the subject of observability has garnered a lot of interest and is frequently found in lists of hot new topics. But, as things seem to inevitably go when a hot new topic sees a surging level of interest in adoption, complex ideas become all too ripe for misunderstanding without a deeper look at the many nuances encapsulated by a simple topical label. This chapter looks at the mathematical origins of the term "observability" and examines how software development practitioners adapted it to describe characteristics of production software systems.

We also look at why the adaptation of observability for use in production software systems is necessary. Traditional practices for debugging the internal state of software applications were designed for legacy systems that were much simpler than those we typically manage today. As systems architecture, infrastructure platforms, and user expectations have continued to evolve, the tools we use to reason about those components have not. By and large, the debugging practices developed decades ago with nascent monitoring tools are still the same as those used by many engineering teams today—even though the systems they manage are infinitely more complex. Observability tools were born out of sheer necessity, when traditional tools and debugging methods simply were not up to the task of quickly finding deeply hidden and elusive problems.

This chapter will help you understand what "observability" means, how to determine if a software system is observable, why observability is necessary, and how observability is used to find problems in ways that are not possible with other approaches.

The Mathematical Definition of Observability

The term "observability" was coined by engineer Rudolf E. Kálmán in 1960. It has since grown to mean many different things in different communities. Let's explore the landscape before turning to our own definition for modern software systems.

In his 1960 paper, Kálmán introduced a characterization he called *observability* to describe mathematical control systems.[1] In control theory (*https://w.wiki/4wHw*), observability is defined as a measure of how well internal states of a system (*https://w.wiki/55Pc*) can be inferred from knowledge of its external outputs.

This definition of observability would have you study observability and controllability as mathematical duals, along with sensors, linear algebra equations, and formal methods. This traditional definition of observability is the realm of mechanical engineers and those who manage physical systems with a specific end state in mind.

If you are looking for a mathematical and process engineering oriented textbook, you've come to the wrong place. Those books definitely exist, and any mechanical engineer or control systems engineer will inform you (usually passionately and at great length) that observability has a formal meaning in traditional systems engineering terminology. However, when that same concept is adapted for use with squishier virtual software systems, it opens up a radically different way of interacting with and understanding the code you write.

Applying Observability to Software Systems

Kálmán's definition of observability can be applied to modern software systems. When adapting the concept of observability to software, we must also layer additional considerations that are specific to the software engineering domain. For a software application to have observability, you must be able to do the following:

- Understand the inner workings of your application
- Understand any system state your application may have gotten itself into, even new ones you have never seen before and couldn't have predicted
- Understand the inner workings and system state solely by observing and interrogating with external tools
- Understand the internal state *without* shipping any new custom code to handle it (because that implies you needed prior knowledge to explain it)

---

1 Rudolf E. Kálmán, "On the General Theory of Control Systems" (*https://oreil.ly/u7BM4*), *IFAC Proceedings Volumes* 1, no. 1 (August 1960): 491–502.

A good litmus test for determining whether those conditions are true is to ask yourself the following questions:

- Can you continually answer open-ended questions about the inner workings of your applications to explain any anomalies, without hitting investigative dead ends (i.e., the issue might be in a certain group of things, but you can't break it down any further to confirm)?
- Can you understand what any particular user of your software may be experiencing at any given time?
- Can you quickly see any cross-section of system performance you care about, from top-level aggregate views, down to the single and exact user requests that may be contributing to any slowness (and anywhere in between)?
- Can you compare any arbitrary groups of user requests in ways that let you correctly identify which attributes are commonly shared by all users who are experiencing unexpected behavior in your application?
- Once you do find suspicious attributes within one individual user request, can you search across all user requests to identify similar behavioral patterns to confirm or rule out your suspicions?
- Can you identify which system user is generating the most load (and therefore slowing application performance the most), as well as the 2nd, 3rd, or 100th most load-generating users?
- Can you identify which of those most-load-generating users only recently started impacting performance?
- If the 142nd slowest user complained about performance speed, can you isolate their requests to understand why exactly things are slow for that specific user?
- If users complain about timeouts happening, but your graphs show that the 99th, 99.9th, even 99.99th percentile requests are fast, can you find the hidden timeouts?
- Can you answer questions like the preceding ones without first needing to predict that you might need to ask them someday (and therefore set up specific monitors in advance to aggregate the necessary data)?
- Can you answer questions like these about your applications even if you have never seen or debugged this particular issue before?
- Can you get answers to questions like the preceding ones quickly, so that you can iteratively ask a new question, and another, and another, until you get to the correct source of issues, without losing your train of thought (which typically means getting answers within seconds instead of minutes)?
- Can you answer questions like the preceding ones even if that particular issue has never happened before?

- Do the results of your debugging investigations often surprise you by revealing new, perplexing, and bizarre findings, or do you generally find only the issues you suspected that you might find?
- Can you quickly (within minutes) isolate any fault in your system, no matter how complex, deeply buried, or hidden within your stack?

Meeting all of the preceding criteria is a high bar for many software engineering organizations to clear. If you can clear that bar, you, no doubt, understand why observability has become such a popular topic for software engineering teams.

Put simply, our definition of "observability" for software systems is a measure of how well you can understand and explain any state your system can get into, no matter how novel or bizarre. You must be able to comparatively debug that bizarre or novel state across all dimensions of system state data, and combinations of dimensions, in an ad hoc iterative investigation, without being required to define or predict those debugging needs in advance. If you can understand any bizarre or novel state *without needing to ship new code*, you have observability.

We believe that adapting the traditional concept of observability for software systems in this way is a unique approach with additional nuances worth exploring. For modern software systems, observability is not about the data types or inputs, nor is it about mathematical equations. It is about how people interact with and try to understand their complex systems. Therefore, observability requires recognizing the interaction between both people and technology to understand how those complex systems work together.

If you accept that definition, many additional questions emerge that demand answers:

- How does one gather that data and assemble it for inspection?
- What are the technical requirements for processing that data?
- What team capabilities are necessary to benefit from that data?

We will get to these questions and more throughout the course of this book. For now, let's put some additional context behind observability as it applies to software.

The application of observability to software systems has much in common with its control theory roots. However, it is far less mathematical and much more practical. In part, that's because software engineering is a much younger and more rapidly evolving discipline than its more mature mechanical engineering predecessor. Production software systems are much less subject to formal proofs. That lack of rigor is, in part, a betrayal from the scars we, as an industry, have earned through operating the software code we write in production.

As engineers attempting to understand how to bridge the gap between theoretical practices encoded in clinical tests and the impacts of what happens when our code runs at scale, we did not go looking for a new term, definition, or functionality to describe how we got there. It was the circumstances of managing our systems and teams that led us to evolving our practices away from concepts, like monitoring, that simply no longer worked. As an industry, we need to move beyond the current gaps in tooling and terminology to get past the pain and suffering inflicted upon us by outages and a lack of more proactive solutions.

Observability is the solution to that gap. Our complex production software systems are a mess for a variety of both technical and social reasons. So it will take both social and technical solutions to dig us out of this hole. Observability alone is not the entire solution to all of our software engineering problems. But it does help you clearly see what's happening in all the obscure corners of your software, where you are otherwise typically stumbling around in the dark and trying to understand things.

Imagine you wake up one Saturday morning with grand plans to make brunch for the entire extended family. You have multiple dishes in mind, including a complex recipe for cheese souffle, a list of everyone's known allergens and food sensitivities, and a tight timeline—Grandma has to make it to the airport by noon. This is a nontrivial challenge on its own. Now imagine you can't find your glasses (and that you're as near-sighted as we are). When it comes to solving practical and time-sensitive problems in software engineering, observability is a darn good place to start.

Mischaracterizations About Observability for Software

Before proceeding, we need to address another definition of "observability," the definition popularly being promoted by software-as-a-service (SaaS) developer tool vendors. These vendors insist that "observability" has no special meaning whatsoever—that it is simply another synonym for "telemetry," indistinguishable from "monitoring." Proponents of this definition relegate observability to being another generic term for understanding how software operates. You will hear this contingent explain away observability as "three pillars" of things they can sell you that they already do today: metrics, logs, and traces.[2]

It is hard to decide which is worse about this definition: its redundancy (why exactly do we need another synonym for "telemetry"?) or its epistemic confusion (why assemble a list of one data type, one anti-data type slash mess of strings, and one… way of visualizing things in order by time?). Regardless, the logical flaw of this definition becomes clear when you realize its proponents have a vested interest in

---

2 Sometimes these claims include time spans to signify "discrete occurrences of change" as a fourth pillar of a generic synonym for "telemetry."

selling you the tools and mindsets built around the siloed collection and storage of data with their existing suite of metrics, logging, and tracing tools. The proponents of this definition let their business models constrain how they think about future possibilities.

In fairness, we—the authors of this book—are also vendors in the observability space. However, this book is not created to sell you on our tools. We have written this book to explain how and why we adapted the original concept of observability to managing modern software systems. You can apply the concepts in this book, regardless of your tool choices, to practice building production software systems with observability. Observability is not achieved by gluing together disparate tools with marketing. You don't have to adopt one specific tool to get observability in your software systems. *Rather, we believe that observability requires evolving the way we think about gathering the data needed to debug effectively.* We believe that, as an industry, it is time to evolve the practices we use to manage modern software systems.

Why Observability Matters Now

Now that we're on the same page about what observability does and doesn't mean in the context of modern software systems, let's talk about why this shift in approach matters now. In short, the traditional approach of using metrics and monitoring of software to understand what it's doing falls drastically short. This approach is fundamentally reactive. It may have served the industry well in the past, but modern systems demand a better methodology.

For the past two or three decades, the space between hardware and its human operators has been regulated by a set of tools and conventions most call "monitoring." Practitioners have, by and large, inherited this set of tools and conventions and accepted it as the best approach for understanding that squishy virtual space between the physical and their code. And they have accepted this approach despite the knowledge that, in many cases, its inherent limitations have taken them hostage late into many sleepless nights of troubleshooting. Yet, they still grant it feelings of trust, and maybe even affection, because that captor is the best they have.

With monitoring, software developers can't fully see their systems. They squint at the systems. They try, in vain, to size them up and to predict all the myriad ways they could possibly fail. Then they watch—they monitor—for those known failure modes. They set performance thresholds and arbitrarily pronounce them "good" or "bad." They deploy a small robot army to check and recheck those thresholds on their behalf. They collect their findings into dashboards. They then organize themselves around those robots into teams, rotations, and escalations. When those robots tell them performance is bad, they alert themselves. Then, over time, they tend to those arbitrary thresholds like gardeners: pruning, tweaking, and fussing over the noisy signals they grow.

Is This Really the Best Way?

For decades, that's how developers and operators have done it. Monitoring has been the de facto approach for so long that they tend to think of it as *the only way* of understanding their systems, instead of just *one way*. Monitoring is such a default practice that it has become mostly invisible. As an industry, we generally don't question whether *we should* do it, but *how*.

The practice of monitoring is grounded in many unspoken assumptions about systems (which we'll detail next). But as systems continue to evolve—as they become more abstract and more complex, and as their underlying components begin to matter less and less—those assumptions become less true. As developers and operators continue to adopt modern approaches to deploying software systems (SaaS dependencies, container orchestration platforms, distributed systems, etc.), the cracks in those assumptions become more evident.

More people, therefore, are finding themselves slamming into the wall of inherent limitations and realizing that monitoring approaches simply do not work for the new modern world. Traditional monitoring practices are catastrophically ineffective for understanding systems. The assumptions of metrics and monitoring are now falling short. To understand why they fail, it helps to examine their history and intended context.

Why Are Metrics and Monitoring Not Enough?

In 1988, by way of the Simple Network Management Protocol (SNMPv1 as defined in RFC 1157), the foundational substrate of monitoring was born: the metric. A *metric* is a single number, with tags optionally appended for grouping and searching those numbers. Metrics are, by their very nature, disposable and cheap. They have a predictable storage footprint. They're easy to aggregate along regular time-series buckets. And, thus, the metric became the base unit for a generation or two of telemetry—the data we gather from remote endpoints for automatic transmission to monitoring systems.

Many sophisticated apparatuses have been built atop the metric: time-series databases (TSDBs), statistical analyses, graphing libraries, fancy dashboards, on-call rotations, ops teams, escalation policies, and a plethora of ways to digest and respond to what that small army of robots is telling you.

But an upper bound exists to the complexity of the systems you can understand with metrics and monitoring tools. And once you cross that boundary, the change is abrupt. What worked well enough last month simply does not work anymore. You begin falling back to low-level commands like `strace`, `tcpdump`, and hundreds of `print` statements to answer questions about how your system is behaving on a daily basis.

It's hard to calculate exactly when that tipping point will be reached. Eventually, the sheer number of possible states the system could get itself into will outstrip your team's ability to pattern-match based on prior outages. Too many brand-new, novel states are needing to be understood constantly. Your team can no longer guess which dashboards should be created to display the innumerable failure modes.

Monitoring and metrics-based tools were built with certain assumptions about your architecture and organization, assumptions that served in practice as a cap on complexity. These assumptions are usually invisible until you exceed them, at which point they cease to be hidden and become the bane of your ability to understand what's happening. Some of these assumptions might be as follows:

- Your application is a monolith.
- There is one stateful data store ("the database"), which you run.
- Many low-level system metrics are available (e.g., resident memory, CPU load average).
- The application runs on containers, virtual machines (VMs), or bare metal, which you control.
- System metrics and instrumentation metrics are the primary source of information for debugging code.
- You have a fairly static and long-running set of nodes, containers, or hosts to monitor.
- Engineers examine systems for problems only after problems occur.
- Dashboards and telemetry exist to serve the needs of operations engineers.
- Monitoring examines "black-box" applications in much the same way as local applications.
- The focus of monitoring is uptime and failure prevention.
- Examination of correlation occurs across a limited (or small) number of dimensions.

When compared to the reality of modern systems, it becomes clear that traditional monitoring approaches fall short in several ways. The reality of modern systems is as follows:

- Your application has many services.
- There is polyglot persistence (i.e., many databases and storage systems).
- Infrastructure is extremely dynamic, with capacity flicking in and out of existence elastically.

- Many far-flung and loosely coupled services are managed, many of which are not directly under your control.

- Engineers actively check to see how changes to production code behave, in order to catch tiny issues early, before they create user impact.

- Automatic instrumentation is insufficient for understanding what is happening in complex systems.

- Software engineers own their own code in production and are incentivized to proactively instrument their code and inspect the performance of new changes as they're deployed.

- The focus of reliability is on how to tolerate constant and continuous degradation, while building resiliency to user-impacting failures by utilizing constructs like error budget, quality of service, and user experience.

- Examination of correlation occurs across a virtually unlimited number of dimensions.

The last point is important, because it describes the breakdown that occurs between the limits of correlated knowledge that one human can be reasonably expected to think about and the reality of modern system architectures. So many possible dimensions are involved in discovering the underlying correlations behind performance issues that no human brain, and in fact no schema, can possibly contain them.

With observability, comparing high-dimensionality and high-cardinality data becomes a critical component of being able to discover otherwise hidden issues buried in complex system architectures.

Debugging with Metrics Versus Observability

Beyond that tipping point of system complexity, it's no longer possible to fit a model of the system into your mental cache. By the time you try to reason your way through its various components, your mental model is already likely to be out-of-date.

As an engineer, you are probably used to debugging via intuition. To get to the source of a problem, you likely feel your way along a hunch or use a fleeting reminder of an outage long past to guide your investigation. However, the skills that served you well in the past are no longer applicable in this world. The intuitive approach works only as long as most of the problems you encounter are variations of the same few predictable themes you've encountered in the past.[3]

---

3 For a more in-depth analysis, see Pete Hodgson's blog post "Why Intuitive Troubleshooting Has Stopped Working for You" (*https://oreil.ly/JXx0c*).

Similarly, the metrics-based approach of monitoring relies on having encountered known failure modes in the past. Monitoring helps detect when systems are over or under predictable thresholds that someone has previously deemed an anomaly. But what happens when you *don't know that type of anomaly is even possible*?

Historically, the majority of problems that software engineers encounter have been variants of somewhat predictable failure modes. Perhaps it wasn't known that your software could fail in quite the manner that it did, but if you reasoned about the situation and its components, discovering a novel bug or failure mode didn't require a logical leap. Most software developers rarely encounter truly unpredictable leaps of logic because they haven't typically had to deal with the type of complexity that makes those leaps commonplace (until now, most of the complexity for developers has been bundled up inside the monolithic app).

> *Every application has an inherent amount of irreducible complexity. The only question is: who will have to deal with it—the user, the application developer, or the platform developer?*
> —Larry Tesler

Modern distributed systems architectures notoriously fail in novel ways that no one is able to predict and that no one has experienced before. This condition happens often enough that an entire set of assertions has been coined about the false assumptions (*https://w.wiki/56wa*) that programmers new to distributed computing often make. Modern distributed systems are also made accessible to application developers as *abstracted infrastructure platforms*. As users of those platforms, application developers are now left to deal with an inherent amount of irreducible complexity that has landed squarely on their plates.

The previously submerged complexity of application code subroutines that interacted with one another inside the hidden random access memory internals of one physical machine have now surfaced as service requests between hosts. That newly exposed complexity then hops across multiple services, traversing an unpredictable network many times over the course of a single function. When modern architectures started to favor decomposing monoliths into microservices, software engineers lost the ability to step through their code with traditional debuggers. Meanwhile, their tools have yet to come to grips with that seismic shift.

In short: we blew up the monolith. Now every request has to hop the network multiple times, and every software developer needs to be better versed in systems and operations just to get their daily work done.

Examples of this seismic shift can be seen with the trend toward containerization, the rise of container orchestration platforms, the shift to microservices, the common use of polyglot persistence, the introduction of the service mesh, the popularity of ephemeral autoscaling instances, serverless computing, lambda functions, and any other myriad SaaS applications in a software developer's typical tool set. Stringing these various tools together into a modern system architecture means that a request may perform 20 to 30 hops after it reaches the edge of things you control (and likely multiply that by a factor of two if the request includes database queries).

In modern cloud native systems, the hardest thing about debugging is no longer understanding how the code runs but *finding where in your system* the code with the problem even lives. Good luck looking at a dashboard or a service map to see which node or service is slow, because distributed requests in these systems often loop back on themselves. Finding performance bottlenecks in these systems is incredibly challenging. When something gets slow, *everything gets slow*. Even more challenging, because cloud native systems typically operate as platforms, the code may live in a part of the system that this team doesn't even control.

In a modern world, debugging with metrics requires you to connect dozens of disconnected metrics that were recorded over the course of executing any one particular request, across any number of services or machines, to infer what might have occurred over the various hops needed for its fulfillment. The helpfulness of those dozens of clues depends entirely upon whether someone was able to predict, in advance, if that measurement was over or under the threshold that meant this action contributed to creating a previously unknown anomalous failure mode that had never been previously encountered.

By contrast, debugging with observability starts with a very different substrate: a deep context of what was happening when this action occurred. Debugging with observability is about preserving as much of the context around any given request as possible, so that you can reconstruct the environment and circumstances that triggered the bug that led to a novel failure mode. Monitoring is for the known-unknowns, but observability is for the unknown-unknowns.

The Role of Cardinality

In the context of databases, *cardinality* refers to the uniqueness of data values contained in a set. *Low cardinality* means that a column has a lot of duplicate values in its set. *High cardinality* means that the column contains a large percentage of completely unique values. A column containing a single value will always have the lowest possible cardinality. A column containing unique IDs will always have the highest possible cardinality.

For example, in a collection of a hundred million user records, you can assume that any universally unique identifier (UUID) will have the highest possible cardinality. Another example of high cardinality might be a public-key signature. First Name and Last Name would have high cardinality, though lower than UUIDs since some names repeat. A field like Gender would have low-cardinality if the schema were written 50 years ago, but given more recent understanding of gender, perhaps no longer. A field like Species would have the lowest possible cardinality—presuming all of your users are humans.

Cardinality matters for observability, because *high-cardinality information is almost always the most useful* in identifying data for debugging or understanding a system. Consider the usefulness of sorting by fields such as user IDs, shopping cart IDs, request IDs, or any other myriad IDs like instances, container, hostname, build number, spans, and so forth. Being able to query against unique IDs is the best way to pinpoint individual needles in any given haystack. You can always downsample a high-cardinality value into something with lower cardinality (for example, bucketing last names by prefix), but you can never do the reverse.

Unfortunately, metrics-based tooling systems can deal with only low-cardinality dimensions at any reasonable scale. Even if you have only merely hundreds of hosts to compare, with metrics-based systems, you can't use the hostname as an identifying tag without hitting the limits of your cardinality key-space.

These inherent limitations place unintended restrictions on the ways that data can be interrogated. When debugging with metrics, for every question you may want to ask of your data, you have to decide—*in advance*, before a bug occurs—what you need to inquire about so that its value can be recorded when that metric is written.

This has two big implications. First, if during the course of investigation, you decide that an additional question must be asked to discover the source of a potential problem, that cannot be done after the fact. You must first go set up the metrics that might answer that question and wait for the problem to happen again. Second, because answering that additional question requires another set of metrics, most metrics-based tooling vendors will charge you for recording that data. Your cost increases linearly with every new way you decide to interrogate your data to find hidden issues you could not have possibly predicted in advance.

The Role of Dimensionality

While *cardinality* refers to the uniqueness of the values within your data, *dimensionality* refers to the number of keys within that data. In observable systems, telemetry data is generated as an arbitrarily wide structured event (see Chapter 8). These events are described as "wide" because they can and should contain hundreds or even thousands of key-value pairs (or dimensions). The wider the event, the richer the context captured when the event occurred, and thus the more you can discover about what happened when debugging it later.

Imagine that you have an event schema that defines six high-cardinality dimensions per event: `time`, `app`, `host`, `user`, `endpoint`, and `status`. With those six dimensions, you can create queries that analyze any combination of dimensions to surface relevant patterns that may be contributing to anomalies. For example, you could retrieve, "all of the 502 errors that occurred in the last half hour for host foo," or, "all of the 403 errors generated by requests to the /export endpoint made by user bar," or, "all of the timeouts that occurred with requests sent to the /payments endpoint by application baz and which host they came from."

With just six basic dimensions, you can examine a useful set of conditions to determine what might be happening in your application system. Now imagine that instead of just six dimensions, you could examine hundreds or thousands of dimensions that contain any detail, value, counter, or string that seems like it might be helpful to your debugging purposes at some point in the future. For example, you could include dimensions that look something like this:

```
app.api_key
app.batch
app.batch_num_data_sets
app.batch_total_data_points
app.dataset.id
app.dataset.name
app.dataset.partitions
app.dataset.slug
app.event_handler
app.raw_size_bytes
app.sample_rate
app.team.id
...
response.content_encoding
response.content_type
response.status_code
service_name
trace.span_id
trace.trace_id
```

With many more dimensions available, you can examine events to make highly sophisticated correlations between any group of service requests (see Chapter 8). The more highly dimensional your data is, the more likely you will be able to find hidden or elusive patterns in application behavior. In modern systems, where the permutations of failures that can occur are effectively limitless, capturing only a few basic dimensions in your telemetry data is insufficient.

You must gather incredibly rich detail about everything happening at the intersection of users, code, and your systems. High-dimensionality data provides greater context about how those intersections unfold. In later chapters, we cover how high-dimensionality data (which often contains high-cardinality data) is analyzed in order to reveal where the issues you care about in a system are happening and why.

Debugging with Observability

Instead of limiting the cardinality and dimensionality of telemetry data, observability tools encourage developers to gather rich telemetry for every possible event that could occur, passing along the full context of any given request and storing it for possible use at some point down the line. Observability tools are specifically designed to query against high-cardinality, high-dimensionality data.

Therefore, for debugging, you can interrogate your event data in any number of arbitrary ways. With observability, you iteratively investigate conditions you care about by exploring your data to see what it can reveal about the state of your system. You ask a question that you did not need to predict in advance to find answers or clues that will lead you to ask the next question, and the next, and the next. You repeat that pattern again and again until you find the needle in the proverbial haystack that you're looking for. A key function of observable systems is the ability to explore your system in open-ended ways.

The explorability of a system is measured by how well you can ask any question and inspect its corresponding internal state. *Explorability* means you can iteratively investigate and eventually understand any state your system has gotten itself into— even if you have never seen that state before—without needing to predict what those states might be in advance. Again, observability means that you can understand and explain any state your system can get into—no matter how novel or bizarre—without shipping new code.

The reason monitoring worked so well for so long is that systems tended to be simple enough that engineers could reason about exactly where they might need to look for problems and how those problems might present themselves. For example, it's relatively simple to connect the dots that when sockets fill up, CPU would overload, and the solution is to add more capacity by scaling application node instances, or by tuning your database, or so forth. Engineers could, by and large, predict the majority of possible failure states up front and discover the rest the hard way once their applications were running in production.

However, monitoring creates a fundamentally reactive approach to system management. You can catch failure conditions that you predicted and knew to check for. If you know to expect it, you check for it. For every condition you don't know to look for, you have to see it first, deal with the unpleasant surprise, investigate it to the best of your abilities, possibly reach a dead end that requires you to see that same condition multiple times before properly diagnosing it, and then you can develop a check for it. In that model, engineers are perversely incentivized to have a strong aversion to situations that could cause unpredictable failures. This is partially why some teams are terrified of deploying new code (more on that topic later).

One subtle additional point: hardware/infrastructure problems are simple compared to the ones generated by your code or your users. The shift from "most of my problems are component failures" to "most of my questions have to do with user behavior or subtle code bugs and interactions" is why even people with monoliths and simpler architectures may pursue the shift from monitoring to observability.

Observability Is for Modern Systems

A production software system is observable to the extent that you can understand new internal system states without having to make arbitrary guesses, predict those failure modes in advance, or ship new code to understand that state. In this way, we extend the control theory concept of observability to the field of software engineering.

In its software engineering context, observability does provide benefits for those on more traditional architectures or monolithic systems. It's *always* helpful to be able to trace your code and see where the time is being spent, or to reproduce behavior from a user's perspective. This capability can certainly save teams from having to discover unpredictable failure modes in production no matter what your architecture is like. But it is with modern distributed systems that the scalpel and searchlight afforded by observability tooling becomes absolutely nonnegotiable.

In distributed systems, the ratio of somewhat predictable failure modes to novel and never-before-seen failure modes is heavily weighted toward the bizarre and unpredictable. Those unpredictable failure modes happen so commonly, and repeat rarely enough, that they outpace the ability for most teams to set up appropriate and relevant enough monitoring dashboards to easily show that state to the engineering teams responsible for ensuring the continuous uptime, reliability, and acceptable performance of their production applications.

We wrote this book with these types of modern systems in mind. Any system consisting of many components that are loosely coupled, dynamic in nature, and difficult to reason about are a good fit for realizing the benefits of observability versus traditional management approaches. If you manage production software systems that fit that description, this book describes what observability can mean for you, your team, your customers, and your business. We also focus on the human factors necessary to develop a practice of observability in key areas of your engineering processes.

Conclusion

Although the term *observability* has been defined for decades, its application to software systems is a new adaptation that brings with it several new considerations and characteristics. Compared to their simpler early counterparts, modern systems have introduced such additional complexity that failures are harder than ever to predict, detect, and troubleshoot.

To mitigate that complexity, engineering teams must now be able to constantly gather telemetry in flexible ways that allow them to debug issues without first needing to predict how failures may occur. Observability enables engineers to slice and dice that telemetry data in flexible ways that allow them to get to the root of any issues that occur in unparalleled ways.

Observability is often mischaracterized as being achieved when you have "three pillars" of different telemetry data types, so we aren't fans of that model. However, if we must have three pillars of observability, then what they should be is tooling that supports high cardinality, high-dimensionality, and explorability. Next, we'll examine how observability differs from the traditional systems monitoring approach.

CHAPTER 2

How Debugging Practices Differ Between Observability and Monitoring

In the previous chapter, we covered the origins and common use of the metrics data type for debugging. In this chapter, we'll more closely examine the specific debugging practices associated with traditional monitoring tools and how those differ from the debugging practices associated with observability tools.

Traditional monitoring tools work by checking system conditions against known thresholds that indicate whether previously known error conditions are present. That is a fundamentally reactive approach because it works well only for identifying previously encountered failure modes.

In contrast, observability tools work by enabling iterative exploratory investigations to systematically determine where and why performance issues may be occurring. Observability enables a proactive approach to identifying any failure mode, whether previously known or unknown.

In this chapter, we focus on understanding the limitations of monitoring-based troubleshooting methods. First, we unpack how monitoring tools are used within the context of troubleshooting software performance issues in production. Then we examine the behaviors institutionalized by those monitoring-based approaches. Finally, we show how observability practices enable teams to identify both previously known and unknown issues.

How Monitoring Data Is Used for Debugging

The *Oxford English Dictionary* defines *monitoring* as observing and checking the progress or quality of (something) over a period of time, to keep under systematic review. Traditional monitoring systems do just that by way of metrics: they check the performance of an application over time; then they report an aggregate measure of performance over that interval. Monitoring systems collect, aggregate, and analyze metrics to sift through known patterns that indicate whether troubling trends are occurring.

This monitoring data has two main consumers: machines and humans. Machines use monitoring data to make decisions about whether a detected condition should trigger an alert or a recovery should be declared. A *metric* is a numerical representation of system state over the particular interval of time when it was recorded. Similar to looking at a physical gauge, we might be able to glance at a metric that conveys whether a particular resource is over- or underutilized at a particular moment in time. For example, CPU utilization might be at 90% right now.

But is that behavior changing? Is the measure shown on the gauge going up or going down? Metrics are typically more useful in aggregate. Understanding the trending values of metrics over time provides insights into system behaviors that affect software performance. Monitoring systems collect, aggregate, and analyze metrics to sift through known patterns that indicate trends their humans want to know about.

If CPU utilization continues to stay over 90% for the next two minutes, someone may have decided that's a condition they want to be alerted about. For clarity, it's worth noting that to the machines, a metric is just a number. System state in the metrics world is very binary. Below a certain number and interval, the machine will not trigger an alert. Above a certain number and interval, the machine will trigger an alert. Where exactly that threshold lies is a human decision.

When monitoring systems detect a trend that a human identified as important, an alert is sent. Similarly, if CPU utilization drops below 90% for a preconfigured time-span, the monitoring system will determine that the error condition for the triggered alert no longer applies and therefore declare the system recovered. It's a rudimentary system, yet so many of our troubleshooting capabilities rely on it.

The way humans use that same data to debug issues is a bit more interesting. Those numerical measurements are fed into TSDBs, and a graphical interface uses that database to source graphical representations of data trends. Those graphs can be collected and assembled into progressively more complicated combinations, known as *dashboards*.

Static dashboards are commonly assembled one per service, and they're a useful starting point for an engineer to begin understanding particular aspects of the underlying system. This is the original intent for dashboards: to provide an overview of how a set of metrics is tracking and to surface noteworthy trends. However, dashboards are a poor choice for discovering new problems with debugging.

When dashboards were first built, we didn't have many system metrics to worry about. So it was relatively easy to build a dashboard that showed the critical data anyone should know about for any given service. In modern times, storage is cheap, processing is powerful, and the data we can collect about a system seems virtually limitless. Modern services typically collect so many metrics that it's impossible to fit them all into the same dashboard. Yet that doesn't stop many engineering teams from trying to fit those all into a singular view. After all, that's the promise of the dashboard!

To make everything fit in a dashboard, metrics are often aggregated and averaged. These aggregate values may convey a specific condition—for example, mean CPU across your cluster is above 90%. But these aggregated measures no longer provide meaningful visibility into what's happening in their corresponding underlying systems—they don't tell you which processes are responsible for that condition. To mitigate that problem, some vendors have added filters and drill-downs to their dashboarding interfaces that allow you to dive deeper and narrow down visualizations in ways that improve their function as a debugging tool.

However, your ability to troubleshoot effectively using dashboards is limited by your ability to pre-declare conditions that describe what you might be looking for. In advance, you need to specify that you want the ability to break down values along a certain small set of dimensions. That has to be done in advance so that your dashboarding tool can create the indexes necessary on those columns to allow the type of analysis you want. That indexing is also strictly stymied by groups of data with high cardinality. You can't just load a dashboard with high cardinality data across multiple graphs if you're using a metrics-based tool.

Requiring the foresight to define necessary conditions puts the onus of data discovery on the user. Any efforts to discover new system insights throughout the course of debugging are limited by conditions you would have had to predict prior to starting your investigation. For example, during the course of your investigation, you might discover that it's useful to group CPU utilization by instance type. But you can't do that because you didn't add the necessary labels in advance.

In that respect, using metrics to surface new system insights is an inherently reactive approach. Yet, as a whole, the software industry has seemingly been conditioned to rely on dashboards for debugging despite these limitations. That reactiveness is a logical consequence of metrics being the best troubleshooting tool the industry had available for many years. Because we're so accustomed to that limitation as the default way troubleshooting is done, the impact that has on our troubleshooting behavior may not be immediately clear at a glance.

Troubleshooting Behaviors When Using Dashboards

The following scenario should be familiar to engineers responsible for managing production services. If you're such an engineer, put yourself in these shoes and use that perspective to examine the assumptions that you also make in your own work environment. If you're not an engineer who typically manages services in production, examine the following scenario for the types of limitations described in the previous section.

It's a new morning, and your workday is just getting started. You walk over to your desk, and one of the first things you do is glance at a collection of readily displayed dashboards. Your dashboarding system aspires to be a "single pane of glass," behind which you can quickly see every aspect of your application system, its various components, and their health statuses. You also have a few dashboards that act as high-level summaries to convey important top-line business metrics—so you can see, for example, whether your app is breaking any new traffic records, if any of your apps have been removed from the App Store overnight, and a variety of other critical conditions that require immediate attention.

You glance at these dashboards to seek familiar conditions and reassure yourself that you are free to start your day without the distraction of firefighting production emergencies. The dashboard displays a collection of two to three dozen graphs. You don't know what many of those graphs actually show. Yet, over time, you've developed confidence in the predictive powers that these graphs give you. For example, if the graph at the bottom of this screen turns red, you should drop whatever you're doing and immediately start investigating before things get worse.

Perhaps you don't know what all the graphs actually measure, but they pretty reliably help you predict where the problems are happening in the production service you're intimately familiar with. When the graphs turn a certain way, you almost acquire a psychic power of prediction. If the left corner of the top graph dips while the bottom-right graph is growing steadily, a problem exists with your message queues. If the box in the center is spiking every five minutes and the background is a few shades redder than normal, a database query is acting up.

Just then, as you're glancing through the graphs, you notice a problem with your caching layer. Nothing on the dashboard clearly says, "Your primary caching server is getting hot." But you've gotten to know your system so well that by deciphering patterns on the screen, you can immediately leap into action to do things that are not at all clearly stated by the data available. You've seen this type of issue before and, based on those past scars, you know that this particular combination of measures indicates a caching problem.

Seeing that pattern, you quickly pull up the dashboard for the caching component of your system to confirm your suspicion. Your suspicion is confirmed, and you jump right into fixing the problem. Similarly, you can do this with more than a handful of patterns. Over time, you've learned to divine the source of problems by reading the tea leaves of your particular production service.

The Limitations of Troubleshooting by Intuition

Many engineers are intimately familiar with this troubleshooting approach. Ask yourself, just how much intuition do you rely on when hopping around various components of your system throughout the course of investigating problems? Typically, as an industry, we value that intuition, and it has provided us with much benefit throughout the years. Now ask yourself: if you were placed in front of those same dashboarding tools, but with an entirely different application, written in a different language, with a different architecture, could you divine those same answers? When the lower-left corner turns blue, would you know what you were supposed to do or if it was even necessary to take action?

Clearly, the answer to that question is no. The expressions of various system problems as seen through dashboards is quite different from app stack to app stack. Yet, as an industry, this is our primary way of interacting with systems. Historically, engineers have relied on static dashboards that are densely populated with data that is an interpretive layer or two away from the data needed to make proper diagnoses when things go wrong. But we start seeing the limitations of their usefulness when we discover novel problems. Let's consider a few examples.

Example 1: Insufficient correlation

An engineer adds an index and wants to know if that achieved their goal of faster query times. They also want to know whether any other unexpected consequences occurred. They might want to ask the following questions:

- Is a particular query (which is known to be a pain point) scanning fewer rows than before?

- How often is the new index getting chosen by the query planner, and for which queries?

- Are write latencies up overall, on average, or at the 95th/99th percentiles?

- Are queries faster or slower when they use this index than their previous query plan?

- What other indexes are also used along with the new index (assuming index intersection)?

- Has this index made any other indexes obsolete, so we can drop those and reclaim some write capacity?

Those are just a few example questions, and they can ask more. However, what they have available is a dashboard and graphs for CPU load average, memory usage, index counters, and lots of other internal statistics for the host and running database. They cannot slice and dice or break down by user, query, destination or source IP, or anything like that. All they can do is eyeball the broad changes and hazard a sophisticated guess, mostly based on timestamps.

Example 2: Not drilling down

An engineer discovers a bug that inadvertently expires data and wants to know if it's affecting *all* the users or just some shards. Instead, what they have available in a dashboard is the ability to see disk space dropping suspiciously fast…on just one data shard. They briskly assume the problem is confined to that shard and move on, not realizing that disk space appeared to be holding steady on the other shard, thanks to a simultaneous import operation.

Example 3: Tool-hopping

An engineer sees a spike in errors at a particular time. They start paging through dashboards, looking for spikes in other metrics at the same time, and they find some, but they can't tell which are the cause of the error and which are the effects. So they jump over into their logging tool and start grepping for errors. Once they find the request ID of an error, they turn to their tracing tool and copy-paste the error ID into the tracing tool. (If that request isn't traced, they repeat this over and over until they catch one that is.)

These monitoring tools can get better at detecting finer-grained problems over time—if you have a robust tradition of always running restrospectives after outages and adding custom metrics where possible in response. Typically, the way this happens is that the on-call engineer figures it out or arrives at a reasonable hypothesis, and also figures out exactly which metric(s) would answer the question if it exists. They ship a change to create that metric and begin gathering it. Of course, it's too late now to see if your last change had the impact you're guessing it did—you can't go back in time and capture that custom metric a second time unless you can replay the whole exact scenario—but if it happens again, the story goes, next time you'll know for sure.

The engineers in the preceding examples might go back and add custom metrics for each query family, for expiration rates per collection, for error rates per shards, etc. (They might go nuts and add custom metrics for every single query family's lock usage, hits for each index, buckets for execution times, etc.—and then find out they doubled their entire monitoring budget the next billing period.)

Traditional Monitoring Is Fundamentally Reactive

The preceding approach is entirely reactive, yet many teams accept this as the normal state of operations—that is simply how troubleshooting is done. At best, it's a way of playing whack-a-mole with critical telemetry, always playing catch-up after the fact. It's also quite costly, since metrics tools tend to price out custom metrics in a way that scales up linearly with each one. Many teams enthusiastically go all-in on custom metrics, then keel over when they see the bill, and end up going back to prune the majority of them.

Is your team one of those teams? To help determine that, watch for these indicators as you perform your work maintaining your production service throughout the week:

- When issues occur in production, are you determining where you need to investigate based on an actual visible trail of system information breadcrumbs? Or are you following your intuition to locate those problems? Are you looking in the place where you know you found the answer last time?

- Are you relying on your expert familiarity of this system and its past problems? When you use a troubleshooting tool to investigate a problem, are you exploratively looking for clues? Or are you trying to confirm a guess? For example, if latency is slow across the board and you have dozens of databases and queues that could be producing it, are you able to use data to determine where the latency is coming from? Or do you guess it must be your MySQL database, per usual, and then go check your MySQL graphs to confirm your hunch?

  How often do you intuitively jump to a solution and then look for confirmation that it's right and proceed accordingly—but actually miss the real issue because that confirmed assumption was only a symptom, or an effect rather than the cause?

- Are your troubleshooting tools giving you precise answers to your questions and leading you to direct answers? Or are you performing translations based on system familiarity to arrive at the answer you actually need?

- How many times are you leaping from tool to tool, attempting to correlate patterns between observations, relying on yourself to carry the context between disparate sources?

- Most of all, is the best debugger on your team always the person who has been there the longest? This is a dead giveaway that most of your knowledge about your system comes not from a democratized method like a tool, but through personal hands-on experience alone.

Guesses aren't good enough. Correlation is not causation. A vast disconnect often exists between the specific questions you want to ask and the dashboards available to provide answers. You shouldn't have to make a leap of faith to connect cause and effect.

It gets even worse when you consider the gravity-warping impact that confirmation bias can have. With a system like this, you can't find what you don't know to look for. You can't ask questions that you didn't predict you might need to ask, far in advance.

Historically, engineers have had to stitch together answers from various data sources, along with the intuitions they've developed about their systems in order to diagnose issues. As an industry, we have accepted that as the normal state of operations. But as systems have grown in complexity, beyond the ability for any one person or team to intuitively understand their various moving parts, the need to grow beyond this reactive and limiting approach becomes clear.

How Observability Enables Better Debugging

As we've seen in the preceding section, monitoring is a reactive approach that is best suited for detecting known problems and previously identified patterns; this model centers around the concept of alerts and outages. Conversely, observability lets you explicitly discover the source of any problem, along any dimension or combination of dimensions, without needing to first predict where and how that problem might be happening; this model centers around questioning and understanding.

Let's comparatively examine the differences between monitoring and observability across three axes: relying on institutional knowledge, finding hidden issues, and having confidence in diagnosing production issues. We provide more in-depth examples of how and why these differences occur in upcoming chapters. For now, we will make these comparative differences at a high level.

Institutional knowledge is unwritten information that may be known to some but is not commonly known by others within an organization. With monitoring-based approaches, teams often orient themselves around the idea that seniority is the key to knowledge: the engineer who has been on the team longest is often the best debugger on the team and the debugger of last resort. When debugging is derived from an individual's experience deciphering previously known patterns, that predilection should be unsurprising.

Conversely, teams that practice observability are inclined in a radically different direction. With observability tools, the best debugger on the team is typically the engineer who is the most curious. Engineers practicing observability have the ability to interrogate their systems by asking exploratory questions, using the answers discovered to lead them toward making further open-ended inquiries (see Chapter 8). Rather than valuing intimate knowledge of one particular system to provide an investigative hunch, observability rewards skilled investigative abilities that translate across different systems.

The impact of that shift becomes most evident when it comes to finding issues that are buried deep within complex systems. A reactive monitoring-based approach that rewards intuition and hunches is also prone to obscuring the real source of issues with confirmation bias. When issues are detected, they're diagnosed based on how similar their behavioral pattern appears to previously known problems. That can lead to treating symptoms of a problem without ever getting to the actual source. Engineers guess at what might be occurring, jump to confirm that guess, and alleviate the symptom without ever fully investigating why it was happening in the first place. Worse, by introducing a fix for the symptom instead of its cause, teams will now have two problems to contend with instead of one.

Rather than leaning on expert foreknowledge, observability allows engineers to treat every investigation as new. When issues are detected, even if the triggering conditions appear similar to past problems, an engineer should be able to put one metaphorical foot in front of the other to follow the clues provided by breadcrumbs of system information. You can follow the data toward determining the correct answer—every time, step by step. That methodical approach means that any engineer can diagnose any issue without needing a vast level of system familiarity to reason about impossibly complex systems to intuitively divine a course of action. Further, the objectivity afforded by that methodology means engineers can get to the source of the specific problem they're trying to solve rather than treating the symptoms of similar problems in the past.

The shift toward objective and methodological investigation also serves to increase the confidence of entire teams to diagnose production issues. In monitoring-based systems, humans are responsible for leaping from tool to tool and correlating observations between them, because the data is pre-aggregated and does not support flexible exploration. If they want to zoom in closer, or ask a new question, they must mentally carry the context when moving from looking at dashboards to reading logs. They must do so once more when moving from logs to looking at a trace, and back again. This context switching is error-prone, exhausting, and often impossible given the inherent incompatibilities and inconsistencies encountered when dealing with multiple sources of data and truth. For example, if you're responsible for drawing correlations between units like TCP/IP packets and HTTP errors experienced by your app, or resource starvation errors and high memory-eviction rates, your investigation likely has such a high degree of conversion error built in that it might be equally effective to take a random guess.

Observability tools pull high-cardinality, high-dimensionality context from telemetry data into a single location where investigators can easily slice and dice to zoom in, zoom out, or follow breadcrumbs to find definitive answers. Engineers should be able to move through an investigation steadily and confidently, without the distraction of constant context switching. Further, by holding that context within one tool, implicit understandings that were often stitched together by experience and institutional knowledge instead become explicit data about your system. Observability allows critical knowledge to move out of the minds of the most experienced engineers and into a shared reality that can be explored by any engineer as needed. You will see how to unlock these benefits as we explore more detailed features of observability tools throughout this book.

Conclusion

The monitoring-based debugging methods of using metrics and dashboards in tandem with expert knowledge to triage the source of issues in production is a prevalent practice in the software industry. In the previous era of elementary application architectures with limited data collection, an investigative practice that relies on the experience and intuition of humans to detect system issues made sense, given the simplicity of legacy systems. However, the complexity and scale of the systems underlying modern applications has quickly made that approach untenable.

Observability-based debugging methods offer a different approach. They are designed to enable engineers to investigate any system, no matter how complex, without leaning on experience or intimate system knowledge to generate a hunch. With observability tools, engineers can approach the investigation of any problem methodically and objectively. By interrogating their systems in an open-ended manner, engineers practicing observability can find the source of deeply hidden problems and confidently diagnose issues in production, regardless of their prior exposure to any given system.

Next, let's look at a concrete experience that ties these concepts together by looking at past lessons learned from scaling an application without observability.

CHAPTER 3

Lessons from Scaling Without Observability

So far, we've defined *observability* and how it differs from traditional monitoring. We've covered some of the limitations of traditional monitoring tools when managing modern distributed systems and how observability solves them. But an evolutionary gap remains between the traditional and modern world. What happens when trying to scale modern systems without observability?

In this chapter, we look at a real example of slamming into the limitations of traditional monitoring and architectures, along with why different approaches are needed when scaling applications. Coauthor Charity Majors shares her firsthand account on lessons learned from scaling without observability at her former company, Parse (*https://w.wiki/56wb*). This story is told from her perspective.

An Introduction to Parse

Hello, dear reader. I'm Charity, and I've been on call since I was 17 years old. Back then, I was racking servers and writing shell scripts at the University of Idaho. I remember the birth and spread of many notable monitoring systems: Big Brother, Nagios, RRDtool and Cacti, Ganglia, Zabbix, and Prometheus. I've used most—not quite all—of them. They were incredibly useful in their time. Once I got a handle on TSDBs and their interfaces, every system problem suddenly looked like a nail for the time-series hammer: set thresholds, monitor, rinse, and repeat.

During my career, my niche has been coming in as the first infrastructure engineer (or one of the first) to join an existing team of software engineers in order to help mature their product to production readiness. I've made decisions about how best to understand what's happening in production systems many, many times.

That's what I did at Parse. Parse was a mobile-backend-as-a-service (MBaaS) platform, providing mobile-app developers a way to link their apps to backend cloud storage systems, and APIs to backend systems. The platform enabled features like user management, push notifications, and integration with social networking services. In 2012, when I joined the team, Parse was still in beta. At that time, the company was using a bit of Amazon CloudWatch and, somehow, was being alerted by five different systems. I switched us over to using Icinga/Nagios and Ganglia because those were the tools I knew best.

Parse was an interesting place to work because it was so ahead of its time in many ways (we would go on to be acquired by Facebook in 2013). We had a microservice architecture before we had the name "microservices" and long before that pattern became a movement. We were using MongoDB as our data store and very much growing up alongside it: when we started, it was version 2.0 with a single lock per replica set. We were developing with Ruby on Rails and we had to monkey-patch Rails to support multiple database shards.

We had complex multitenant architectures with shared tenancy pools. In the early stages, we were optimizing for development speed, full stop.

I want to pause here to stress that optimizing for development speed was *the right thing to do*. With that decision, we made many early choices that we later had to undo and redo. But most start-ups don't fail because they make the wrong tooling choices. And let's be clear: most start-ups do fail. They fail because there's no demand for their product, or because they can't find product/market fit, or because customers don't love what they built, or any number of reasons where time is of the essence. Choosing a stack that used MongoDB and Ruby on Rails enabled us to get to market quickly enough that we delighted customers, and they wanted a lot more of what we were selling.

Around the time Facebook acquired Parse, we were hosting over 60,000 mobile apps. Two and a half years later, when I left Facebook, we were hosting over a million mobile apps. But even when I first joined, in 2012, the cracks were already starting to show.

Parse officially launched a couple of months after I joined. Our traffic doubled, then doubled, and then doubled again. We were the darling of Hacker News, and every time a post about us showed up there, we'd get a spike of new sign-ups.

In August of 2012, one of our hosted apps moved into a top 10 spot in the iTunes Store for the first time. The app was marketing a death-metal band from Norway. The band used the app to livestream broadcasts. For the band, this was in the evening; for Parse, it was the crack of dawn. Every time the band livestreamed, Parse went down in seconds flat. We had a scaling problem.

Scaling at Parse

At first, figuring out what was happening to our services was difficult. Our diagnosis was challenging because (thanks to our co-tenancy model) whenever something got slow, *everything* got slow, even if it had nothing to do with whatever was causing the problem.

Solving that collective set of problems took a lot of trial-and-error tinkering. We had to level up our MongoDB database administration skills. Then, finally, after a lot of work, we figured out the source of the problem. To mitigate that same problem again in the future, we wrote tooling that let us selectively throttle particular apps or rewrite/limit poorly structured queries on the fly. We also generated custom Ganglia dashboards for the user ID of this Norwegian death-metal band so that, in the future, we could swiftly tell whether it was to blame for an outage.

Getting there was tough. But we got a handle on it. We all heaved a collective sigh of relief, but that was only the beginning.

Parse made it easy for mobile-app developers to spin up new apps and quickly ship them to an app store. Our platform was a hit! Developers loved the experience. So, day after day, that's what they did. Soon, we were seeing new Parse-hosted apps skyrocket to the top of the iTunes Store or the Android Market several times a week. Those apps would do things like use us to send push notifications, save game state, perform complex geolocation queries—the workload was utterly unpredictable. Millions of device notifications were being dumped onto the Parse platform at any time of the day or night, with no warning.

That's when we started to run into many of the fundamental flaws in the architecture we'd chosen, the languages we were using, and the tools we were using to understand those choices. I want to reiterate: each choice was *the right thing to do*. We got to market fast, we found a niche, and we delivered. Now, we had to figure out how to grow into the next phase.

I'll pause here to describe some of those decisions we made, and the impact they now had at this scale. When incoming API requests came in, they were load-balanced and handed off to a pool of Ruby on Rails HTTP workers known as Unicorns (*https://w.wiki/56wc*). Our infrastructure was in Amazon Web Services (AWS), and all of our Amazon Elastic Compute Cloud (EC2) instances hosted a Unicorn primary, which would fork a couple of dozen Unicorn child processes; those then handled the API requests themselves. The Unicorns were configured to hold a socket open to multiple backends—MySQL for internal user data, Redis for push notifications, MongoDB for user-defined application data, Cloud Code for executing user-provided code in containers server-side, Apache Cassandra for Parse analytics, and so on.

It's important to note here that Ruby is not a threaded language. So that pool of API workers was a fixed pool. Whenever any one of the backends got just a little bit slower at fulfilling requests, the pool would rapidly fill itself up with pending requests to that backend. Whenever a backend became very slow (or completely unresponsive), the pools would fill up within seconds—and all of Parse would go down.

At first, we attacked that problem by overprovisioning instances: our Unicorns ran at 20% utilization during their normal steady state. That approach allowed us to survive some of the gentler slowdowns. But at the same time, we also made the painful decision to undergo a complete rewrite from Ruby on Rails to Go. We realized that the only way out of this hellhole was to adopt a natively threaded language. It took us over two years to rewrite the code that had taken us one year to write. In the meantime, we were on the bleeding edge of experiencing all the ways that traditional operational approaches were fundamentally incompatible with modern architectural problems.

This was a particularly brutal time all around at Parse. We had an experienced operations engineering team doing all the "right things." We were discovering that the best practices we all knew, which were born from using traditional approaches, simply weren't up to the task of tackling problems in the modern distributed microservices era.

At Parse, we were all-in on infrastructure as code. We had an elaborate system of Nagios checks, PagerDuty alerts, and Ganglia metrics. We had tens of thousands of Ganglia graphs and metrics. But those tools were failing us because they were valuable only when we already knew what the problem was going to be—when we knew which thresholds were good and where to check for problems.

For instance, TSDB graphs were valuable when we knew which dashboards to carefully curate and craft—if we could predict which custom metrics we would need in order to diagnose problems. Our logging tools were valuable when we had a pretty good idea of what we were looking for—if we'd remembered to log the right things in advance, and if we knew the right regular expression to search for. Our application performance management (APM) tools were great when problems manifested as one of the top 10 bad queries, bad users, or bad endpoints that they were looking for.

But we had a whole host of problems that those solutions couldn't help us solve. That previous generation of tools was falling short under these circumstances:

- Every other day, we had a brand-new user skyrocketing into the top 10 list for one of the mobile-app stores.
- Load coming from any of the users identified in any of our top 10 lists wasn't the cause of our site going down.

- The list of slow queries were all just symptoms of a problem and not the cause (e.g., the read queries were getting slow because of a bunch of tiny writes, which saturated the lock collectively while individually returning almost instantly).

- We needed help seeing that our overall site reliability was 99.9%, but that 0.1% wasn't evenly distributed across all users. That 0.1% meant that just one shard was 100% down, and it just happened to be the shard holding all data that belonged to a famed multibillion-dollar entertainment company with a mousey mascot.

- Every day, a new bot account might pop up and do things that would saturate the lock percentage on our MySQL primary.

These types of problems are all categorically different from the last generation of problems: the ones for which that set of tools was built. Those tools were built for a world where predictability reigned. In those days, production software systems had "the app"—with all of its functionality and complexity contained in one place—and "the database." But now, scaling meant that we blew up those monolithic apps into many services used by many different tenants. We blew up the database into a diverse range of many storage systems.

At many companies, including Parse, our business models turned our products into platforms. We invited users to run any code they saw fit to run on our hosted services. We invited them to run any query they felt like running against our hosted databases. And in doing so, suddenly, all of the control we had over our systems evaporated in a puff of market dollars to be won.

In this era of services as platforms, our customers love how powerful we make them. That drive has revolutionized the software industry. And for those of us running the underlying systems powering those platforms, it meant that everything became massively—and exponentially—harder not just to operate and administer, but also to *understand*.

How did we get here, and when did the industry seemingly change overnight? Let's look at the various small iterations that created such a seismic shift.

The Evolution Toward Modern Systems

In the beginning—back in those early days of the dot-com era—there was "the app" and "the database." They were simple to understand. They were either *up* or *down*. They were either slow or not slow. And we had to monitor them for aliveness and acceptable responsiveness thresholds.

That task was not always simple. But, operationally, it was straightforward. For quite some time, we even centered around a pinnacle of architectural simplicity. The most popular architectural pattern was the LAMP stack: Linux, Apache, MySQL, and PHP or Python. You've probably heard this before, and I feel obligated to say it again now: *if you can solve your problem with a LAMP stack (or equivalent), you probably should.*

When architecting a service, the first rule is to not *add unnecessary complexity.* You should carefully identify the problems you need to solve, and solve *only those problems.* Think carefully about the options you need to keep open, and keep those options open. Therefore, most of the time, you should choose boring technology (*https://mcfunley.com/choose-boring-technology*). Don't confuse boring with bad. Boring technology simply means that its edge cases and failure scenarios are well understood by many people.

However, with the demands of today's users, more of us are discovering that many of the problems we need to solve cannot be solved by the humble-yet-mighty LAMP stack. This could be the case for a multitude of reasons. You might have higher reliability needs requiring resiliency guarantees that a LAMP stack can't provide. Maybe you have too much data or data that's too complex to be well served by a LAMP stack. Usually, we reach the edges of that simple architectural model in service of scale, reliability, or speed—that's what drives us to shard, partition, or replicate our stacks.

The way we manage our code also matters. In larger or more complex settings, the monorepo creates organizational pressures that can drive technical change. Splitting up a code base can create clearer areas of ownership in ways that allow an organization to move more swiftly and autonomously than it could if everyone was contributing to The One Big App.

These types of needs—and more—are part of what has driven modern shifts in systems architecture that are clear and pronounced. On a technical level, these shifts include several primary effects:

- The decomposition of everything, from one to many
- The need for a variety of data stores, from one database to many storage systems
- A migration from monolithic applications toward many smaller microservices
- A variety of infrastructure types away from "big iron" servers toward containers, functions, serverless, and other ephemeral, elastic resources

These technical changes have also had powerful ripple effects at the human and organizational level: our systems are *sociotechnical.* The complexity introduced by these shifts at the social level (and their associated feedback loops) have driven further changes to the systems and the way we think about them.

Consider some of the prevalent social qualities we think of in conjunction with the computing era during the LAMP stack's height of popularity. A tall organizational barrier existed between operations and development teams, and from time to time, code would get lobbed over that wall. Ops teams notoriously resisted introducing changes to production systems. Deploying changes led to unpredictable behavior that could often lead to downtime. So they'd prevent developers from ever directly touching production—tending closely to their uptime. In that type of "glass castle" approach, deployment freezes were a commonly used method for keeping production services stable.

In the LAMP stack era, that protective approach to production wasn't entirely wrong either. Back then, much of the chaos in production systems was indeed inflicted when introducing bad code. When new code was deployed, the effects were pretty much binary: the site was up or it was down (maybe, sometimes if you were unlucky, it had a third state: inexplicably slow).

Very few architectural constructs (which are commonplace today) existed back then to control the side effects of dealing with bad code. There was no such thing as a graceful degradation of service. If developers introduced a bug to a small, seemingly trivial system component (for example, export functionality), it might crash the entire system every time someone used it. No mechanisms were available to temporarily disable those turns-out-not-so-trivial subcomponents. It wasn't possible to fix just that one broken subsystem while the rest of the service ran unaffected. Some teams would attempt to add that sort of granular control to their monoliths. But that path was so fraught and difficult that most didn't even try.

Regardless, many of those monolithic systems continued to get bigger. As more and more people tried to collaborate on the same paths, problems like lock contention, cost ceilings, and dynamic resource needs became showstoppers. The seismic shift from one to many became a necessity for these teams. Monoliths were quickly decomposed into distributed systems and, with that shift, came second-order effects:

- The binary simplicity of service availability as up or down shifted to complex availability heuristics to represent any number of partial failures or degraded availability.
- Code deployments to production that had relatively simple deployment schemes shifted toward progressive delivery.
- Deployments that immediately changed code paths and went live shifted to promotion schemes where code deployments were decoupled from feature releases (via feature flags).
- Applications that had one current version running in production shifted toward typically having multiple versions baking in production at any given time.

- Having an in-house operations team running your infrastructure shifted toward many critical infrastructure components being run by other teams at other companies abstracted behind an API, where they may not even be accessible to you, the developer.

- Monitoring systems that worked well for alerting against and troubleshooting previously encountered known failures shifted to being woefully inadequate in a distributed world, where unknown failures that had never been previously encountered (and may never be encountered again) were the new type of prevalent problem.

 Progressive delivery, a term coined by RedMonk cofounder James Governor, refers to a basket of skills and technologies concerned with controlled, partial deployment of code or changes made to production (for example, canarying, feature flags, blue/green deploys, and rolling deploys).

The tools and techniques needed to manage monolithic systems like the LAMP stack were radically ineffective for running modern systems. Systems with applications deployed in one "big bang" release are managed rather differently than microservices. With microservices, applications are often rolled out piece by piece, and code deployments don't necessarily release features because feature flags now enable or disable code paths with no deployment required.

Similarly, in a distributed world, staging systems have become less useful or reliable than they used to be. Even in a monolithic world, replicating a production environment to staging was always difficult. Now, in a distributed world, it's effectively impossible. That means debugging and inspection have become ineffective in staging, and we have shifted to a model requiring those tasks to be accomplished in production itself.

The Evolution Toward Modern Practices

The technical and social aspects of our systems are interrelated. Given these sociotechnical systems, the emphasis on shifting our technology toward different performance models also requires a shift in the models that define the ways our teams perform.

Furthermore, these shifts are so interrelated that it's impossible to draw a clean boundary between them. Many of the technology shifts described in the preceding section influenced how teams had to reorganize and change practices in order to support them.

In one area, however, a radical shift in social behavior is absolutely clear. The evolution toward modern distributed systems also brings with it third-order effects that change the relationship that engineers must have with their production environment:

- User experience can no longer be generalized as being the same for all service users. In the new model, different users of a service may be routed through the system in different ways, using different components, providing experiences that can vary widely.

- Monitoring alerts that look for edge cases in production that have system conditions exceeding known thresholds generate a tremendous number of false positives, false negatives, and meaningless noise. Alerting has shifted to a model in which fewer alerts are triggered, by focusing only on symptoms that directly impact user experience.

- Debuggers can no longer be attached to one specific runtime. Fulfilling service requests now requires hopping across a network, spanning multiple runtimes, often multiple times per individual request.

- Known recurring failures that require manual remediation and can be defined in a runbook are no longer the norm. Service failures have shifted from that model toward one in which known recurring failures can be recovered automatically. Failures that cannot be automatically recovered, and therefore trigger an alert, likely mean the responding engineer will be facing a novel problem.

These tertiary signals mean that a massive gravitational shift in focus is happening away from the importance of preproduction and toward the importance of being intimately familiar with production. Traditional efforts to harden code and ensure its safety *before* it goes to production are starting to be accepted as limiting and somewhat futile. Test-driven development and running tests against staging environments still have use. But they can never replicate the wild and unpredictable nature of how that code will be used in production.

As developers, we all have a fixed number of cycles we can devote to accomplishing our work. The limitation of the traditional approach is that it focuses on preproduction hardening first and foremost. Any leftover scraps of attention, if they even exist, are then given to focusing on production systems. If we want to build reliable services in production, that ordering must be reversed.

In modern systems, we *must* focus the bulk of our engineering attention and tooling on production systems, first and foremost. The leftover cycles of attention should be applied to staging and preproduction systems. There is value in staging systems. But it is secondary in nature.

Staging systems are not production. They can never replicate what is happening in production. The sterile lab environment of preproduction systems can never mimic the same conditions under which real paying users of your services will test that code in the real world. Yet many teams still treat production as a glass castle.

Engineering teams must reprioritize the value of production and change their practices accordingly. By not shifting production systems to their primary focus, these teams will be relegated to toiling away on production systems with subpar tooling, visibility, and observability. They will continue to treat production as a fragile environment where they hesitate to tread—instinctively and comfortably rolling back deployments at the slightest sight of potential issues—because they lack the controls to make small tweaks, tune settings, gently degrade services, or progressively deploy changes in response to problems they intimately understand.

The technological evolution toward modern systems also brings with it a social evolution that means engineering teams must change their relationship with production. Teams that do not change that relationship will more acutely suffer the pains of not doing so. The sooner that production is no longer a glass castle in modern systems, the sooner the lives of the teams responsible for those systems—and the experience of the customers using them—will improve.

Shifting Practices at Parse

At Parse, we had to undergo those changes rather painfully as we worked to quickly scale. But those changes didn't happen overnight. Our traditional practices were all we knew. Personally, I was following the well-known production system management path I had used at other companies many times before.

When novel problems happened, as with the Norwegian death-metal band, I would dive in and do a lot of investigation until the source of the problem was discovered. My team would run a retrospective to dissect the issue, write a runbook to instruct our future selves on how to deal with it, craft a custom dashboard (or two) that would surface that problem instantly next time, and then move on and consider the problem resolved.

That pattern works well for monoliths, where truly novel problems are rare. It worked well in the earliest days at Parse. But that pattern is completely ineffective for modern systems, where truly novel problems are likely to be the bulk of all the problems encountered. Once we started encountering a barrage of categorically different problems on a daily basis, the futility of that approach became undeniable. In that setting, all the time we spent on restrospectives, creating runbooks, and crafting custom dashboards was little more than wasted time. We would never see those same problems again.

The reality of this traditional approach is that so much of it involves guessing. In other systems, I had gotten so good at guessing what might be wrong that it felt almost effortless. I was intuitively in tune with my systems. I could eyeball a complex set of dashboards and confidently tell my team, "The problem is Redis," even though Redis was represented nowhere on that screen. I took pride in that sort of technical intuition. It was fun! I felt like a hero.

I want to underline this aspect of hero culture in the software industry. In monolithic systems, with LAMP-stack-style operations, the debugger of last resort is generally the person who has been there the longest, who built the system from scratch. The engineer with the most seniority is the ultimate point of escalation. They have the most scar tissue and the largest catalog of outages in their mental inventory, and they are the ones who inevitably swoop in to save the day.

As a result, these heroes also can never take a real vacation. I remember being on my honeymoon in Hawaii, getting paged at 3 a.m. because MongoDB had somehow taken down the Parse API service. My boss, the CTO, was overwhelmingly apologetic. But the site was down. It had been down for over an hour, and no one could figure out why. So they paged me. Yes, I complained. But also, deep down, it secretly felt great. I was *needed*. I was necessary.

If you've ever been on call to manage a production system, you might recognize that pattern. Hero culture is terrible. It's not good for the company. It's not good for the hero (it leads to savage burnout). It's horribly discouraging for every engineer who comes along later and feels they have no chance of ever being the "best" debugger unless a more senior engineer leaves. That pattern is completely unnecessary. But most important, it *doesn't scale*.

At Parse, to address our scaling challenges, we needed to reinvest the precious time we were effectively wasting by using old approaches to novel problems. So many of the tools that we had at that time—and that the software industry still relies on—were geared toward pattern matching. Specifically, they were geared toward helping the expert-level and experienced engineer pattern-match previously encountered problems to newer variants on the same theme. I never questioned that because it was the best technology and process we had.

After Facebook acquired Parse in 2013, I came to discover Scuba, the data management system Facebook uses for most real-time analysis. This fast, scalable, distributed, in-memory database ingests millions of rows (events) per second. It stores live data completely in memory and aggregates it across hundreds of servers when processing queries. My experience with it was rough. I thought Scuba had an aggressively ugly, even hostile, user experience. But it did one thing extremely well that permanently changed my approach to troubleshooting a system: it let me slice and dice data, in near real time, on dimensions of infinitely high cardinality.

We started sending some of our application telemetry data sets into Scuba and began experimenting with its analytical capabilities. The time that it took us to discover the source of novel problems dropped dramatically. Previously, with the traditional pattern-matching approach, it would take us days—or possibly never?—to understand what was happening. With real-time analytics that could be arbitrarily sliced and diced along any dimension of high cardinality, that time dropped to mere minutes—possibly seconds.

We could investigate a novel problem by starting with the symptoms and following a "trail of breadcrumbs" to the solution, no matter where it led, no matter whether it was the first time we had experienced that problem. We didn't have to be familiar with the problem in order to solve it. Instead, we now had an analytical and repeatable method for asking a question, getting answers, and using those answers to ask the next question until we got to the source. Troubleshooting issues in production meant starting with the data and relentlessly taking one methodical step after another until we arrived at a solution.

That newfound ability irrevocably shifted our practices. Rather than relying on intricate knowledge and a catalog of outages locked up in the mental inventory of individual engineers—inaccessible to their teammates—we now had data and a methodology that was visible and accessible by everyone in a shared tool. For the team, that meant we could follow each other's footsteps, retrace each other's paths, and understand what others were thinking. That ability freed us from the trap of relying on tools geared toward pattern matching.

With metrics and traditional monitoring tools, we could easily see performance spikes or notice that a problem might be occurring. But those tools didn't allow us to arbitrarily slice, dice, and dig our way down our stack to identify the source of problems or see correlations among errors that we had no other possible way of discovering. Those tools also required us to predict what data might be valuable in advance of investigating a novel problem (as if we knew which questions we would need to ask before the novel problem ever presented itself). Similarly, with logging tools, we had to remember to log anything useful in advance—and know exactly what to search for when that was relevant to the investigation. With our APM tools, we could quickly see problems that our tool vendor predicted would be the most useful to know, but that did very little when novel problems were the norm.

Once we made that paradigm shift, the best debugger was no longer the person who had been there the longest. The best debugger became whoever was the most curious, the most persistent, and the most literate with our new analytical tools. This effectively democratized access to our system and the shared wisdom of its engineers.

By approaching every problem as novel, we could determine what was truly happening anytime an issue arose in production instead of simply pattern-matching it to the nearest analogous previous problem. That made it possible to effectively troubleshoot systems that presented the biggest challenges with a traditional approach.

We could now quickly and effectively diagnose problems with the following:

- Microservices and requests that spanned multiple runtimes.
- Polyglot storage systems, without requiring expertise in each.
- Multitenancy and running both server-side code and queries; we could easily drill down into individual user experiences to see exactly what was happening.

Even with our few remaining monolithic systems that used boring technology, where all possible problems were pretty well understood, we still experienced some gains. We didn't necessarily discover anything new, but we were able to ship software more swiftly and confidently as a result.

At Parse, what allowed us to scale our approach was learning how to work with a system that was *observable*. By gathering application telemetry, at the right level of abstraction, aggregated around the user's experience, with the ability to analyze it in real time, we gained magical insights. We removed the limitations of our traditional tools once we had the capability to ask any question, trace any sequence of steps, and understand any internal system state, simply by observing the outputs of our applications. We were able to modernize our practices once we had *observability*.

Conclusion

This story, from my days at Parse, illustrates how and why organizations make a transition from traditional tools and monitoring approaches to scaling their practices with modern distributed systems and observability. I departed Facebook in 2015, shortly before it announced the impending shutdown of the Parse hosting service. Since then, many of the problems my team and I faced in managing modern distributed systems have only become more common as the software industry has shifted toward adopting similar technologies.

Liz, George, and I believe that shift accounts for the enthusiasm behind, and the rise in popularity of, observability. Observability is the solution to problems that have become prevalent when scaling modern systems. In further chapters, we'll explore the many facets, impacts, and benefits that observability delivers.

CHAPTER 4

How Observability Relates to DevOps, SRE, and Cloud Native

So far, we've referenced observability in the context of modern software systems. Therefore, it's important to unpack how observability fits into the landscape of other modern practices such as the DevOps, site reliability engineering (SRE), and cloud native movements. This chapter examines how these movements have both magnified the need for observability and integrated it into their practices.

Observability does not exist in a vacuum; instead, it is both a consequence and an integral part of the DevOps, SRE, and cloud native movements. Like testability, observability is a property of these systems that improves understanding of them. Observability and testability require continuous investment rather than being a one-time addition, or having a one-size-fits-all solution. As they improve, benefits accrue for you, as a developer, and for end users of your systems. By examining why these movements created a need for observability and integrated its use, you can better understand why observability has become a mainstream topic and why increasingly diverse teams are adopting this practice.

Cloud Native, DevOps, and SRE in a Nutshell

In contrast with the monolithic and waterfall development approaches that software delivery teams employed in the 1990s to early 2000s, modern software development and operations teams increasingly use cloud native and Agile methodologies. In particular, these methodologies enable teams to autonomously release features without tightly coupling their impact to other teams. Loose coupling unlocks several key business benefits, including higher productivity and better profitability. For example, the ability to resize individual service components upon demand and pool resources across a large number of virtual and physical servers means the business benefits from better cost controls and scalability.

For more examples of the benefits of Agile and cloud native methodologies, see the DevOps Research and Assessment (DORA) 2019 *Accelerate State of DevOps* Report (*https://oreil.ly/2Gqjz*) by Nicole Forsgren et al.

However, cloud native has significant trade-offs in complexity. An often overlooked aspect of introducing these capabilities is the management cost. Abstracted systems with dynamic controls introduce new challenges of emergent complexity and non-hierarchical communications patterns. Older monolithic systems had less emergent complexity, and thus simpler monitoring approaches sufficed; you could easily reason about what was happening inside those systems and where unseen problems might be occurring. Today, running cloud native systems feasibly at scale demands more advanced sociotechnical practices like continuous delivery and observability.

The Cloud Native Computing Foundation (CNCF) defines *cloud native* (*https://github.com/cncf/toc/blob/main/DEFINITION.md*) as "building and running scalable applications in modern, dynamic environments...[Cloud native] techniques enable loosely coupled systems that are *resilient, manageable,* and *observable.* Combined with robust automation, they allow engineers to *make high-impact changes frequently and predictably with minimal toil.*" By minimizing toil (repetitive manual human work) and emphasizing observability, cloud native systems empower developers to be creative. This definition focuses not just on scalability, but also on development velocity and operability as goals.

For a further look at what it means to eliminate toil, we recommend Chapter 5 of *Site Reliability Engineering* (*https://sre.google/sre-book/eliminating-toil*), edited by Betsy Beyer et al. (O'Reilly).

The shift to cloud native doesn't only require adopting a complete set of new technologies, but also changing how people work. That shift is inherently sociotechnical. On the surface, using the microservices toolchain itself has no explicit requirement to adopt new social practices. But to achieve the promised benefits of the technology, changing the work habits also becomes necessary. Although this should be evident from the stated definition and goals, teams typically get several steps in before realizing that their old work habits do not help them address the management costs introduced by this new technology. That is why successful adoption of cloud native design patterns is inexorably tied to the need for observable systems and for DevOps and SRE practices.

Similarly, DevOps and SRE both highlight a desire to shorten feedback loops and reduce operational toil in their definitions and practices. DevOps provides "Better Value, Sooner, Safer, and Happier"[1] through culture and collaboration between development and operations groups. SRE joins together systems engineering and software skill sets to solve complex operational problems through developing software systems rather than manual toil. As we'll explore in this chapter, the combination of cloud native technology, DevOps and SRE methodologies, and observability are stronger together than each of their individual parts.

Observability: Debugging Then Versus Now

The goal of observability is to provide a level of introspection that helps people reason about the internal state of their systems and applications. That state can be achieved in various ways. For example, you could employ a combination of logs, metrics, and traces as debugging signals. But the goal of observability itself is agnostic in terms of how it's accomplished.

In monolithic systems, you could anticipate the potential areas of failure and therefore could debug your systems by yourself and achieve appropriate observability by using verbose application logging, or coarse system-level metrics such as CPU/disk utilization combined with flashes of insight. However, these legacy tools and instinctual techniques no longer work for the new set of management challenges created by the opportunities of cloud native systems.

Among the example technologies that the cloud native definition mentions are containers, service meshes, microservices, and immutable infrastructure. Compared to legacy technologies like virtual machines and monolithic architectures, containerized microservices inherently introduce new problems such as cognitive complexity from interdependencies between components, transient state discarded after container restart, and incompatible versioning between separately released components. Immutable infrastructure means that it's no longer feasible to ssh into a host for debugging, as it may perturb the state on that host. Service meshes add an additional routing layer that provides a powerful way to collect information about how service calls are happening, but that data is of limited use unless you can analyze it later.

Debugging anomalous issues requires a new set of capabilities to help engineers detect and understand problems from *within* their systems. Tools such as distributed tracing can help capture the state of system internals when specific events occurred. By adding context in the form of many key-value pairs to each event, you will create a

---

1 Jonathan Smart, "Want to Do an Agile Transformation? Don't. Focus on Flow, Quality, Happiness, Safety, and Value" (*https://oreil.ly/KQEy9*), July 21, 2018.

wide, rich view of what is happening in all the parts of your system that are typically hidden and impossible to reason about.

For example, in a distributed, cloud native system, you may find it difficult to debug an issue occurring across multiple hosts by using logs or other noncorrelated signals. But by utilizing a combination of signals, you could systematically drill down into anomalous behavior starting from the high level of your service metrics, iterating until you discover which hosts are most relevant. Sharding logs by host means you no longer need centralized retention and indexing of all logs as you would for a monolith. To understand the relationships among subcomponents and services in a monolith or distributed system, you previously may have needed to keep the relationships of all system components in your head.

Instead, if you can use distributed tracing to break down and visualize each individual step, you need to understand the complexity of your dependencies only as they impact execution of a specific request. Understanding which calling and receiving code paths are associated with which versions of each service allows you to find reverse compatibility problems and any changes that broke compatibility.

Observability provides a shared context that enables teams to debug problems in a cohesive and rational way, regardless of a system's complexity, rather than requiring one person's mind to retain the entire state of the system.

Observability Empowers DevOps and SRE Practices

It's the job of DevOps and SRE teams to understand production systems and tame complexity. So it's natural for them to care about the observability of the systems they build and run. SRE focuses on managing services according to service level objectives (SLOs) and error budgets (see Chapters 12 and 13). DevOps focuses on managing services through cross-functional practices, with developers maintaining responsibility for their code in production. Rather than starting with a plethora of alerts that enumerate potential causes of outages, mature DevOps and SRE teams both measure any visible symptoms of user pain and then drill down into understanding the outage by using observability tooling.

The shift away from cause-based monitoring and toward symptom-based monitoring means that you need the ability to explain the failures you see in practice, instead of the traditional approach of enumerating a growing list of known failure modes. Rather than burning a majority of their time responding to a slew of false alarms that have no bearing on the end-user visible performance, teams can focus on systematically winnowing hypotheses and devising mitigations for actual system failures. We cover this in greater detail in Chapter 12.

Beyond the adoption of observability for break/fix use cases, forward-thinking DevOps and SRE teams use engineering techniques such as feature flagging, continuous verification, and incident analysis. Observability supercharges these use cases by providing the data required to effectively practice them. Let's explore how observability empowers each:

Chaos engineering and continuous verification
> These require you to have observability to "detect when the system is normal and how it deviates from that steady-state as the experiment's method is executed."[2] You cannot meaningfully perform chaos experiments without the ability to understand the system's baseline state, to predict expected behavior under test, and to explain deviations from expected behavior. "There is no point in doing chaos engineering when you actually don't know how your system is behaving at your current state before you inject chaos."[3]

Feature flagging
> This introduces novel combinations of flag states in production that you cannot test exhaustively in preproduction environments. Therefore, you need observability to understand the individual and collective impact of each feature flag, user by user. The notion of monitoring behavior component by component no longer holds when an endpoint can execute in multiple ways depending on which user is calling it and which feature flags are enabled.

Progressive release patterns
> These patterns, such as canarying and blue/green deployment, require observability to effectively know when to stop the release and to analyze whether the system's deviations from the expected are a result of the release.

Incident analysis and blameless postmortem
> These require you to construct clear models about your sociotechnical systems— not just what was happening inside the technical system at fault, but also what the human operators *believed* was happening during the incident. Thus, robust observability tooling facilitates performing excellent retrospectives by providing an ex post facto paper trail and details to cue retrospective writers.

---

2 Russ Miles, *Chaos Engineering Observability* (Sebastopol, CA: O'Reilly, 2019).

3 Ana Medina, "Chaos Engineering with Ana Medina of Gremlin" (*https://oreil.ly/KdUW9*), *o11ycast* podcast, August 15, 2019.

Conclusion

As the practices of DevOps and SRE continue to evolve, and as platform engineering grows as an umbrella discipline, more innovative engineering practices will inevitably emerge in your toolchains. But all of those innovations will depend upon having observability as a core sense to understand your modern complex systems. The shift toward DevOps, SRE, and cloud native practices have created a need for a solution like observability. In turn, observability has also supercharged the capabilities of teams that have adopted its practice.

PART II

Fundamentals of Observability

In the first part of this book, we examined the definition of "observability," its necessity in modern systems, its evolution from traditional practices, and the way it is currently being used in practice. This second section delves deeper into technical aspects and details why particular requirements are necessary in observable systems.

Chapter 5 introduces the basic data type necessary to build an observable system—the arbitrarily wide structured event. It is this fundamental data type for telemetry that makes the analysis described later in this part possible.

Chapter 6 introduces distributed tracing concepts. It breaks down how tracing systems work in order to illustrate that trace data is simply a series of interrelated arbitrarily wide structured events. This chapter walks you through manually creating a minimal trace with code examples.

Chapter 7 introduces the OpenTelemetry project. While the manual code examples in Chapter 6 help illustrate the concept, you would more than likely start with an instrumentation library. Rather than choosing a proprietary library or agent that locks you into one vendor's particular solution, we recommend starting with an open source and vendor-neutral instrumentation framework that allows you to easily switch between observability tools of your choice.

Chapter 8 introduces the core analysis loop. Generating and collecting telemetry data is only a first step. Analyzing that data is what helps you achieve observability. This chapter introduces the workflow required to sift through your telemetry data in order to surface relevant patterns and quickly locate the source of issues. It also covers approaches for automating the core analysis loop.

Chapter 9 reintroduces the role of metrics as a data type, and where and when to best use metrics-based traditional monitoring approaches. This chapter also shows how traditional monitoring practices can coexist with observability practices.

This part focuses on technical requirements in relation to the workflow necessary to shift toward observability-based debugging practices. In Part III, we'll examine how those individual practices impact team dynamics and how to tackle adoption challenges.

CHAPTER 5

Structured Events Are the Building Blocks of Observability

In this chapter, we examine the fundamental building block of observability: the structured event. Observability is a measure of how well you can understand and explain any state your system can get into, no matter how novel or bizarre. To do that, you must be able to get answers to any question you can ask, without anticipating or predicting a need to answer that question in advance. For that to be possible, several technical prerequisites must first be met.

Throughout this book, we address the many technical prerequisites necessary for observability. In this chapter, we start with the telemetry needed to understand and explain any state your system may be in. Asking *any* question, about any combination of telemetry details, requires the ability to arbitrarily slice and dice data along any number of dimensions. It also requires that your telemetry be gathered in full resolution, down to the lowest logical level of granularity that also retains the context in which it was gathered. For observability, that means gathering telemetry at the per service or per request level.

With old-fashioned-style metrics, you had to define custom metrics up front if you wanted to ask a new question and gather new telemetry to answer it. In a metrics world, the way to get answers to any possible question is to gather and store every possible metric—which is simply impossible (and, even if it were possible, prohibitively expensive). Further, metrics do not retain the context of the event, simply an aggregate measurement of what occurred at a particular time. With that aggregate view, you could not ask new questions or look for new outliers in the existing data set.

With observability, you can ask new questions of your existing telemetry data at any time, without needing to first predict what those questions might be. In an observable system, you must be able to iteratively explore system aspects ranging from high-level aggregate performance all the way down to the raw data used in individual requests.

The technical requirement making that possible starts with the data format needed for observability: the arbitrarily wide structured event. Collecting these events is not optional. It is not an implementation detail. It is a requirement that makes any level of analysis possible within that wide-ranging view.

Debugging with Structured Events

First, let's start by defining an event. For the purpose of understanding the impact to your production services, an *event* is a record of everything that occurred while one particular request interacted with your service.

To create that record, you start by initializing an empty map right at the beginning, when the request first enters your service. During the lifetime of that request, any interesting details about what occurred—unique IDs, variable values, headers, every parameter passed by the request, the execution time, any calls made to remote services, the execution time of those remote calls, or any other bit of context that may later be valuable in debugging—get appended to that map. Then, when the request is about to exit or error, that entire map is captured as a rich record of what just happened. The data written to that map is organized and formatted, as key-value pairs, so that it's easily searchable: in other words, the data should be structured. That's a *structured event*.

As you debug problems in your service, you will compare structured events to one another to find anomalies. When some events behave significantly differently from others, you will then work to identify what those outliers have in common. Exploring those outliers requires filtering and grouping by different dimensions—and combinations of dimensions—contained within those events that might be relevant to your investigation.

The data that you feed into your observability system as structured events needs to capture the right level of abstraction to help observers determine the state of your applications, no matter how bizarre or novel. Information that is helpful for investigators may have runtime information not specific to any given request (such as container information or versioning information), as well as information about each request that passes through the service (such as shopping cart ID, user ID, or session token). Both types of data are useful for debugging.

The sort of data that is relevant to debugging a request will vary, but it helps to think about that by comparing the type of data that would be useful when using a conventional debugger. For example, in that setting, you might want to know the values of variables during the execution of the request and to understand when function calls are happening. With distributed services, those function calls may happen as multiple calls to remote services. In that setting, any data about the values of variables during request execution can be thought of as the *context* of the request.

All of that data should be accessible for debugging and stored in your events. They are *arbitrarily wide events*, because the debugging data you need may encompass a significant number of fields. There should be no practical limit to the details you can attach to your events. We'll delve further into the types of information that should be captured in structured events, but first let's compare how capturing system state with structured events differs from traditional debugging methods.

The Limitations of Metrics as a Building Block

First, let's define *metrics*. Unfortunately, this term requires disambiguation because often it is used as a generic synonym for "telemetry" (e.g., "all of our metrics are up and to the right, boss!"). For clarity, when we refer to metrics, we mean the scalar values collected to represent system state, with tags optionally appended for grouping and searching those numbers. Metrics are the staple upon which traditional monitoring of software systems has been built (refer to Chapter 1 for a more detailed look at the origin of metrics in this sense).

However, the fundamental limitation of a metric is that it is a pre-aggregated measure. The numerical values generated by a metric reflect an aggregated report of system state over a predefined period of time. When that number is reported to a monitoring system, that pre-aggregated measure now becomes the lowest possible level of granularity for examining system state. That aggregation obscures many possible problems. Further, a request into your service may be represented by having a part in hundreds of metrics over the course of its execution. Those metrics are all distinct measures—disconnected from one another—that lack the sort of connective tissue and granularity necessary to reconstruct exactly which metrics belong to the same request.

For example, a metric for `page_load_time` might examine the average time it took for all active pages to load during the trailing five-second period. Another metric for `requests_per_second` might examine the number of HTTP connections any given service had open during the trailing one-second period. Metrics reflect system state, as expressed by numerical values derived by measuring any given property over a given period of time. The behavior of all requests that were active during that period are aggregated into one numerical value. In this example, investigating what occurred during the lifespan of any one particular request flowing through that system would provide a trail of breadcrumbs that leads to both of these metrics. However, the level of available granularity necessary to dig further is unavailable.

Delving into how metrics are stored in TSDBs is beyond the scope of this chapter, but it is partially addressed in Chapter 16. For a more in-depth look at how metrics and TSDBs are incompatible with observability, we recommend Alex Vondrak's 2021 blog post, "How Time Series Databases Work—and Where They Don't" (*https://hny.co/blog/time-series-database*).

In an event-based approach, a web server request could be instrumented to record each parameter (or dimension) submitted with the request (for example, `userid`), the intended subdomain (`www`, `docs`, `support`, `shop`, `cdn`, etc.), total duration time, any dependent child requests, the various services involved (`web`, `database`, `auth`, `billing`) to fulfill those child requests, the duration of each child request, and more. Those events can then be arbitrarily sliced and diced across various dimensions, across any window of time, to present any view relevant to an investigation.

In contrast to metrics, events are snapshots of what happened at a particular point in time. One thousand discrete events may have occurred within that same trailing five-second period in the preceding example. If each event recorded its own `page_load_time`, when aggregated along with the other 999 events that happened in that same five-second period, you could still display the same average value as shown by the metric. Additionally, with the granularity provided by events, an investigator could also compute that same average over a one-second period, or subdivide queries by fields like user ID or hostname to find correlations with `page_load_time` in ways that simply aren't possible when using the aggregated value provided by metrics.

An extreme counterargument to this analysis could be that, given enough metrics, the granularity needed to see system state on the level of individual requests could be achieved. Putting aside the wildly impractical nature of that approach, ignoring that concurrency could never completely be accounted for, and that investigators would still be required to stitch together which metrics were generated along the path of a request's execution, the fact remains that metrics-based monitoring systems are simply not designed to scale to the degree necessary to capture those measures. Regardless, many teams relying on metrics for debugging find themselves in an escalating arms race of continuously adding more and more metrics in an attempt to do just that.

As aggregate numerical representations of predefined relationships over predefined periods of time, metrics serve as only one narrow view of one system property. Their granularity is too large and their ability to present system state in alternate views is too rigid to achieve observability. Metrics are too limiting to serve as the fundamental building block of observability.

The Limitations of Traditional Logs as a Building Block

As seen earlier, structured data is clearly defined and searchable. Unstructured data isn't organized in an easily searchable manner and is usually stored in its native format. When it comes to debugging production software systems, the most prevalent use of unstructured data is from a construct older than metrics. Let's examine the use of logs.

Before jumping into this section, we should note that it is modern logging practice to use structured logs. But just in case you haven't transitioned to using structured logs, let's start with a look at what unstructured logs are and how to make them more useful.

Unstructured Logs

Log files are essentially large blobs of unstructured text, designed to be readable by humans but difficult for machines to process. These files are documents generated by applications and various underlying infrastructure systems that contain a record of all notable events—as defined by a configuration file somewhere—that have occurred. For decades, they have been an essential part of system debugging applications in any environment. Logs typically contain tons of useful information: a description of the event that happened, an associated timestamp, a severity-level type associated with that event, and a variety of other relevant metadata (user ID, IP address, etc.).

Traditional logs are *unstructured* because they were designed to be human readable. Unfortunately, for purposes of human readability, logs often separate the vivid details of one event into multiple lines of text, like so:

```
6:01:00 accepted connection on port 80 from 10.0.0.3:63349
6:01:03 basic authentication accepted for user foo
6:01:15 processing request for /super/slow/server
6:01:18 request succeeded, sent response code 200
6:01:19 closed connection to 10.0.0.3:63349
```

While that sort of narrative structure can be helpful when first learning the intricacies of a service in development, it generates huge volumes of noisy data that becomes slow and clunky in production. In production, these chunks of narrative are often interspersed throughout millions upon millions of other lines of text. Typically, they're useful in the course of debugging once a cause is already suspected and an investigator is verifying their hypothesis by digging through logs for verification.

However, modern systems no longer run at an easily comprehensible human scale. In traditional monolithic systems, human operators had a very small number of services to manage. Logs were written to the local disk of the machines where applications ran. In the modern era, logs are often streamed to a centralized aggregator, where they're dumped into very large storage backends.

Searching through millions of lines of unstructured logs can be accomplished by using some type of log file parser. *Parsers* split log data into chunks of information and attempt to group them in meaningful ways. However, with unstructured data, parsing gets complicated because different formatting rules (or no rules at all) exist for different types of log files. Logging tools are full of different approaches to solving this problem, with varying degrees of success, performance, and usability.

Structured Logs

The solution is to instead create *structured* log data designed for machine parsability. From the preceding example, a structured version might instead look something like this:

```
time="6:01:00" msg="accepted connection" port="80" authority="10.0.0.3:63349"
time="6:01:03" msg="basic authentication accepted" user="foo"
time="6:01:15" msg="processing request" path="/super/slow/server"
time="6:01:18" msg="sent response code" status="200"
time="6:01:19" msg="closed connection" authority="10.0.0.3:63349"
```

Many logs are only portions of events, regardless of whether those logs are structured. When connecting observability approaches to logging, it helps to think of an event as a unit of work within your systems. A structured event should contain information about what it took for a service to perform a unit of work. A *unit of work* can be seen as somewhat relative. For example, a unit of work could be downloading a single file, parsing it, and extracting specific pieces of information. Yet other times, it could mean processing an answer after extracting specific pieces of information from dozens of files. In the context of services, a unit of work could be accepting an HTTP request and doing everything necessary to return a response. Yet other times, one HTTP request can generate many other events during its execution.

Ideally, a structured event should be scoped to contain everything about what it took to perform that unit of work. It should record the input necessary to perform the work, any attributes gathered—whether computed, resolved, or discovered—along the way, the conditions of the service as it was performing the work, and details about the result of the work performed.

It's common to see anywhere from a few to a few dozen log lines or entries that, when taken together, represent what could be considered one unit of work. So far, the example we've been using does just that: one unit of work (the handling of one connection) is represented by five separate log entries. Rather than being helpfully grouped into one event, the messages are spread out into many messages. Sometimes, a common field—like a request ID—might be present in each entry so that the separate entries can be stitched together. But typically there won't be.

The log lines in our example could instead be rolled up into one singular event. Doing so would make it look like this:

```
time="2019-08-22T11:56:11-07:00" level=info msg="Served HTTP request"
authority="10.0.0.3:63349" duration_ms=123 path="/super/slow/server" port=80
service_name="slowsvc" status=200 trace.trace_id=eafdf3123 user=foo
```

That representation can be formatted in different ways, including JavaScript Object Notation (JSON). Most commonly, this type of event information could appear as a JSON object, like so:

```
{
"authority":"10.0.0.3:63349",
"duration_ms":123,
"level":"info",
"msg":"Served HTTP request",
"path":"/super/slow/server",
"port":80,
"service_name":"slowsvc",
"status":200,
"time":"2019-08-22T11:57:03-07:00",
"trace.trace_id":"eafdf3123",
"user":"foo"
}
```

The goal of observability is to enable you to interrogate your event data in arbitrary ways to understand the internal state of your systems. Any data used to do so must be machine-parsable in order to facilitate that goal. Unstructured data is simply unusable for that task. Log data can, however, be useful when redesigned to resemble a structured event, the fundamental building block of observability.

Properties of Events That Are Useful in Debugging

Earlier in this chapter, we defined a structured event as a record of everything that occurred while one particular request interacted with your service. When debugging modern distributed systems, that is approximately the right scope for a unit of work. To create a system where an observer can understand any state of the system—no matter how novel or complex—an event must contain ample information that may be relevant to an investigation.

The backend data store for an observable system must allow your events to be arbitrarily wide. When using structured events to understand service behavior, remember that the model is to initialize an empty blob and record anything that may be relevant for later debugging. That can mean pre-populating the blob with data known as the request enters your service: request parameters, environmental information, runtime internals, host/container statistics, etc. As the request is executing, other valuable information may be discovered: user ID, shopping cart ID, other remote services to be called to render a result, or any various bits of information that may help you find and identify this request in the future. As the request exits your service, or returns an error, there are several bits of data about how the unit of work was performed: duration, response code, error messages, etc. It is common for events generated with mature instrumentation to contain 300 to 400 dimensions per event.

Debugging novel problems typically means discovering previously unknown failure modes (*unknown-unknowns*) by searching for events with outlying conditions and finding patterns or correlating them. For example, if a spike of errors occurs, you may need to slice across various event dimensions to find out what they all have in common. To make those correlations, your observability solution will need the ability to handle fields with high cardinality.

 Cardinality refers to the number of unique elements in a set, as you remember from Chapter 1. Some dimensions in your events will have very low or very high cardinality. Any dimension containing unique identifiers will have the highest possible cardinality. Refer back to "The Role of Cardinality" on page 13 for more on this topic.

An observability tool must be able to support high-cardinality queries to be useful to an investigator. In modern systems, many of the dimensions that are most useful for debugging novel problems have high cardinality. Investigation also often requires stringing those high-cardinality dimensions together (i.e., high dimensionality) to find deeply hidden problems. Debugging problems is often like trying to find a needle in a haystack. High cardinality and high dimensionality are the capabilities that enable you to find very fine-grained needles in deeply complex distributed system haystacks.

For example, to get to the source of an issue, you may need to create a query that finds "all Canadian users, running iOS11 version 11.0.4, using the French language pack, who installed the app last Tuesday, running firmware version 1.4.101, who are storing photos on shard3 in region us-west-1." Every single one of those constraints is a high-cardinality dimension.

As mentioned earlier, to enable that functionality, events must be *arbitrarily wide*: fields within an event cannot be limited to known or predictable fields. Limiting ingestible events to containing known fields may be an artificial constraint imposed by the backend storage system used by a particular analysis tool. For example, some backend data stores may require predefining data schemas. Predefining a schema requires that users of the tool be able to predict, in advance, which dimensions may need to be captured. Using schemas or other strict limitations on data types, or shapes, are also orthogonal to the goals of observability (see Chapter 16).

Conclusion

The fundamental building block of observability is the arbitrarily wide structured event. Observability requires the ability to slice and dice data along any number of dimensions, in order to answer any question when iteratively stepping your way through a debugging process. Structured events must be arbitrarily wide because they need to contain sufficient data to enable investigators to understand everything that was happening when a system accomplished one unit of work. For distributed services, that typically means scoping an event as the record of everything that happened during the lifetime of one individual service request.

Metrics aggregate system state over a predefined period of time. They serve as only one narrow view of one system property. Their granularity is too large, and their ability to present system state in alternate views is too rigid, to stitch them together to represent one unit of work for any particular service request. Metrics are too limiting to serve as the fundamental building block of observability.

Unstructured logs are human readable but computationally difficult to use. Structured logs are machine parsable and can be useful for the goals of observability, presuming they are redesigned to resemble a structured event.

For now, we'll simply concentrate on the data type necessary for telemetry. In the next few chapters, we'll more closely examine why analyzing high-cardinality and high-dimensionality data is important. We will also further define the necessary capabilities for a tool to enable observability. Next, let's start by looking at how structured events can be stitched together to create traces.

CHAPTER 6

Stitching Events into Traces

In the previous chapter, we explored why events are the fundamental building blocks of an observable system. This chapter examines how you can stitch events together into a trace. Within the last decade, distributed tracing has become an indispensable troubleshooting tool for software engineering teams.

Distributed traces are simply an interrelated series of events. Distributed tracing systems provide packaged libraries that "automagically" create and manage the work of tracking those relationships. The concepts used to create and track the relationships between discrete events can be applied far beyond traditional tracing use cases. To further explore what's possible with observable systems, we must first explore the inner workings of tracing systems.

In this chapter, we demystify distributed tracing by examining its core components and why they are so useful for observable systems. We explain the components of a trace and use code examples to illustrate the steps necessary to assemble a trace by hand and how those components work. We present examples of adding relevant data to a trace event (or span) and why you may want that data. Finally, after showing you how a trace is assembled manually, we'll apply those same techniques to nontraditional tracing use cases (like stitching together log events) that are possible with observable systems.

Distributed Tracing and Why It Matters Now

Tracing is a fundamental software debugging technique wherein various bits of information are logged throughout a program's execution for the purpose of diagnosing problems. Since the very first day that two computers were linked together to exchange information, software engineers have been discovering the gremlins lurking within our programs and protocols. Those issues in the seams persist despite our best efforts, and in an age when distributed systems are the norm, the debugging techniques we use must adapt to meet more complex needs.

Distributed tracing is a method of tracking the progression of a single request—called a *trace*—as it is handled by various services that make up an application. Tracing in this sense is "distributed" because in order to fulfill its functions, a singular request must often traverse process, machine, and network boundaries. The popularity of microservice architectures has led to a sharp increase in debugging techniques that pinpoint where failures occur along that route and what might be contributing to poor performance. But anytime a request traverses boundaries—such as from on-premises to cloud infrastructure, or from infrastructure you control to SaaS services you don't, and back again—distributed tracing can be incredibly useful to diagnose problems, optimize code, and build more reliable services.

The rise in popularity of distributed tracing also means that several approaches and competing standards for accomplishing that task have emerged. Distributed tracing first gained mainstream traction after Google's publication of the Dapper paper (*https://ai.google/research/pubs/pub36356*) by Ben Sigelman et al. in 2010. Two notable open source tracing projects emerged shortly after: Twitter's Zipkin in 2012 (*https://zipkin.io*) and Uber's Jaeger in 2017 (*https://eng.uber.com/distributed-tracing*), in addition to several commercially available solutions such as Honeycomb (*https://hny.co*) or Lightstep (*https://lightstep.com*).

Despite the implementation differences in these tracing projects, the core methodology and the value they provide are the same. As explored in Part I, modern distributed systems have a tendency to scale into a tangled knot of dependencies. Distributed tracing is valuable because it clearly shows the relationships among various services and components in a distributed system.

Traces help you understand system interdependencies. Those interdependencies can obscure problems and make them particularly difficult to debug unless the relationships between them are clearly understood. For example, if a downstream database service experiences performance bottlenecks, that latency can cumulatively stack up. By the time that latency is detected three or four layers upstream, identifying which component of the system is the root of the problem can be incredibly difficult because now that same latency is being seen in dozens of other services.

In an observable system, a trace is simply a series of interconnected events. To understand how traces relate to the fundamental building blocks of observability, let's start by looking at how traces are assembled.

The Components of Tracing

To understand the mechanics of how tracing works in practice, we'll use an example to illustrate the various components needed to collect the data necessary for a trace. First, we'll consider the outcome we want from a trace: to clearly see relationships among various services. Then we'll look at how we might modify our existing code to get that outcome.

To quickly understand where bottlenecks may be occurring, it's useful to have waterfall-style visualizations of a trace, as shown in Figure 6-1. Each stage of a request is displayed as an individual chunk in relation to the start time and duration of a request being debugged.

 Waterfall visualizations (*https://w.wiki/56wd*) show how an initial value is affected by a series of intermediate values, leading to a final cumulative value.

service_name	name	1s	17.21s	34.43s	51.64s	68.85s	86.06s
3 saas-update	start	86.063s					
67 saas-update	UpdateIntercom	20.389s					
9K+ saas-update	UpdateSalesforce			64.097s			
31 saas-update	UpdateStripe						1.576s

Figure 6-1. This waterfall-style trace visualization displays four trace spans during one request

Each chunk of this waterfall is called a *trace span*, or *span* for short. Within any given trace, spans are either the *root span*—the top-level span in that trace—or are nested within the root span. Spans nested within the root span may also have nested spans of their own. That relationship is sometimes referred to as *parent-child*. For example, in Figure 6-2, if Service A calls Service B, which calls Service C, then for that trace, Span A is the parent of Span B, which is in turn the parent of Span C.

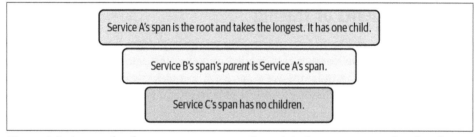

Figure 6-2. A trace that has two parent spans. Span A is the root span and is also the parent of Span B. Span B is a child of Span A and also the parent of Span C. Span C is a child of Span B and has no child spans of its own.

Note that a service might be called and appear multiple times within a trace as separate spans, such as in the case of circular dependencies or intense calculations broken into parallel functions within the same service hop. In practice, requests often traverse messy and unpredictable paths through a distributed system. To construct the view we want for any path taken, no matter how complex, we need five pieces of data for each component:

Trace ID
    We need a unique identifier for the trace we're about to create so that we can map it back to a particular request. This ID is created by the root span and propagated throughout each step taken to fulfill the request.

Span ID
    We also need a unique identifier for each individual span created. Spans contain information captured while a unit of work occurred during a single trace. The unique ID allows us to refer to this span whenever we need it.

Parent ID
    This field is used to properly define nesting relationships throughout the life of the trace. A Parent ID is absent in the root span (that's how we know it's the root).

Timestamp
    Each span must indicate when its work began.

Duration
    Each span must also record how long that work took to finish.

Those fields are absolutely required in order to assemble the structure of a trace. However, you will likely find a few other fields helpful when identifying these spans or how they relate to your system. Any additional data added to a span is essentially a series of tags.

These are some examples:

Service Name
> For investigative purposes, you'll want to indicate the name of the service where this work occurred.

Span Name
> To understand the relevancy of each step, it's helpful to give each span a name that identifies or differentiates the work that was being done—e.g., names could be `intense_computation1` and `intense_computation2` if they represent different work streams within the same service or network hop.

With that data, we should be able to construct the type of waterfall visualization we want for any request in order to quickly diagnose any issues. Next, let's look at how we would instrument our code to generate that data.

Instrumenting a Trace the Hard Way

To understand how the core components of a trace come together, we'll create a manual example of an overly simple tracing system. In any distributed tracing system, quite a bit more information is being added to traces to make the data more usable. For example, you may wish to enrich a trace with additional metadata prior to sending it to a backend data store (see Chapter 16).

> *If you wish to make an apple pie from scratch, you must first invent the universe.*
> —Carl Sagan

For illustration purposes, we'll presume that a backend for collection of this data already exists and will focus on just the client-side instrumentation necessary for tracing. We'll also presume that we can send data to that system via HTTP.

Let's say that we have a simple web endpoint. For quick illustrative purposes, we will create this example with Go as our language. When we issue a GET request, it makes calls to two other services to retrieve data based on the payload of the request (such as whether the user is authorized to access the given endpoint) and then it returns the results:

```
func rootHandler(r *http.Request, w http.ResponseWriter) {
    authorized := callAuthService(r)
    name := callNameService(r)

    if authorized {
        w.Write([]byte(fmt.Sprintf(`{"message": "Waddup %s"}`, name)))
    } else {
        w.Write([]byte(`{"message": "Not cool dawg"}`))
    }
}
```

The main purpose of distributed tracing is to follow a request as it traverses multiple services. In this example, because this request makes calls to two other services, we would expect to see a minimum of three spans when making this request:

- The originating request to `rootHandler`
- The call to our authorization service (to authenticate the request)
- The call to our name service (to get the user's name)

First, let's generate a unique *trace ID* so we can group any subsequent spans back to the originating request. We'll use UUIDs (*https://w.wiki/8G6*) to avoid any data duplication issues and store the attributes and data for this span in a map (we could then later serialize that data as JSON to send it to our data backend). We'll also generate a *span ID* that can be used as an identifier for relating different spans in the same trace together:

```
func rootHandler(...) {
    traceData := make(map[string]interface{})
    traceData["trace_id"] = uuid.String()
    traceData["span_id"] = uuid.String()

    // ... main work of request ...
}
```

Now that we have IDs that can be used to string our requests together, we'll also want to know when this span started and how long it took to execute. We do that by capturing a *timestamp*, both when the request starts and when it ends. Noting the difference between those two timestamps, we will calculate *duration* in milliseconds:

```
func rootHandler(...) {
    // ... trace id setup from above ...

    startTime := time.Now()
    traceData["timestamp"] = startTime.Unix()

    // ... main work of request ...

    traceData["duration_ms"] = time.Now().Sub(startTime)
}
```

Finally, we'll add two descriptive fields: `service_name` indicates which service the work occurred in, and span `name` indicates the type of work we did. Additionally, we'll set up this portion of our code to send all of this data to our tracing backend via a remote procedure call (RPC) once it's all complete:

```
func loginHandler(...) {
    // ... trace id and duration setup from above ...

    traceData["name"] = "/oauth2/login"
    traceData["service_name"] = "authentication_svc"
```

```
    // ... main work of request ...

    sendSpan(traceData)
}
```

We have the portions of data we need for this one singular trace span. However, we don't yet have a way to relay any of this trace data to the other services that we're calling as part of our request. At the very least, we need to know which span this is within our trace, which parent this span belongs to, and that data should be propagated throughout the life of the request.

The most common way that information is shared in distributed tracing systems is by setting it in HTTP headers on outbound requests. In our example, we could expand our helper functions `callAuthService` and `callNameService` to accept the `traceData` map and use it to set special HTTP headers on their outbound requests.

You could call those headers anything you want, as long as the programs on the receiving end understand those same names. Typically, HTTP headers follow a particular standard, such as those of the World Wide Web Consortium (W3C (*https:// www.w3.org/TR/trace-context*)) or B3 (*https://github.com/openzipkin/b3-propagation*). For our example, we'll use the B3 standard. We would need to send the following headers (as in Figure 6-3) to ensure that child spans are able to build and send their spans correctly:

X-B3-TraceId
    Contains the trace ID for the entire trace (from the preceding example)

X-B3-ParentSpanId
    Contains the current span ID, which will be set as the parent ID in the child's generated span

Now let's ensure that those headers are sent in our outbound HTTP request:

```
func callAuthService(req *http.Request, traceData map[string]interface{}) {
    aReq, _ = http.NewRequest("GET", "http://authz/check_user", nil)
    aReq.Header.Set("X-B3-TraceId", traceData["trace.trace_id"])
    aReq.Header.Set("X-B3-ParentSpanId", traceData["trace.span_id"])

    // ... make the request ...
}
```

We would also make a similar change to our `callNameService` function. With that, when each service is called, it can pull the information from these headers and add them to `trace_id` and `parent_id` in their own generation of `traceData`. Each of those services would also send their generated spans to the tracing backend. On the backend, those traces are stitched together to create the waterfall-type visualization we want to see.

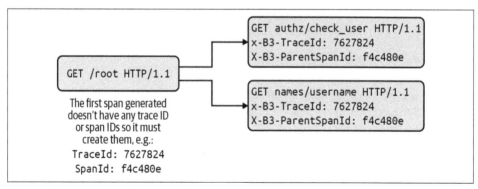

Figure 6-3. Our example app would now propagate `traceID` *and* `parentID` *to each child span*

Now that you've seen what goes into instrumenting and creating a useful trace view, let's see what else we might want to add to our spans to make them more useful for debugging.

Adding Custom Fields into Trace Spans

Understanding parent-child relationships and execution duration is a good start. But you may want to add other fields in addition to the necessary trace data to better understand what's happening in each span whose operation is typically buried deeply within your distributed systems.

For example, in addition to storing the service name for ease of identification , it might be useful to know the exact host on which the work was executed and whether it was related to a particular user. Let's modify our example to capture those details as part of our trace span by adding them as key-value pairs:

```
hostname, _ := os.Hostname()
traceData["tags"] = make(map[string]interface{})
traceData["tags"]["hostname"] = hostname
traceData["tags"]["user_name"] = name
```

You could further extend this example to capture any other system information you might find relevant for debugging such as the application's `build_id`, `instance_type`, information about your runtime, or any plethora of details like any of the examples in Chapter 5. For now, we'll keep it simple.

Putting this all together, our full example app that creates a trace from scratch would look something like this (the code is repetitive and verbose for clarity):

```
func rootHandler(r *http.Request, w http.ResponseWriter) {

    traceData := make(map[string]interface{})
    traceData["tags"] = make(map[string]interface{})
```

```
        hostname, _ := os.Hostname()
        traceData["tags"]["hostname"] = hostname
        traceData["tags"]["user_name"] = name

        startTime := time.Now()
        traceData["timestamp"] = startTime.Unix()
        traceData["trace_id"] = uuid.String()
        traceData["span_id"] = uuid.String()
        traceData["name"] = "/oauth2/login"
        traceData["service_name"] = "authentication_svc"

        func callAuthService(req *http.Request, traceData map[string]interface{}) {
            aReq, _ = http.NewRequest("GET", "http://authz/check_user", nil)
            aReq.Header.Set("X-B3-TraceId", traceData["trace.trace_id"])
            aReq.Header.Set("X-B3-ParentSpanId", traceData["trace.span_id"])

            // ... make the auth request ...
        }

        func callNameService(req *http.Request, traceData map[string]interface{}) {
            nReq, _ = http.NewRequest("GET", "http://authz/check_user", nil)
            nReq.Header.Set("X-B3-TraceId", traceData["trace.trace_id"])
            nReq.Header.Set("X-B3-ParentSpanId", traceData["trace.span_id"])

            // ... make the name request ...
        }

        authorized := callAuthService(r)
        name := callNameService(r)

        if authorized {
            w.Write([]byte(fmt.Sprintf(`{"message": "Waddup %s"}`, name)))
        } else {
            w.Write([]byte(`{"message": "Not cool dawg"}`))
        }

        traceData["duration_ms"] = time.Now().Sub(startTime)
        sendSpan(traceData)
    }
```

The code examples used in this section are a bit contrived to illustrate how these concepts come together in practice. The good news is that you would typically not have to generate all of this code yourself. Distributed tracing systems commonly have their own supporting libraries to do most of this boilerplate setup work.

These shared libraries are typically unique to the particular needs of the tracing solution you wish to use. Unfortunately, vendor-specific solutions do not work well with other tracing solutions, meaning that you have to re-instrument your code if you want to try a different solution. In the next chapter, we'll look at the open source

OpenTelemetry project and how it enables you to instrument only once and use a wide variety of solutions.

Now that you have a complete view of what goes into instrumenting and creating useful trace views, let's apply that to what you learned in the preceding chapter to understand why tracing is such a key element in observable systems.

Stitching Events into Traces

In Chapter 5, we examined the use of structured events as the building blocks of an observable system. We defined an *event* as a record of everything that occurred while one particular request interacted with your service. During the lifetime of that request, any interesting details about what occurred in order to return a result should be appended to the event.

In the code examples, our functions were incredibly simple. In a real application, each service call made throughout the execution of a single request would have its own interesting details about what occurred: variable values, parameters passed, results returned, associated context, etc. Each event would capture those details along with the `traceData` that later allows you to see and debug the relationships among various services and components in your distributed systems.

In our examples—as well as in distributed tracing systems in general—the instrumentation we used was added at the remote-service-call level. However, in an observable system, you could use the same approach to tie together any number of correlated events from different sources. For example, you could take a first step toward observability by migrating your current single-line logging solution toward a more cohesive view by applying these same trace concepts.

To do that, you could migrate from generating unstructured multiline logs to generating structured logs (see Chapter 5). Then you could add the same required fields for `traceData` to your structured logs. Having done so, you could generate the same waterfall-style view from your log data. We wouldn't recommend that as a long-term approach, but it can be useful, especially when first getting started (see Chapter 10 for more tips).

A more common scenario for a nontraditional use of tracing is to do a chunk of work that is not distributed in nature, but that you want to split into its own span for a variety of reasons. For example, perhaps you find that your application is bottlenecked by JSON unmarshaling (or some other CPU-intensive operation) and you need to identify when that causes a problem.

One approach is to wrap these "hot blocks" of code into their own separate spans to get an even more detailed waterfall view (see Chapter 7 for more examples). That approach can be used to create traces in non-distributed (monolithic) or non-service-oriented programs. For example, you could create a span for every chunk of work in a batch job (e.g., every object uploaded to Amazon Simple Storage Service, or S3) or for each distinct phase of an AWS Lambda-based pipeline. Indeed, AWS software development kits (SDKs) do this by default; see the AWS Developer Guide (*https:// oreil.ly/tQtvk*) for more details.

In an observable system, any set of events can be stitched into traces. Tracing doesn't have to be limited to service-to-service calls. So far, we've focused only on gathering the data in these events and sending them to our observability backend. In later chapters, we'll look at the analysis methods that allow you to arbitrarily slice and dice that data to find patterns along any dimension you choose.

Conclusion

Events are the building blocks of observability, and traces are simply an interrelated series of events. The concepts used to stitch together spans into a cohesive trace are useful in the setting of service-to-service communication. In observable systems, those same concepts can also be applied beyond making RPCs to any discrete events in your systems that are interrelated (like individual file uploads all created from the same batch job).

In this chapter, we instrumented a trace the hard way by coding each necessary step by hand. A more practical way to get started with tracing is to use an instrumentation framework. In the next chapter, we'll look at the open source and vendor-neutral OpenTelemetry project as well as how and why you would use it to instrument your production applications.

CHAPTER 7

Instrumentation with OpenTelemetry

In the previous two chapters, we described the principles of structured events and tracing. Events and traces are the building blocks of observability that you can use to understand the behavior of your software applications. You can generate those fundamental building blocks by adding instrumentation code into your application to emit telemetry data alongside each invocation. You can then route the emitted telemetry data to a backend data store, so that you can later analyze it to understand application health and help debug issues.

In this chapter, we'll show you how to instrument your code to emit telemetry data. The approach you choose might depend on the instrumentation methods your observability backend supports. It is common for vendors to create proprietary APM, metrics, or tracing libraries to generate telemetry data for their specific solutions. However, for the purposes of this vendor-neutral book, we will describe how to implement instrumentation with open source standards that will work with a wide variety of backend telemetry stores.

This chapter starts by introducing the OpenTelemetry standard and its approach for automatically generating telemetry from applications. Telemetry from automatic instrumentation is a fine start, but the real power of observability comes from custom attributes that add context to help you debug how your intended business logic is actually working. We'll show you how to use custom instrumentation to augment the out-of-the-box instrumentation included with OpenTelemetry. By the end of the chapter, you'll have an end-to-end instrumentation strategy to generate useful telemetry data. And in later sections of this book, we'll show you how to analyze that telemetry data to find the answers you need.

A Brief Introduction to Instrumentation

It is a well-established practice in the software industry to instrument applications to send data about system state to a central logging or monitoring solution. That data, known as *telemetry*, records what your code did when processing a particular set of requests. Over the years, software developers have defined various overlapping categories of telemetry data, including logs, metrics, and, more recently, traces and profiles.

As discussed in Chapter 5, arbitrarily wide events are the ideal building blocks for observability. But wide events are not new; they are just a special kind of log that consists of many structured data fields rather than fewer, more ambiguous blobs. And a trace (see Chapter 6) comprises multiple wide events with embedded fields to connect disparate events.

However, the approach to application instrumentation has typically been proprietary. Sometimes producing the data requires manually adding code to generate telemetry data within your services; other times, an agent can assist in gathering data automatically. Each distinct monitoring solution (unless it's `printf()`) has its own custom set of necessary steps to generate and transmit telemetry data in a format appropriate for that product's backend data store.

In the past, you may have installed instrumentation libraries or agents in their applications that are backend-specific. You would then add in your own custom instrumentation to capture any data you deem relevant to understanding the internal state of your applications, using the functions made available by those client libraries. However, the product-specific nature of those instrumentation approaches also creates vendor lock-in. If you wanted to send telemetry data to a different product, you needed to repeat the entire instrumentation process using a different library, wastefully duplicating code and doubling the measurement overhead.

Open Instrumentation Standards

The monitoring and observability community has created several open source projects over the years in an attempt to address the vendor lock-in problem. OpenTracing (under the Cloud Native Computing Foundation) and OpenCensus (sponsored by Google) emerged in 2016 and 2017, respectively. These competing open standards provided a set of libraries for the most popular programming languages to allow collection of telemetry data for transfer to a backend of your choice in real time. Eventually, in 2019, both groups combined efforts to form the OpenTelemetry project under the CNCF umbrella.

> *The good thing about standards is that there are so many to choose from.*
>   —Andrew S. Tanenbaum

OpenTelemetry (*OTel*) represents the next major version of both OpenTracing and OpenCensus, providing full replacement and preserving compatibility. OTel captures traces, metrics, logs, and other application telemetry data and lets you send it to the backend of your choice. OTel has become the single open source standard for application instrumentation among observability solutions. With OTel, you can instrument your application code only once and send your telemetry data to any backend system of your choice, whether it is open source or proprietary.

This chapter will show you how to jumpstart your observability journey with the flexibility and power of OTel. You can use these lessons to quickly instrument your applications and use that data in any number of observability solutions.

Instrumentation Using Code-Based Examples

At the time of publication, OTel supports instrumenting code written in many languages (including Go, Python, Java, Ruby, Erlang, PHP, JavaScript, .NET, Rust, C++, and Swift), and also includes a common message standard and collector agent.

To provide practical examples of instrumentation rather than confining ourselves to abstract concepts, we need to utilize one specific language that OTel supports. We use the Go programming language for these examples because it is the language Kubernetes is written in and a lingua franca of modern distributed microservices and cloud native systems. However, you can apply these concepts to any language because OTel offers standard terminology and API design (when possible) in each language it supports.

You shouldn't need to be a Go programmer to understand these examples. However, we'll also explain what each of the following code snippets does in detail.

A Crash-Course in OpenTelemetry Concepts

OpenTelemetry provides the libraries, agents, tooling, and other components designed for the creation and management of telemetry data from your services. OTel brings together APIs for different telemetry data types and manages the distributed context propagation common to all of them. It combines concepts and components from each of its predecessor projects to retain their advantages while still being backward compatible with previously written instrumentation.

To do this, OTel breaks functionality into several components with a distinct set of terminology. Useful concepts to keep in mind with OTel are as follows:

API
> The specification portion of OTel libraries that allows developers to add instrumentation to their code without concern for the underlying implementation.

SDK

The concrete implementation component of OTel that tracks state and batches data for transmission.

Tracer

A component within the SDK that is responsible for tracking which span is currently active in your process. It also allows you to access and modify the current span to perform operations like adding attributes, events, or finishing it when the work it tracks is complete.

Meter

A component within the SDK that is responsible for tracking which metrics are available to report on in your process. It also allows you to access and modify the current metrics to perform operations like adding values, or retrieving those values at periodic intervals.

Context propagation

An integral part of the SDK that deserializes context about the current inbound request from headers such as W3C `TraceContext` or B3M, tracks what the current request context is within the process, and serializes it to pass downstream to a new service.

Exporter

A plug-in for the SDK that translates OTel in-memory objects into the appropriate format for delivery to a specific destination. Destinations may be local (such as a log file or `stdout`) or may be remote (backends can be open source, such as Jaeger, or proprietary commercial solutions, like Honeycomb or Lightstep). For remote destinations, OTel defaults to using an exporter speaking the wire protocol known as OpenTelemetry Protocol (OTLP), which can be used to send data to the OpenTelemetry Collector.

Collector

A standalone binary process that can be run as a proxy or sidecar that receives telemetry data (by default in OTLP format), processes it, and tees it to one or more configured destinations.

A deep dive into OTel components is beyond the scope of this book, but you can find out more about these concepts by reading the OpenTelemetry documentation (*https://docs.opentelemetry.io*).

Start with Automatic Instrumentation

One of the largest challenges of adopting distributed tracing is getting enough useful data to be able to map it to the knowledge you already have about your systems. How can you teach your observability systems about the services, endpoints, and dependencies you have so that you can start gaining insight? While you *could* manually start and end trace spans for each request, there's a better way to decrease the friction and get insight in hours or days, not months.

For this purpose, OTel includes automatic instrumentation to minimize the time to first value for users. Because OTel's charter is to ease adoption of the cloud native ecosystem and microservices, it supports the most common frameworks for interactions between services. For example, OTel automatically generates trace spans for incoming and outgoing gRPC, HTTP, and database/cache calls from instrumented services. This will provide you with at least the skeleton of who calls whom in the tangled web of microservices and downstream dependencies.

To provide you with that automatic instrumentation of request properties and timings, the framework needs to call OTel before and after handling each request. Thus, common frameworks often support wrappers, interceptors, or middleware that OTel can hook into in order to automatically read context propagation metadata and create spans for each request. In Go, this configuration is explicit because Go requires explicit type safety and compile-time configuration; however, in languages such as Java and .NET, you can attach a standalone OpenTelemetry Agent at runtime that will infer which frameworks are running and automatically register itself.

To illustrate the wrapper pattern, in Go, the common denominator for Go is the `http.Request`/`http.Response` `HandlerFunc` interface. You can use the `otelhttp` package to wrap an existing HTTP handler function before passing it into the HTTP server's default request router (known as a *mux* in Go):

```
import "go.opentelemetry.io/contrib/instrumentation/net/http/otelhttp"

mux.Handle("/route",
otelhttp.NewHandler(otelhttp.WithRouteTag("/route",
http.HandlerFunc(h)), "handler_span_name"))
```

In contrast, gRPC provides an `Interceptor` interface that you can provide OTel with to register its instrumentation:

```
import (
  "go.opentelemetry.io/contrib/instrumentation/google.golang.org/grpc/otelgrpc"
)

s := grpc.NewServer(
  grpc.UnaryInterceptor(otelgrpc.UnaryServerInterceptor()),
  grpc.StreamInterceptor(otelgrpc.StreamServerInterceptor()),
)
```

Armed with this automatically generated data, you will be able to find problems such as uncached hot database calls, or downstream dependencies that are slow for a subset of their endpoints, from a subset of your services. But this is only the very beginning of the insight you'll get.

Add Custom Instrumentation

Once you have automatic instrumentation, you have a solid foundation for making an investment in custom instrumentation specific to your business logic. You can attach fields and rich values, such as client IDs, shard IDs, errors, and more to the auto-instrumented spans inside your code. These annotations make it easier in the future to understand what's happening at each layer.

By adding custom spans within your application for particularly expensive, time-consuming steps internal to your process, you can go beyond the automatically instrumented spans for outbound calls to dependencies and get visibility into all areas of your code. This type of custom instrumentation is what helps you practice observability-driven development, where you create instrumentation alongside new features in your code so that you can verify it operates as you expect in production in real time as it is being released (see Chapter 11). Adding custom instrumentation to your code helps you work proactively to make future problems easier to debug by providing full context—that includes business logic—around a particular code execution path.

Starting and finishing trace spans

As detailed in Chapter 6, trace spans should cover each individual unit of work performed. Usually, that unit is an individual request passing through one microservice, and it can be instantiated at the HTTP request or RPC layer. However, in certain circumstances, you might want to add additional details to understand where execution time is being spent, record information about subprocessing that is happening, or surface any number of additional details.

OTel's tracers store information on which span is currently active inside a key of the context.Context (or in thread-locals, as appropriate to the language). When referring to context in OTel, we should disambiguate the term. *Context* may be referring not only to its logical usage—the circumstances surrounding an event in your service—but also to specific types of context, like a trace's span context. Thus, to start a new span, we must obtain from OTel an appropriate tracer for our component, and pass it the current context to update:

```
import "go.opentelemetry.io/otel"

// Within each module, define a private tracer once for easy identification
var tr = otel.Tracer("module_name")

func funcName(ctx context.Context) {
  sp := tr.Start(ctx, "span_name")
  defer sp.End()
  // do work here
}
```

This snippet allows you to create and name a child span of whatever span already existed in the context (for instance, from an HTTP or gRPC context), start the timer running, calculate the span duration, and then finalize the span for transmission to a backend in the `defer` performed at the end of the function call.

Adding wide fields to an event

As you've seen in earlier chapters, observability is best served by batching up data from the execution of each function into one singular wide event per request. That means you can, and should, add in any custom field you find worthwhile for determining the health of your services or the set of users impacted, or understanding the state of your code during its execution.

OTel makes it easy to add custom fields to any gathered telemetry data by transiently buffering and collating any fields added by your instrumentation during the execution of each request. The OTel data model retains open spans until they're marked finished. Therefore, you can attach numerous distinct fields of metadata to the telemetry that is ultimately written as one single span. At smaller scales, you can handle schema management informally with constants in your code, but at larger scales you'll want to see Chapter 18 for how to normalize schemas with telemetry pipelines.

Anywhere you have an active span in the process or thread context, you can make a call like `sp := trace.SpanFromContext(ctx)` to get the currently active span from the active context object. In languages with implicit thread-local context, no explicit context argument need be passed.

Once you have the current active span, you can add fields or events to it. In Go, you must explicitly specify the type for maximum performance and type safety:

```
import "go.opentelemetry.io/otel/attribute"
sp.SetAttributes(attribute.Int("http.code", resp.ResponseCode))
sp.SetAttributes(attribute.String("app.user", username))
```

This snippet sets two key-value pair attributes. The attribute `http.code` contains an integer value (the HTTP response code), and `app.user` contains a string including the current username in the execution request.

Recording process-wide metrics

In general, most metrics such as measures and counters should be recorded as attributes on the trace span to which they pertain. For instance, Value in Cart is probably best associated with a span in which the user's cart is processed rather than being aggregated and scraped by a metrics system. However, if you absolutely need an exact, unsampled count that is pre-aggregated by specific dimensions, or need a non-request-specific, process-wide value that is periodically scraped, you can update a measure or counter with a collection of tags:

```
import "go.opentelemetry.io/otel"
import "go.opentelemetry.io/otel/metric"

// similar to instantiating a tracer, you will want a meter per package.
var meter = otel.Meter("example_package")

// predefine our keys so we can reuse them and avoid overhead
var appKey = attribute.Key("app")
var containerKey = attribute.Key("container")

goroutines, _ := metric.Must(meter).NewInt64Measure("num_goroutines",
  metric.WithKeys(appKey, containerKey),
  metric.WithDescription("Amount of goroutines running."),
)

// Then, within a periodic ticker goroutine:
meter.RecordBatch(ctx, []attribute.KeyValue{
  appKey.String(os.Getenv("PROJECT_DOMAIN")),
  containerKey.String(os.Getenv("HOSTNAME"))},
  goroutines.Measurement(int64(runtime.NumGoroutine())),
  // insert other measurements performed on a measure here.
)
```

This periodically records the number of running goroutines and exports the data via OTel.

When following the path of observability, we strongly recommend that you not box yourself into using the rigid and inflexible measures provided by most application-level metrics. We explore that topic further in Chapter 9. For now, a similar method to the preceding one could be used if you find that you absolutely need to record the value of a metric.

Send Instrumentation Data to a Backend System

By default, OTel assumes you will be sending data to a local sidecar running on a default port; however, you may want to explicitly specify how to route the data in your application start-up code.

After creating telemetry data by using the preceding methods, you'll want to send it somewhere. OTel supports two primary methods for exporting data from your process to an analysis backend; you can proxy it through the OpenTelemetry Collector (see Chapter 18) or you can export it directly from your process to the backend.

Exporting directly from your process requires you to import, depend on, and instantiate one or more exporters. *Exporters* are libraries that translate OTel's in-memory span and metric objects into the appropriate format for various telemetry analysis tools.

Exporters are instantiated once, on program start-up, usually in the main function. Typically, you'll need to emit telemetry to only one specific backend. However, OTel allows you to arbitrarily instantiate and configure many exporters, allowing your system to emit the same telemetry to more than one telemetry sink at the same time. One possible use case for exporting to multiple telemetry sinks might be to ensure uninterrupted access to your current production observability tool, while using the same telemetry data to test the capabilities of a different observability tool you're evaluating.

With the ubiquity of OTLP, the most sensible default is to always configure the OTLP gRPC exporter to either your vendor or to an OpenTelemetry Collector (see Chapter 18) rather than use the vendor's custom code:

```
driver := otlpgrpc.NewClient(
  otlpgrpc.WithTLSCredentials(credentials.NewClientTLSFromCert(nil, "")),
  otlpgrpc.WithEndpoint("my.backend.com:443"),
)
otExporter, err := otlp.New(ctx, driver)
tp := sdktrace.NewTracerProvider(
  sdktrace.WithSampler(sdktrace.AlwaysSample()),
  sdktrace.WithResource(resource.NewWithAttributes(
    semconv.SchemaURL, semconv.ServiceNameKey.String(serviceName))),
  sdktrace.WithBatcher(otExporter))
```

But if you must configure multiple custom exporters for backends that are neither an OpenTelemetry Collector nor support the common OTLP standard, here is an example of instantiating two exporters in the application start-up code:

```
import (
  x "github.com/my/backend/exporter"
  y "github.com/some/backend/exporter"
  "go.opentelemetry.io/otel"
  sdktrace "go.opentelemetry.io/otel/sdk/trace"
)

func main() {
  exporterX = x.NewExporter(...)
  exporterY = y.NewExporter(...)
  tp, err := sdktrace.NewTracerProvider(
    sdktrace.WithSampler(sdktrace.AlwaysSample()),
    sdktrace.WithSyncer(exporterX),
    sdktrace.WithBatcher(exporterY),
  )
  otel.SetTracerProvider(tp)
```

In this example code, we import both *my/backend/exporter* and *some/backend/ exporter*, configure them to synchronously or in batches receive trace spans from a tracer provider, and then set the tracer provider as the default tracer provider. This machinery causes all subsequent calls to otel.Tracer() to retrieve an appropriately configured tracer.

Conclusion

While several approaches to instrument your applications for observability are possible, OTel is an open source standard that enables you to send telemetry data to any number of backend data stores you choose. OTel is emerging as a new vendor-neutral approach to ensure that you can instrument your applications to emit telemetry data, regardless of which observability system you choose.

The code-based examples in this chapter are written in Go, but the same terminology and concepts apply to any of the current languages supported by OTel. You can find an extended, compilable version of our example code online (*https://oreil.ly/7IcWz*). You would use the same steps to leverage the power of automatic instrumentation, add custom fields to your events, start and finish trace spans, and instantiate exporters. You can even add metrics to your traces if necessary.

But that begs the question; why is the caveat—if necessary—added when considering metrics? Metrics are a data type with inherent limitations. In the next two chapters, we'll explore the use of events and metrics to shed further light on this consideration.

CHAPTER 8

Analyzing Events to Achieve Observability

In the first two chapters of this part, you learned about telemetry fundamentals that are necessary to create a data set that can be properly debugged with an observability tool. While having the right data is a fundamental requirement, observability is measured by what you can learn about your systems from that data. This chapter explores debugging techniques applied to observability data and what separates them from traditional techniques used to debug production systems.

We'll start by closely examining common techniques for debugging issues with traditional monitoring and application performance monitoring tools. As highlighted in previous chapters, traditional approaches presume a fair amount of familiarity with previously known failure modes. In this chapter, that approach is unpacked a bit more so that it can then be contrasted with debugging approaches that don't require the same degree of system familiarity to identify issues.

Then, we'll look at how observability-based debugging techniques can be automated and consider the roles that both humans and computers play in creating effective debugging workflows. When combining those factors, you'll understand how observability tools help you analyze telemetry data to identify issues that are impossible to detect with traditional tools.

This style of hypothesis-driven debugging—in which you form hypotheses and then explore the data to confirm or deny them—is not only more scientific than relying on intuition and pattern matching, but it also democratizes the act of debugging. As opposed to traditional debugging techniques, which favor those with the most system familiarity and experience to quickly find answers, debugging with observability favors those who are the most curious or the most diligent about checking up on their code in production. With observability, even someone with very little knowledge of the system should be able to jump in and debug an issue.

Debugging from Known Conditions

Prior to observability, system and application debugging mostly occurred by building upon what you know about a system. This can be observed when looking at the way the most senior members of an engineering team approach troubleshooting. It can seem downright magical when they know which questions are the right ones to ask and instinctively know the right place to look. That magic is born from intimate familiarity with their application and systems.

To capture this magic, managers urge their senior engineers to write detailed runbooks in an attempt to identify and solve every possible "root cause" they might encounter out in the wild. In Chapter 2, we covered the escalating arms race of dashboard creation embarked upon to create just the right view that identifies a newly encountered problem. But that time spent creating runbooks and dashboards is largely wasted, because modern systems rarely fail in precisely the same way twice. And when they do, it's increasingly common to configure an automated remediation that can correct that failure until someone can investigate it properly.

Anyone who has ever written or used a runbook can tell you a story about just how woefully inadequate they are. Perhaps they work to temporarily address technical debt: there's one recurring issue, and the runbook tells other engineers how to mitigate the problem until the upcoming sprint when it can finally be resolved. But more often, especially with distributed systems, a long thin tail of problems that *almost never happen* are responsible for cascading failures in production. Or, five seemingly impossible conditions will align just right to create a large-scale service failure in ways that might happen only once every few years.

On the Topic of Runbooks

The assertion that time spent creating runbooks is largely wasted may seem a bit harsh at first. To be clear, there is a place for documentation meant to quickly orient your team with the needs of a particular service and its jumping-off points. For example, every service should have documentation that contains basic information including which team owns and maintains the service, how to reach the on-call engineer, escalation points, other services this service depends on (and vice versa), and links to good queries or dashboards to understand how this service is performing.

However, maintaining a living document that attempts to contain all possible system errors and resolutions is a futile and dangerous game. That type of documentation can quickly go stale, and *wrong documentation* is perhaps more dangerous than *no documentation*. In fast-changing systems, instrumentation itself is often the best possible documentation, since it combines intention (what are the dimensions that an engineer named and decided to collect?) with the real-time, up-to-date information of live status in production.

Yet engineers typically embrace that dynamic as just the way that troubleshooting is done—because that is how the act of debugging has worked for decades. First, you must intimately understand all parts of the system—whether through direct exposure and experience, documentation, or a runbook. Then you look at your dashboards and then you…intuit the answer? Or maybe you make a guess at the root cause, and then start looking through your dashboards for evidence to confirm your guess.

Even after instrumenting your applications to emit observability data, you might still be debugging from known conditions. For example, you could take that stream of arbitrarily wide events and pipe it to `tail -f` and `grep` it for known strings, just as troubleshooting is done today with unstructured logs. Or you could take query results and stream them to a series of infinite dashboards, as troubleshooting is done today with metrics. You see a spike on one dashboard, and then you start flipping through dozens of other dashboards, visually pattern-matching for other similar shapes.

It's not just that you're now collecting event data that enables you to debug unknown conditions. It's the way you approach the act of instrumentation and debugging.

At Honeycomb, it took us quite some time to figure this out, even after we'd built our own observability tool. Our natural inclination as engineers is to jump straight to what we know about our systems. In Honeycomb's early days, before we learned how to break away from debugging from known conditions, what observability helped us do was just jump to the right high-cardinality questions to ask.

If we'd just shipped a new frontend feature and were worried about performance, we'd ask, "How much did it change our CSS and JS asset sizes?" Having just written the instrumentation ourselves, we would know to figure that out by calculating maximum `css_asset_size` and `js_asset_size`, then breaking down performance by `build_id`. If we were worried about a new customer who was starting to use our services, we'd ask, "Are their queries fast?" Then we would just know to filter by `team_id` and calculate p95 response time.

But what happens when you don't know what's wrong or where to start looking, and haven't the faintest idea of what could be happening? When debugging conditions are completely unknown to you, *then* you must instead debug from first principles.

Debugging from First Principles

As laid out in the previous two chapters, gathering telemetry data as events is the first step. Achieving observability also requires that you unlock a new understanding of your system by analyzing that data in powerful and objective ways. Observability enables you to debug your applications from first principles.

A first principle (*https://w.wiki/56we*) is a basic assumption about a system that was not deduced from another assumption. In philosophy, a first principle is defined as the first basis from which a thing is known. To *debug from first principles* is basically a methodology to follow in order to understand a system scientifically. Proper science requires that you do not assume anything. You must start by questioning what has been proven and what you are absolutely sure is true. Then, based on those principles, you must form a hypothesis and validate or invalidate it based on observations about the system.

Debugging from first principles is a core capability of observability. While intuitively jumping straight to the answer is wonderful, it becomes increasingly impractical as complexity rises and the number of possible answers skyrockets. (And it *definitely* doesn't scale…not everyone can or should have to be a systems wizard to debug their code.)

In Chapters 2 and 3, you saw examples of elusive issues that were incredibly difficult to diagnose. What happens when you don't know a system's architecture like the back of your hand? Or what happens when you don't even know what data is being collected about this system? What if the source of an issue is multicausal: you're wondering what went wrong, and the answer is "13 different things"?

The real power of observability is that you shouldn't have to know so much in advance of debugging an issue. You should be able to systematically and scientifically take one step after another, to methodically follow the clues to find the answer, even when you are unfamiliar (or less familiar) with the system. The magic of instantly jumping to the right conclusion by inferring an unspoken signal, relying on past scar tissue, or making some leap of familiar brilliance is instead replaced by methodical, repeatable, verifiable process.

Putting that approach into practice is demonstrated with the core analysis loop.

Using the Core Analysis Loop

Debugging from first principles begins when you are made aware that something is wrong (we'll look at alerting approaches that are compatible with observability in Chapter 12). Perhaps you received an alert, but this could also be something as simple as receiving a customer complaint: you know that something is slow, but you do not know what is wrong. Figure 8-1 is a diagram representing the four stages of the *core analysis loop*, the process of using your telemetry to form hypotheses and to validate or invalidate them with data, and thereby systematically arrive at the answer to a complex problem.

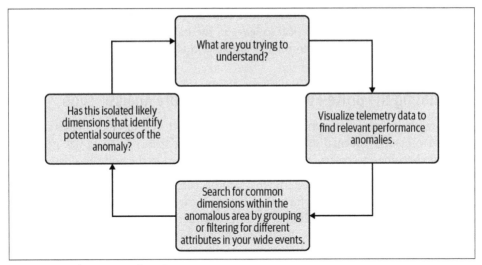

Figure 8-1. The core analysis loop

The core analysis loop works like this:

1. Start with the overall view of what prompted your investigation: what did the customer or alert tell you?

2. Verify that what you know so far is true: is a notable change in performance happening somewhere in this system? Data visualizations can help you identify changes of behavior as a change in a curve somewhere in the graph.

3. Search for dimensions that might drive that change in performance. Approaches to accomplish that might include:

   a. Examining sample rows from the area that shows the change: are there any outliers in the columns that might give you a clue?

   b. Slicing those rows across various dimensions looking for patterns: do any of those views highlight distinct behavior across one or more dimensions? Try an experimental group by on commonly useful fields, like status_code.

   c. Filtering for particular dimensions or values within those rows to better expose potential outliers.

4. Do you now know enough about what might be occurring? If so, you're done! If not, filter your view to isolate this area of performance as your next starting point. Then return to step 3.

This is the basis of debugging from first principles. You can use this loop as a brute-force method to cycle through all available dimensions to identify which ones explain or correlate with the outlier graph in question, with no prior knowledge or wisdom about the system required.

Of course, that brute-force method could take an inordinate amount of time and make such an approach impractical to leave in the hands of human operators alone. An observability tool should automate as much of that brute-force analysis for you as possible.

Automating the Brute-Force Portion of the Core Analysis Loop

The core analysis loop is a method to objectively find a signal that matters within a sea of otherwise normal system noise. Leveraging the computational power of machines becomes necessary in order to swiftly get down to the bottom of issues.

When debugging slow system performance, the core analysis loop has you isolate a particular area of system performance that you care about. Rather than manually searching across rows and columns to coax out patterns, an automated approach would be to retrieve the values of all dimensions, both inside the isolated area (the anomaly) and outside the area (the system baseline), diff them, and then sort by the difference. Very quickly, that lets you see a list of things that are different in your investigation's areas of concern as compared to everything else.

For example, you might isolate a spike in request latency and, when automating the core analysis loop, get back a sorted list of dimensions and how often they appear within this area. You might see the following:

- `request.endpoint` with value `batch` is in 100% of requests in the isolated area, but in only 20% of the baseline area.
- `handler_route` with value `/1/markers/` is in 100% of requests in the isolated area, but only 10% of the baseline area.
- `request.header.user_agent` is populated in 97% of requests in the isolated area, but 100% of the baseline area.

At a glance, this tells you that the events in this specific area of performance you care about are different from the rest of the system in all of these ways, whether that be one deviation or dozens. Let's look at a more concrete example of the core analysis loop by using Honeycomb's BubbleUp feature.

With Honeycomb, you start by visualizing a heatmap to isolate a particular area of performance you care about. Honeycomb automates the core analysis loop with the BubbleUp feature: you point and click at the spike or anomalous shape in the graph that concerns you, and draw a box around it. BubbleUp computes the values of *all* dimensions both inside the box (the anomaly you care about and want to explain) and outside the box (the baseline), and then compares the two and sorts the resulting view by percent of differences, as shown in Figure 8-2.

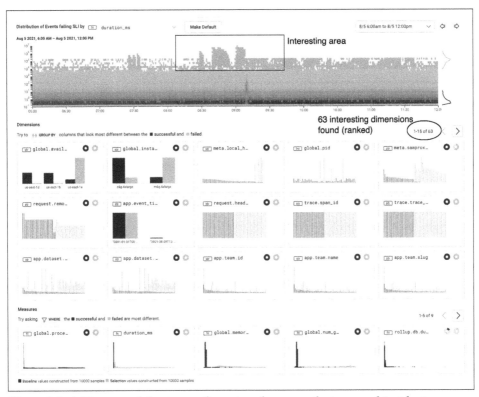

Figure 8-2. A Honeycomb heatmap of event performance during a real incident. BubbleUp surfaces results for 63 interesting dimensions and ranks the results by largest percentage difference.

In this example, we're looking at an application with high-dimensionality instrumentation that BubbleUp can compute and compare. The results of the computation are shown in histograms using two primary colors: blue for baseline dimensions and orange for dimensions in the selected anomaly area (blue appears as dark gray in the print image, and orange as lighter gray). In the top-left corner (the top results in the sort operation), we see a field named `global.availability_zone` with a value of `us-east-1a` showing up in only 17% of baseline events, but in 98% of anomalous events in the selected area (Figure 8-3).

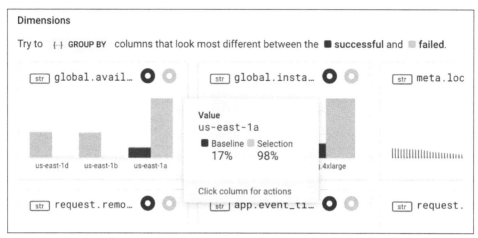

Figure 8-3. In this close-up of the results from Figure 8-2, the orange bar (light gray in the print image) shows that global.availability_zone *appears as* us-east-1a *in 98% of events in the selected area, and the blue bar (dark gray) shows that's the case in only 17% of baseline events.*

In this example, you can quickly see that slow-performing events are mostly originating from one particular availability zone (AZ) from our cloud infrastructure provider. The other information automatically surfaced also points out one particular virtual machine instance type that appears to be more affected than others. Other dimensions surfaced, but in this example the differences tended to be less stark, indicating that they were perhaps not as relevant to our investigation.

This information has been tremendously helpful: we now know the conditions that appear to be triggering slow performance. A particular type of instance in one particular AZ is much more prone to very slow performance than other infrastructure we care about. In that situation, the glaring difference pointed to what turned out to be an underlying network issue with our cloud provider's entire AZ.

Not all issues are as immediately obvious as this underlying infrastructure issue. Often you may need to look at other surfaced clues to triage code-related issues. The core analysis loop remains the same, and you may need to slice and dice across dimensions until one clear signal emerges, similar to the preceding example. In this case, we contacted our cloud provider and were also able to independently verify the unreported availability issue when our customers also reported similar issues in the same zone. If this had instead been a code-related issue, we might decide to reach out to those users, or figure out the path they followed through the UI to see those errors, and fix the interface or the underlying system.

Note that the core analysis loop can be achieved only by using the baseline building blocks of observability, which is to say arbitrarily wide structured events. You cannot achieve this with metrics; they lack the broad context to let you slice and dice and dive in or zoom out in the data. You cannot achieve this with logs unless you have correctly appended all the request ID, trace ID, and other headers, and then done a great deal of postprocessing to reconstruct them into events—and then added the ability to aggregate them at read time and perform complex custom querying.

In other words: yes, an observability tool should automate much of the number crunching for you, but even the manual core analysis loop is unattainable without the basic building blocks of observability. The core analysis loop can be done manually to uncover interesting dimensions. But in this modern era of cheap computing resources, an observability tool should automate that investigation for you. Because debugging from first principles does not require prior familiarity with the system, that automation can be done simply and methodically, without the need to seed "intelligence" about the application being debugged.

That begs a question around how much intelligence should be applied to this number crunching. Is artificial intelligence and machine learning the inevitable solution to all our debugging problems?

This Misleading Promise of AIOps

Since Gartner coined the term in 2017, *artificial intelligence for operations* (*AIOps*) has generated lots of interest from companies seeking to somehow automate common operational tasks. Delving deeply into the misleading promise of AIOps (*https:// thenewstack.io/observability-and-the-misleading-promise-of-aiops*) is beyond the scope of this book. But AIOps intersects observability, reducing alert noise and anomaly detection.

In Chapter 12, we unpack a simpler approach to alerting that makes the need for algorithms to reduce alert noise a moot point. The second intersection, anomaly detection, is the focus of this chapter, so we'll unpack that in this section.

As seen earlier in this chapter, the concept behind using algorithms to detect anomalies is to select a baseline of "normal" events and compare those to "abnormal" events not contained within the baseline window. Selecting the window in which that's done can be incredibly challenging for automated algorithms.

Similar to using BubbleUp to draw a box around the area you care about, AI must decide where to draw its own box. If a system behaved consistently over time, anomalies would be worrisome, unusual cases that could be easily detected. In an innovative environment with system behavior that changes frequently, it's more likely that AI will draw a box of the wrong size. The box will be either too small—identifying a great deal of perfectly normal behavior as anomalies, or too large—miscategorizing anomalies as normal behavior. In practice, both types of mistakes will be made, and detection will be far too noisy or far too quiet.

This book is about the engineering principles needed to manage running production software on modern architectures with modern practices. Any reasonably competitive company in today's world will have engineering teams frequently deploying changes to production. New feature deployments introduce changes in performance that didn't previously exist: that's an anomaly. Fixing a broken build: that's an anomaly. Introducing service optimizations in production that change the performance curve: that's an anomaly too.

AI technology isn't magic. AI can help only if clearly discernible patterns exist and if the AI can be trained to use ever-changing baselines to model its predictions—a training pattern that, so far, has yet to emerge in the AIOps world.

In the meantime, there *is* an intelligence designed to reliably adapt its pattern recognition to ever-changing baselines by applying real-time context to a new problem set: human intelligence. Human intelligence and contextual awareness of a problem to be solved can fill in the gaps when AIOps techniques fall short. Similarly, that adaptive and contextual human intelligence lacks the processing speed achieved by applying algorithms over billions of rows of data.

It's in observability and automating the core analysis loop that both *human and machine intelligence merge* to get the best of both worlds. Let computers do what they do best: churn through massive sets of data to identify patterns that might be interesting. Let the humans do what they do best: add cognitive context to those potentially interesting patterns that reliably sifts out the signals that matter from the noises that don't.

Think of it like this: any computer can crunch the numbers and detect a spike, but only a human can attach meaning to that spike. Was it good or bad? Intended or not? With today's technology, AIOps cannot reliably assign these value judgments for you.

Humans alone can't solve today's most complex software performance issues. But neither can computers or vendors touting AIOps as a magical silver bullet. Leveraging the strengths of humans and machines, in a combined approach, is the best and most pragmatic solution in today's world. Automating the core analysis loop is a prime example of how that can be done.

Conclusion

Collecting the right telemetry data is only the first step in the journey toward observability. That data must be analyzed according to first principles in order to objectively and correctly identify application issues in complex environments. The core analysis loop is an effective technique for fast fault localization. However, that work can be time-consuming for humans to conduct methodically as a system becomes increasingly complex.

When looking for the sources of anomalies, you can leverage compute resources to quickly sift through very large data sets to identify interesting patterns. Surfacing those patterns to a human operator, who can put them into the necessary context and then further direct the investigation, strikes an effective balance that best utilizes the strengths of machines and humans to quickly drive system debugging. Observability systems are built to apply this type of analysis pattern to the event data you've learned how to collect in the previous chapters.

Now that you understand both the types of data needed and the practice of analyzing that data to get fast answers with observability, the next chapter circles back to look at how observability practices and monitoring practices can coexist.

CHAPTER 9

How Observability and Monitoring Come Together

So far in this book, we've examined the differentiating capabilities of observable systems, the technological components necessary for observability, and how observability fits into the technical landscape. Observability is fundamentally distinct from monitoring, and both serve different purposes. In this chapter, we examine how they fit together and the considerations for determining how both may coexist within your organization.

Many organizations have years—if not decades—of accumulated metrics data and monitoring expertise set up around their production software systems. As covered in earlier chapters, traditional monitoring approaches are adequate for traditional systems. But when managing modern systems, does that mean you should throw all that away and start fresh with observability tools? Doing that would be both cavalier and brash. The truth for most organizations is that their approach to coexisting approaches should be dictated by their adopted responsibilities.

This chapter explores how observability and monitoring come together by examining the strengths of each, the domains where they are best suited, and the ways they complement one another. Every organization is different, and a recipe for the coexistence of observability and monitoring cannot be universally prescribed. However, a useful guideline is that observability is best suited to understanding issues at the application level and that monitoring is best for understanding issues at the system level. By considering your workloads, you can figure out how the two come together best for you.

Where Monitoring Fits

In Chapter 2, we focused on differentiating observability and monitoring. That chapter mostly focuses on the shortcomings of monitoring systems and how observability fills in those gaps. But monitoring systems still continue to provide valuable insights. Let's start by examining where traditional monitoring systems continue to be the right tool for the job.

The traditional monitoring approach to understanding system state is a mature and well-developed process. Decades of iterative improvement have evolved monitoring tools beyond their humble beginnings with simple metrics and round-robin databases (RRDs), toward TSDBs and elaborate tagging systems. A wealth of sophisticated options also exist to provide this service—from open source software solutions, to start-ups, to publicly traded companies.

Monitoring practices are well-known and widely understood beyond the communities of specialists that form around specific tools. Across the software industry, monitoring best practices exist that anyone who has operated software in production can likely agree upon.

For example, a widely accepted core tenet of monitoring is that a human doesn't need to sit around watching graphs all day; the system should proactively inform its users when something is wrong. In this way, monitoring systems are reactive. They react to known failure states by alerting humans that a problem is occurring.

Monitoring systems and metrics have evolved to optimize themselves for that job. They automatically report whether known failure conditions are occurring or about to occur. They are optimized for reporting on unknown conditions about known failure modes (in other words, they are designed to detect *known-unknowns*).

The optimization of monitoring systems to find known-unknowns means that it's a best fit for understanding the state of your systems, which change much less frequently and in more predictable ways than your application code. By *systems*, we mean your infrastructure, or your runtime, or counters that help you see when you're about to slam up against an operating constraint.

As seen in Chapter 1, metrics and monitoring were created to examine hardware-level performance. Over time, they've been adapted to encompass a wider range of infrastructure and system-level concerns. Most readers of this book, who work in technology companies, should recognize that the underlying systems are not what matter to your business. At the end of the day, what matters to your business is how the applications you wrote perform in the hands of your customers. The only reason your business is concerned about those underlying systems is that they could negatively impact application performance.

For example, you want to know if CPU utilization is pegged on a virtual instance with a noisy neighbor because that tells you the latency you're seeing isn't an issue inside your code. Or if you see that physical memory is close to being exhausted across your entire fleet, that tells you an impending disaster probably originated from your code. Correlating system constraints with application performance matters, but system performance matters mostly as a warning signal or a way to rule out code-based issues.

Over time, metrics have also been adapted to creep into monitoring application-level concerns. But as you've seen throughout Part I, these aggregate measures are far too coarse because they cannot be decomposed to show the performance of individual requests in your services. In the role of a warning signal, aggregate measures like metrics work well. But metrics aren't, and never have been, a good way to indicate how the code you wrote behaves in the hands of individual users.

Where Observability Fits

In contrast to monitoring, observability has different tenets and use cases. As seen in Chapter 2, observability is more proactive. Its practices demand that engineers should always watch their code as it is deployed, and should spend time every day exploring their code in production, watching users use it, and looking around for outliers and curious trails to follow.

As covered in Chapter 8, the core analysis loop enables debugging from first principles and is tailored to discovering previously unknown failure modes (in other words, it is designed to detect *unknown-unknowns*). The optimization of observability to find unknown-unknowns means it's a best fit for understanding the state of the code you write, which changes much more frequently than your systems (typically, every day) and in far less predictable ways.

Monitoring and observability tools have different best practices and different implementations, and they serve different purposes.

System Versus Software Considerations

In more traditional settings, the distinction between systems and software was clear: bare-metal infrastructure was the system, and everything running inside that system was the software. Modern systems, and their many higher-order abstractions, have made that distinction somewhat less clear. Let's start with some definitions.

For these purposes, *software* is the code you are actively developing that runs a production service delivering value to your customers. Software is what your business *wants* to run to solve a market problem.

System is an umbrella term for everything else about the underlying infrastructure and runtime that is necessary to run that service. Systems are what your business *needs* to run in order to support the software it *wants* to run. By that definition, the system (or infrastructure, as we could use the two terms interchangeably here) includes everything from databases (e.g., MySQL or MongoDB) to compute and storage (e.g., containers or virtual machines) to anything and everything else that has to be provisioned and set up before you can deploy and run your software.

The world of cloud computing has made these definitions somewhat difficult to nail down, so let's drill down further. Let's say that to run your software, you need to run underlying components like Apache Kafka, Postfix, HAProxy, Memcached, or even something like Jira. If you're buying access to those components as a service, they don't count as infrastructure for this definition; you're essentially paying someone else to run it for you. However, if your team is responsible for installing, configuring, occasionally upgrading, and troubleshooting the performance of those components, that's infrastructure you need to worry about.

Compared to software, everything in the system layer is a commodity that changes infrequently, is focused on a different set of users, and provides a different value. Software—the code you write for your customers to use—is a core differentiator for your business: it is the very reason your company exists today. Software, therefore, has a different set of considerations for how it should be managed. Table 9-1 provides a comparison.

Table 9-1. Factors that vary between systems and software

Factor	Your systems	Your software
Rate of change	Package updates (monthly)	Repo commits (daily)
Predictability	High (stable)	Low (many new features)
Value to your business	Low (cost center)	High (revenue generator)
Number of users	Few (internal teams)	Many (your customers)
Core concern	Is the system or service healthy?	Can each request acquire the resources it needs for end-to-end execution in a timely and reliable manner?
Evaluation perspective	The system	Your customers
Evaluation criteria	Low-level kernel and hardware device drivers	Variables and API endpoint
Functional responsibility	Infrastructure operations	Software development
Method for understanding	Monitoring	Observability

With infrastructure, only one perspective really matters: the perspective of the team responsible for its management. The important question to ask about infrastructure is whether the service it provides is essentially healthy. If it's not, that team must quickly take action to restore the infrastructure to a healthy condition. The system may be running out of capacity, or an underlying failure may have occurred; a human should be alerted and respond to take action.

The conditions that affect infrastructure health change infrequently and are relatively easier to predict. In fact, well-established practices exist to predict (e.g., capacity planning) and automatically remediate (e.g., autoscaling) these types of issues. Because of its relatively predictable and slowly changing nature, aggregated metrics are perfectly acceptable to monitor and alert for system-level problems.

With application code, the perspective that matters most is that of your customers. The underlying systems may be essentially healthy, yet user requests may still be failing for any number of reasons. As covered in earlier chapters, distributed systems make these types of problems harder to detect and understand. Suddenly, the ability to use high-cardinality fields (user ID, shopping cart ID, etc.) as a way to observe a specific customer's experience becomes critical. Especially in the modern world of continuous delivery, as new versions of your code are constantly being deployed, software concerns are always shifting and changing. Observability provides a way to ask appropriate questions that address those concerns in real time.

These two approaches are not mutually exclusive. Every organization will have considerations that fall more into one category than the other. Next, let's look at ways those two approaches may coexist, depending on the needs of your organization.

Assessing Your Organizational Needs

Just as systems and software are complementary, so too are the methods for understanding the way each behaves. Monitoring best helps engineers understand system-level concerns. Observability best helps engineers understand application-level concerns. Assessing your own organizational needs means understanding which concerns are most critical to your business.

Observability will help you deeply understand how software you develop and ship is performing when serving your customers. Code that is well instrumented for observability allows you to answer complex questions about user performance, see the inner workings of your software in production, and identify and swiftly remediate issues that are easy to miss when only examining aggregate performance.

If your company writes and ships software as part of its core business strategy, you need an observability solution. If, in addition to providing an overall level of acceptable aggregate performance, your business strategy also relies on providing excellent service to a particular subset of high-profile customers, your need for observability is especially emphasized.

Monitoring will help you understand how well the systems you run in support of that software are doing their job. Metrics-based monitoring tools and their associated alerts help you see when capacity limits or known error conditions of underlying systems are being reached.

If your company provides infrastructure to its customers as part of its core business strategy (e.g., an infrastructure-as-a-service, or IaaS, provider), you will need a substantial amount of monitoring—low-level Domain Name System (DNS) counters, disk statistics, etc. The underlying systems are business-critical for these organizations, and they need to be experts in these low-level systems that they expose to customers. However, if providing infrastructure is not a core differentiator for your business, monitoring becomes less critical. You may need to monitor only the high-level services and end-to-end checks, for the most part. Determining just how much less monitoring your business needs requires several considerations.

Companies that run a significant portion of their own infrastructure need more monitoring. Whether running systems on premises or with a cloud provider, this consideration is less about where that infrastructure lives and more about operational responsibility. Whether you provision virtual machines in the cloud or administer your own databases on premises, the key factor is whether your team takes on the burden of ensuring infrastructure availability and performance.

Organizations that take on the responsibility of running their own bare-metal systems need monitoring that examines low-level hardware performance. They need monitoring to inspect counters for Ethernet ports, statistics on hard drive performance, and versions of system firmware. Organizations that outsource hardware-level operations to an IaaS provider won't need metrics and aggregates that perform at that level.

And so it goes, further up the stack. As more operational responsibility is shifted to a third party, so too are infrastructure monitoring concerns.

Companies that outsource most of their infrastructure to higher-level platform-as-a-service (PaaS) providers can likely get away with little, if any, traditional monitoring solutions. Heroku, AWS Lambda, and others essentially let you pay them to do the job of ensuring the availability and performance of the infrastructure that your business *needs to run*, so it can instead focus on the software it *wants to run*.

Today, your mileage may vary, depending on the robustness of your cloud provider. Presumably, the abstractions are clean enough and high-level enough that the experience of removing your dependence on infrastructure monitoring wouldn't be terribly frustrating. But, in theory, all providers are moving to a model that enables that shift to occur.

Exceptions: Infrastructure Monitoring That Can't Be Ignored

This neat dividing line between monitoring for systems and observability for software has a few exceptions. As mentioned earlier, the evaluation perspective for determining how well your software performs is customer experience. If your software is performing slowly, your customers are experiencing it poorly. Therefore, a primary concern for evaluating customer experience is understanding anything that can cause performance bottlenecks. The exceptions to that neat dividing line are any metrics that directly indicate how your software is interacting with its underlying infrastructure.

From a software perspective, there's little—if any—value in seeing the thousands of graphs for variables discovered in the */proc* filesystem by every common monitoring tool. Metrics about power management and kernel drivers might be useful for understanding low-level infrastructure details, but they get routinely and blissfully ignored (as they should) by software developers because they indicate little useful information about impact on software performance.

However, higher-order infrastructure metrics like CPU usage, memory consumption, and disk activity are indicative of physical performance limitations. As a software engineer, you should be closely watching these indicators because they can be early warning signals of problems triggered by your code. For instance, you want to know if the deployment you just pushed caused resident memory usage to triple within minutes. Being able to see sudden changes like a jump to twice as much CPU consumption or a spike in disk-write activity right after a new feature is introduced can quickly alert you to problematic code changes.

Higher-order infrastructure metrics may or may not be available, depending on how abstracted your underlying infrastructure has become. But if they are, you will certainly want to capture them as part of your approach to observability.

The connection between monitoring and observability here becomes one of correlation. When performance issues occur, you can use monitoring to quickly rule out or confirm systems-level issues. Therefore, it is useful to see systems-level metrics data side by side with your application-level observability data. Some observability tools (like Honeycomb and Lightstep) present that data in a shared context, though others may require you to use different tools or views to make those correlations.

Real-World Examples

While observability is still a nascent category, a few patterns are emerging for the coexistence of monitoring and observability. The examples cited in this section represent the patterns we've commonly seen among our customers or within the larger observability community, but they are by no means exhaustive or definitive. These approaches are included to illustrate how the concepts described in this chapter are applied in the real world.

Our first example customer had a rich ecosystem of tools for understanding the behavior of their production systems. Prior to making a switch to observability, teams were using a combination of Prometheus for traditional monitoring, Jaeger for distributed tracing, and a traditional APM tool. They were looking to improve their incident response times by simplifying their existing multitool approach that required making correlations among data captured in three disparate systems.

Switching to an observability-based approach meant that they were able to consolidate needs and reduce their footprint to a monitoring system and an observability system that coexist. Software engineering teams at this organization report primarily using observability to understand and debug their software in production. The central operations team still uses Prometheus to monitor the infrastructure. However, software engineers report that they can still refer to Prometheus when they have questions about the resource usage impacts of their code. They also report that this need is infrequent and that they rarely need to use Prometheus to troubleshoot application bottlenecks.

Our second example customer is a relatively newer company that was able to build a greenfield application stack. Their production services primarily leverage serverless functions and SaaS platforms to power their applications, and they run almost no infrastructure of their own. Never having had any real infrastructure to begin with, they never started down the path of trying to make monitoring solutions work for their environment. They rely on application instrumentation and observability to understand and debug their software in production. They also export some of that data for longer-term aggregation and warehousing.

Lastly, our third example customer is a mature financial services company undergoing a digital transformation initiative. They have a large heterogeneous mix of legacy infrastructure and applications as well as greenfield applications that are managed across a variety of business units and engineering teams. Many of the older applications are still operating, but the teams that originally built and maintained them have long since disbanded or been reorganized into other parts of the company. Many applications are managed with a mix of metrics-based monitoring paired with dashboarding capabilities (provided by an all-in-one commercial vendor), along with various logging tools to search their unstructured logs.

The business would not realize much, if any, value from ripping out, rearchitecting, and replacing monitoring approaches that work well for stable and working services. Instead, greenfield applications are being developed for observability instead of using the former approach requiring a mix of monitoring, dashboards, and logging. When new applications use company infrastructure, software engineering teams also have access to infrastructure metrics to monitor resource usage impacts. However, some software engineering teams are starting to capture infrastructure metrics in their events in order to reduce their need to use a different system to correlate resource usage with application issues.

Conclusion

The guiding principle for determining how observability and monitoring coexist within your organization should be dictated by the software and infrastructure responsibilities adopted within its walls. Monitoring is best suited to evaluating the health of your systems. Observability is best suited to evaluating the health of your software. Exactly how much of each solution will be necessary in any given organization depends on how much management of that underlying infrastructure has been outsourced to third-party (aka cloud) providers.

The most notable exceptions to that neat dividing line are higher-order infrastructure metrics on physical devices that directly impact software performance, like CPU, memory, and disk. Metrics that indicate consumption of these physical infrastructure constraints are critical for understanding the boundaries imposed by underlying infrastructure. If these metrics are available from your cloud infrastructure provider, they should be included as part of your approach to observability.

By illustrating a few common approaches to balancing monitoring and observability in complementary ways, you can see how the considerations outlined throughout this chapter are implemented in the real world by different teams. Now that we've covered the fundamentals of observability in depth, the next part of this book goes beyond technology considerations to also explore the cultural changes necessary for successfully adopting observability practices and driving that adoption across teams.

PART III

Observability for Teams

In Part II, we examined various technical aspects of observability, how those concepts build on one another to enable the core analysis loop and debugging from first principles, and how that practice can coexist with traditional monitoring. In this part, we switch gears to look at the changes in social and cultural practices that help drive observability adoption across different teams.

Chapter 10 tackles many of the common challenges teams face when first starting down the path of observability. How and where you start will always depend on multiple factors, but this chapter recaps many of the techniques we've seen work effectively.

Chapter 11 focuses on how developer workflows change when using observability. Though we've referenced this topic in earlier chapters, here we walk through more concrete steps. You'll learn about the benefits developers gain by adding custom instrumentation into their code early in the development phase, and how that's used to debug their tests and to ensure that their code works correctly all the way through production.

Chapter 12 looks at the potential that observability unlocks when it comes to using more sophisticated methods for monitoring the health of your services in production. This chapter introduces service-level objectives (SLOs) and how they can be used for more effective alerting.

Chapter 13 builds on the preceding chapter by demonstrating why event data is a key part of creating more accurate, actionable, and debuggle alerts than using SLOs based on metrics data.

Chapter 14 looks at how teams can use observability to debug and better understand other parts of their stack, like their CI/CD build pipelines. This guest-contributed chapter is written by Frank Chen, senior staff software engineer at Slack.

This part of the book focuses on team workflows that can change and benefit from observability practices by detailing various scenarios and use cases to address common pain points for engineering teams managing modern software systems operating at any scale. In Part IV, we'll look at specific and unique challenges that occur when using observability tools at scale.

CHAPTER 10

Applying Observability Practices in Your Team

Let's switch gears to focus on the fundamentals of observability from a social and cultural practice perspective. In this chapter, we provide several tips to help you get started with observability practices. If you're in a leadership role within your engineering team—such as a team lead, a manager, or maybe the resident observability fan/champion—the hardest thing to figure out (after getting management approval) in an observability implementation strategy is knowing where to start.

For us, this is a particularly tricky chapter to write. Having helped many teams start down this path, we know that no universal recipe for success exists. How and where you get started will always depend on many factors. As unsatisfying as "it depends" can be for an answer, the truth is that your journey with observability depends on particulars including the problems most pertinent to you and your team, the gaps in your existing tooling, the level of support and buy-in from the rest of your organization, the size of your team, and other such considerations.

Whatever approach works best for you is, by definition, not wrong. The advice in this chapter is not intended to suggest that this is the one true way to get started with observability (there is no singular path!). That said, we have seen a few emergent patterns and, if you are struggling with where to begin, some of these suggestions may be helpful to you. Feel free to pick and choose from any of the tips in this chapter.

Join a Community Group

Observability is an emerging practice, and the approaches are still relatively young, with plenty of exploration left to do. Whenever the practices and technology behind our sociotechnical systems are rapidly evolving, one of the best ways to learn and improve is by participating in a community of people who are struggling with variations on the same themes as you. Community groups connect you with other professionals who can quickly become a helpful network of friends and acquaintances.

As you and your community face similar challenges, you'll have an opportunity to learn so much very quickly just by hanging out in Slack groups and talking to other people who are banging against the same types of problems. Community groups allow you to connect with people beyond your normal circles from a variety of backgrounds. By actively participating and understanding how other teams handle some of the same challenges you have, you'll make comparative observations and learn from the experiences of others.

Over time, you'll also discover other community members with common similarities in tech stack, team size, organizational dynamics, and so forth. Those connections will give you someone to turn to as a sounding board, for background, or personal experiences with solutions or approaches you might also be considering. Having that type of shared context before you pull the trigger on new experiments can be invaluable. Actively participating in a community group will save you a ton of time and heartbreak.

Participating in a community will also keep you attuned to developments you may have otherwise missed. Different providers of observability tools will participate in different communities to better understand user challenges, gather feedback on new ideas, or just generally get a pulse on what's happening. Participating in a community specific to your observability tool of choice can also give you a pulse on what's happening as it happens.

When joining a community, remember that community relationships are a two-way street. Don't forget to do your share of chopping wood and carrying water: show up and start contributing by helping others first. Being a good community citizen means participating and helping the group for a while before dropping any heavy asks for help. In other words, don't speak up only when you need something from others. Communities are only as strong as you make them.

If you need a place to start, we recommend checking out the CNCF Technical Advisory Group (TAG) for Observability (*https://github.com/cncf/tag-observability*). There you'll find both Slack chat groups as well as regular online meetings. The OpenTelemetry Community page (*https://opentelemetry.io/community*) also lists useful resources. More generally, a lot of conversations around observability happen via Twitter (search for "observability" and you'll find people and topics to follow). More specifically, product-focused Slack groups such as Honeycomb's Pollinators Slack (*https://hny.co/blog/spread-the-love-appreciating-our-pollinators-community*) exist, where you'll find a mix of general and vendor-specific information. We also recommend Michael Hausenblas's newsletter o11y news (*https://o11y.news*).

Start with the Biggest Pain Points

Introducing any new technology can be risky. As a result, new technology initiatives often target small and inconspicuous services as a place to start. Counterintuitively, for observability, starting small is one of the bigger mistakes we often see people make.

Observability tools are designed to help you quickly find elusive problems. Starting with an unobtrusive and relatively unimportant service will have the exact opposite effect of proving the value of observability. If you start with a service that already works relatively well, your team will experience all of the work it takes to get started with observability and get none of the benefits.

When spearheading a new initiative, it's important to get points on the board relatively quickly. Demonstrate value, pique curiosity, and garner interest by solving hard or elusive problems right off the bat. Has a flaky and flappy service been waking people up for weeks, yet nobody can figure out the right fix? Start there. Do you have a problem with constant database congestion, yet no one can figure out the cause? Start there. Are you running a service bogged down by an inexplicable load that's being generated by a yet-to-be-identified user? That's your best place to start.

Quickly demonstrating value will win over naysayers, create additional support, and further drive observability adoption. Don't pick an easy problem to start with. Pick a hard problem that observability is designed to knock out of the park. Start with that service. Instrument the code, deploy it to production, explore with great curiosity, figure out how to find the answer, and then socialize that success. Show off your solution during your weekly team meeting. Write up your findings and methodologies; then share them with the company. Make sure whoever is on call for that service knows how to find that solution.

The fastest way to drive adoption is to solve the biggest pain points for teams responsible for managing their production services. Target those pains. Resist the urge to start small.

Buy Instead of Build

Similar to starting with the biggest pain points, the decision of whether to build your own observability tooling or buy a commercially available solution comes down to proving return on investment (ROI) quickly. We examine this argument more closely in Chapter 15. For now, we'll frame the decision at the outset to favor putting in the least amount of effort to prove the greatest amount of value. Building an entire solution first is the greatest amount of possible effort with the longest possible time to value.

Be prepared to try out multiple observability solutions to see if they meet the functional requirements laid out in Chapter 1. Remember that observability allows you to understand and explain any state your system can get into, no matter how novel or bizarre. You must be able to comparatively debug that bizarre or novel state across all dimensions of system state data, and combinations of dimensions, in an ad hoc manner, without being required to define or predict those debugging needs in advance.

Unfortunately, at the time of this writing, few tools exist that are able to deliver on those requirements. While the marketing departments of various vendors are happy to apply the observability label to tools in their product suites, few are able to unlock the workflows and benefits outlined in this book. Therefore, as a user, you should be prepared to try out many tools to see which actually deliver and which are simply repackaging the same traditional monitoring tools sold for years.

Your best way to do that is to instrument your applications by using OpenTelemetry (see Chapter 7). Using OTel may not be as fast and easy as another vendor's proprietary agent or libraries, but it shouldn't be slow and difficult to use either. The small up-front investment in time necessary to do this right from the start will pay extreme dividends later when you decide to try multiple solutions to see which best meets your needs.

That misinformation and uncertainty is an unfortunate reality of today's vendor ecosystem. As a result, it can be tempting to bypass that entire mess by building your own solution. However, that choice is also fraught with a few unfortunate realities (see Chapter 15).

First, few off-the-shelf open source observability tools are available for you to run yourself, even if you wanted to. The three leading candidates you'll come across are Prometheus, the ELK stack (Elasticsearch, Logstash, and Kibana), and Jaeger. While each provides a specific valuable solution, none offers a complete solution that can deliver on the functional requirements for observability outlined in this book.

Prometheus is a TSDB for metrics monitoring. While Prometheus is arguably one of the most advanced metrics monitoring systems with a vibrant development community, it still operates solely in the world of metrics-based monitoring solutions. It carries with it the inherent limitations of trying to use coarse measures to discover finer-grained problems (see Chapter 2).

The *ELK stack* focuses on providing a log storage and querying solution. Log storage backends are optimized for plain-text search at the expense of other types of searching and aggregation. While useful when searching for known errors, plain-text search becomes impractical when searching for answers to compound questions like "Who is seeing this problem, and when are they seeing it?" Analyzing and identifying relevant patterns among a flood of plain-text logs critical for observability is challenging in an entirely log-based solution (see Chapter 8).

Jaeger is an event-based distributed tracing tool. Jaeger is arguably one of the most advanced open source distributed tracing tools available today. As discussed in Chapter 6, trace events are a fundamental building block for observable systems. However, a necessary component is also the analytical capability to determine which trace events are of interest during your investigation. Jaeger has some support for filtering certain data, but it lacks sophisticated capabilities for analyzing and segmenting all of your trace data (see Chapter 8).

Each of these tools provides different parts of a system view that can be used to achieve observability. The challenges in using them today are either running disparate systems that place the burden of carrying context between them into the minds of their operators, or building your own bespoke solution for gluing those individual components together. Today, no open source tool exists to provide observability capabilities in one out-of-the-box solution. Hopefully, that will not be true forever. But it is today's reality.

Lastly, whichever direction you decide to take, make sure that the end result is actually providing you with observability. Stress-test the solution. Again, resist the urge to start small. Tackle big, difficult problems. Observability requires an ability to debug system state across all high-cardinality fields, with high dimensionality, in interactive and performant real-time exploration. Can this solution deliver the types of analysis and iterative investigation described in earlier chapters? If the answer is yes, congratulations! You found a great observability solution. If the answer is no, the product you are using has likely been misleadingly labeled as an observability solution when it is not.

The key to getting started with observability is to move quickly and demonstrate value early in the process. Choosing to buy a solution will keep your team focused on solving problems with observability tooling rather than on building their own. If you instrument your applications with OTel, you can avoid the trap of vendor lock-in and send your telemetry data to any tool you ultimately decide to use.

Flesh Out Your Instrumentation Iteratively

Properly instrumenting your applications takes time. The automatic instrumentation included with projects like OTel are a good place to start. But the highest-value instrumentation will be specific to the needs of your individual application. Start with as much useful instrumentation as you can but plan to develop your instrumentation as you go.

For more examples of automatic versus manual instrumentation, we recommend "What Is Auto-Instrumentation?" (*https://hny.co/blog/what-is-auto-instrumentation*), a blog post by Mike Goldsmith.

One of the best strategies for rolling out observability across an entire organization is to instrument a painful service or two as you first get started. Use that instrumentation exercise as a reference point and learning exercise for the rest of the pilot team. Once the pilot team is familiar with the new tooling, use any new debugging situation as a way to introduce more and more useful instrumentation.

Whenever an on-call engineer is paged about a problem in production, the first thing they should do is use the new tooling to instrument problem areas of your application. Use the new instrumentation to figure out where issues are occurring. After the second or third time people take this approach, they usually catch on to how much easier and less time-consuming it is to debug issues by introducing instrumentation first. Debugging from instrumentation first allows you to see what's really happening.

Once the pilot team members are up to speed, they can help others learn. They can provide coaching on creating helpful instrumentation, suggest helpful queries, or point others toward more examples of helpful troubleshooting patterns. Each new debugging issue can be used to build out the instrumentation you need. You don't need a fully developed set of instrumentation to get immediate value with observability.

A Note on Instrumentation Conventions

The focus when you get started with instrumentation should be to prove as much value as possible with your chosen observability tool. The fact that you are iteratively fleshing out your instrumentation is more important than how you do it.

However, keep in mind that as your instrumentation grows and as adoption spreads across teams, you should introduce naming conventions for custom telemetry data you are generating. For examples of organization-wide standards, see Chapter 14.

Look for Opportunities to Leverage Existing Efforts

One of the biggest barriers to adopting any new technology is the *sunk-cost fallacy*. Individuals and organizations commit the sunk-cost fallacy when they continue a

---

behavior or endeavor as a result of previously invested time, money, or effort.[1] How much time, money, and effort has your organization already invested in traditional approaches that are no longer serving your needs?

Resistance to fundamental change often hits a roadblock when the perception of wasted resources creeps in. What about all those years invested in understanding and instrumenting for the old solutions? Although the sunk-cost fallacy isn't logical, the feelings behind it are real, and they'll stop your efforts dead in their tracks if you don't do anything about them.

Always be on the lookout for and leap at any chance to forklift other work into your observability initiatives. As examples, if there's an existing stream of data you can tee to a secondary destination or critical data that can be seen in another way, jump on the opportunity to ship that data into your observability solution. Examples of situations you could use to do this include:

- If you're using an ELK stack—or even just the Logstash part—it's trivial to add a snippet of code to fork the output of a source stream to a secondary destination. Send that stream to your observability tool. Invite users to compare the experience.

- If you're already using structured logs, all you need to do is add a unique ID to log events as they propagate throughout your entire stack. You can keep those logs in your existing log analysis tool, while also sending them as trace events to your observability tool.

- Try running observability instrumentation (for example, Honeycomb's Beelines or OTel) alongside your existing APM solution. Invite users to compare and contrast the experience.

- If you're using Ganglia, you can leverage that data by parsing the Extensible Markup Language (XML) dump it puts into /var/tmp with a once-a-minute cronjob that shovels that data into your observability tool as events. That's a less than optimal use of observability, but it certainly creates familiarity for Ganglia users.

- Re-create the most useful of your old monitoring dashboards as easily reference-able queries within your new observability tool. While dashboards certainly have their shortcomings (see Chapter 2), this gives new users a landing spot where they can understand the system performance they care about at a glance, and also gives them an opportunity to explore and know more.

---

1 Hal R. Arkes and Catherine Blumer, "The Psychology of Sunk Costs," *Organizational Behavior and Human Decision Processes* 35 (1985): 124–140.

Anything you can do to blend worlds will help lower that barrier to adoption. Other people need to understand how their concerns map into the new solution. Help them see their current world in the new world you're creating for them. It's OK if this sneak peek isn't perfect. Even if the experience is pretty rough, you're shooting for familiarity. The use of the new tooling in this approach might be terrible, but if the names of things are familiar and the data is something they know, it will still invite people to interact with it more than a completely scratch data set.

Prepare for the Hardest Last Push

Using the preceding strategies to tackle the biggest pain points first and adopt an iterative approach can help you make fast progress as you're getting started. But those strategies don't account for one of the hardest parts of implementing an observability solution: crossing the finish line. Now that you have some momentum going, you also need a strategy for polishing off the remaining work.

Depending on the scope of work and size of your team, rolling out new instrumentation iteratively as part of your on-call approach can typically get most teams to a point where they've done about half to two-thirds of the work required to introduce observability into every part of the stack they intend. Inevitably, most teams discover that some parts of their stack are under less-active development than others. For those rarely touched parts of the stack, you'll need a solid completion plan, or your implementation efforts are likely to lag.

Even with the best of project management intentions, as some of the pain that was driving observability adoption begins to ease, so too can the urgency of completing the implementation work. The reality most teams live in is that engineering cycles are scarce, demands are always competing, and another pain to address is always waiting around the corner once they've dealt with the one in front of them.

The goal of a complete implementation is to have built a reliable go-to debugging solution that can be used to fully understand the state of your production applications whenever anything goes wrong. Before you get to that end state, you will likely have various bits of tooling that are best suited to solving different problems. During the implementation phase, that disconnect can be tolerable because you're working toward a more cohesive future. But in the long-term, not completing your implementation could create a drain of time, cognitive capacity, and attention from your teams.

That's when you need to make a timeline to chug through the rest quickly. Your target milestone should be to accomplish the remaining instrumentation work necessary so that your team can use your observability tool as its go-to option for debugging issues in production. Consider setting up a special push to get to the finish line, like a hack week culminating in a party with prizes (or something equally silly and fun) to bring the project over the top to get it done.

During this phase, it's worth noting that your team should strive to genericize instrumentation as often as possible so that it can be reused in other applications or by other teams within your organization. A common strategy here is to avoid repeating the initial implementation work by creating generic observability libraries that allow you to swap out underlying solutions without getting into code internals, similar to the approach taken by OTel (see Chapter 7).

Conclusion

Knowing exactly where and how to start your observability journey depends on the particulars of your team. Hopefully, these general recommendations are useful to help you figure out places to get started. Actively participating in a community of peers can be invaluable as your first place to dig in. As you get started, focus on solving the biggest pain points rather than starting in places that already operate smoothly enough. Throughout your implementation journey, remember to keep an inclination toward moving fast, demonstrating high value and ROI, and tackling work iteratively. Find opportunities to include as many parts of your organization as possible. And don't forget to plan for completing the work in one big final push to get your implementation project over the finish line.

The tips in this chapter can help you complete the work it takes to get started with observability. Once that work is complete, using observability on a daily basis helps unlock other new ways of working by default. The rest of this part of the book explores those in detail. In the next chapter, we'll examine how observability-driven development can revolutionize your understanding of the way new code behaves in production.

CHAPTER 11

Observability-Driven Development

As a practice, observability fundamentally helps engineers improve their understanding of how the code they've written is experienced by end users (typically, in production). However, that should not imply that observability is applicable only after software is released to production. Observability can, and should, be an early part of the software development life cycle. In this chapter, you will learn about the practice of observability-driven development.

We will start by exploring test-driven development, how it is used in the development cycle, and where it can fall short. Then we'll look at how to use observability in a method similar to test-driven development. We'll examine the ramifications of doing so, look at various ways to debug your code, and more closely examine the nuances of how instrumentation helps observability. Finally, we'll look at how observability-driven development can shift observability left (*https://w.wiki/56wf*) and help speed up software delivery to production.

Test-Driven Development

Today's gold standard for testing software prior to its release in production is test-driven development (*https://w.wiki/Lnw*) (TDD). TDD is arguably one of the more successful practices to take hold across the software development industry within the last two decades. TDD has provided a useful framework for shift-left testing that catches, and prevents, many potential problems long before they reach production. Adopted across wide swaths of the software development industry, TDD should be credited with having uplifted the quality of code running production services.

TDD is a powerful practice that provides engineers a clear way to think about software operability. Applications are defined by a deterministic set of repeatable tests that can be run hundreds of times per day. If these repeatable tests pass, the application must be running as expected. Before changes to the application are produced, they start as a set of new tests that exist to verify that the change would work as expected. A developer can then begin to write new code in order to ensure the test passes.

TDD is particularly powerful because tests run the same way every time. Data typically doesn't persist between test runs; it gets dropped, erased, and re-created from scratch for each run. Responses from underlying or remote systems are stubbed or mocked. With TDD, developers are tasked with creating a specification that precisely defines the expected behaviors for an application in a controlled state. The role of tests is to identify any unexpected deviations from that controlled state so that engineers can then deal with them immediately. In doing so, TDD removes guesswork and provides consistency.

But that very consistency and isolation also limits TDD's revelations about what is happening with your software in production. Running isolated tests doesn't reveal whether customers are having a good experience with your service. Nor does passing those tests mean that any errors or regressions could be quickly and directly isolated and fixed before releasing that code back into production.

Any reasonably experienced engineer responsible for managing software running in production can tell you that production environments are anything but consistent. Production is full of interesting deviations that your code might encounter out in the wild but that have been excised from tests because they're not repeatable, don't quite fit the specification, or don't go according to plan. While the consistency and isolation of TDD makes your code tractable, it does not prepare your code for the interesting anomalies that should be surfaced, watched, stressed, and tested because they ultimately shape your software's behavior when real people start interacting with it.

Observability can help you write and ship better code even before it lands in source control—because it's part of the set of tools, processes, and culture that allows engineers to find bugs in their code quickly.

Observability in the Development Cycle

Catching bugs cleanly, resolving them swiftly, and preventing them from becoming a backlog of technical debt that weighs down the development process relies on a team's ability to find those bugs quickly. Yet, software development teams often hinder their ability to do so for a variety of reasons.

For example, consider that in some organizations, software engineers aren't responsible for operating their software in production. These engineers merge their code into main, cross their fingers in hopes that this change won't be one that breaks production, and essentially wait to get paged if a problem occurs. Sometimes they get paged soon after deployment. The deployment is then rolled back, and the triggering changes can be examined for bugs. But more likely, problems aren't detected for hours, days, weeks, or months after the code is merged. By that time, it becomes extremely difficult to pick out the origin of the bug, remember the context, or decipher the original intent behind why that code was written or why it shipped.

Quickly resolving bugs critically depends on being able to examine the problem *while the original intent is still fresh in the original author's head*. It will never again be as easy to debug a problem as it was right after it was written and shipped. It only gets harder from there; speed is key. (In older deployment models, you might have merged your changes, waited for a release engineer to perform the release at an unknown time, and then waited for operations engineers on the front line to page a software engineer to fix it—and likely not even the engineer who wrote it in the first place.) The more time that elapses between when a bug is inadvertently shipped and when the code containing that bug is examined for problems, the more time that's wasted across many humans by several orders of magnitude.

At first glance, the links between observability and writing better software may not be clear. But it is this need for debugging quickly that deeply intertwines the two.

Determining Where to Debug

Newcomers to observability often make the mistake of thinking that observability is a way to debug your code, similar to using highly verbose logging. While it's possible to debug your code using observability tools, that is not their primary purpose. Observability operates on the order of *systems*, not on the order of *functions*. Emitting enough detail at the line level to reliably debug code would emit so much output that it would swamp most observability systems with an obscene amount of storage and scale. Paying for a system capable of doing that would be impractical, because it could cost from one to ten times as much as your system itself.

Observability is not for debugging your code logic. *Observability is for figuring out where in your systems to find the code you need to debug.* Observability tools help you by swiftly narrowing down where problems may be occurring. From which component did an error originate? Where is latency being introduced? Where did a piece of this data get munged? Which hop is taking up the most processing time? Is that wait time evenly distributed across all users, or is it experienced by only a subset? Observability helps your investigation of problems pinpoint likely sources.

Often, observability will also give you a good idea of what might be happening in or around an affected component, indicate what the bug might be, or even provide hints as to where the bug is happening: in your code, the platform's code, or a higher-level architectural object.

Once you've identified where the bug lives and some qualities about how it arises, observability's job is done. From there, if you want to dive deeper into the code itself, the tool you want is a good old-fashioned debugger (for example, the GNU Debugger, GDB) or a newer generation profiler. Once you suspect how to reproduce the problem, you can spin up a local instance of the code, copy over the full context from the service, and continue your investigation. While they are related, the difference between an observability tool and a debugger is an order of scale; like a telescope and a microscope, they may have some overlapping use cases, but they are primarily designed for different things.

This is an example of different paths you might take with debugging versus observability:

- You see a spike in latency. You start at the edge; group by endpoint; calculate average, 90th-, and 99th-percentile latencies; identify a cadre of slow requests; and trace one of them. It shows the timeouts begin at `service3`. You copy the context from the traced request into your local copy of the `service3` binary and attempt to reproduce it in the debugger or profiler.

- You see a spike in latency. You start at the edge; group by endpoint; calculate average, 90th-, and 99th-percentile latencies; and notice that exclusively write endpoints are suddenly slower. You group by database destination host, and note that the slow queries are distributed across some, but not all, of your database primaries. For those primaries, this is happening only to ones of a certain instance type or in a particular AZ. You conclude the problem is not a code problem, but one of infrastructure.

Debugging in the Time of Microservices

When viewed through this lens, it becomes clear why the rise of microservices is tied so strongly to the rise of observability. Software systems used to have fewer components, which meant they were easier to reason about. An engineer could think their way through all possible problem areas by using only low-cardinality tagging. Then, to understand their code logic, they simply always used a debugger or IDE. But once monoliths started being decomposed into many distributed microservices, the debugger no longer worked as well because it couldn't hop the network.

 As a historical aside, the phrase "`strace` for microservices" was an early attempt to describe this new style of understanding system internals before the word "observability" was adapted to fit the needs of introspecting production software systems.

Once service requests started traversing networks to fulfill their functions, all kinds of additional operational, architectural, infrastructural, and other assorted categories of complexity became irrevocably intertwined with the logic bugs we unintentionally shipped and inflicted on ourselves.

In monolithic systems, it's obvious to your debugger if a certain function slows immediately after code is shipped that modified that function. Now, such a change could manifest in several ways. You might notice that a particular service is getting slower, or a set of dependent services is getting slower, or you might start seeing a spike in timeouts—or the only manifestation might be a user complaining. Who knows.

And regardless of how it manifests, it is likely still incredibly unclear according to your monitoring tooling whether that slowness is being caused by any of the following:

- A bug in your code
- A particular user changing their usage pattern
- A database overflowing its capacity
- Network connection limits
- A misconfigured load balancer
- Issues with service registration or service discovery
- Some combination of the preceding factors

Without observability, all you may see is that all of the performance graphs are either spiking or dipping at the same time.

How Instrumentation Drives Observability

Observability helps pinpoint the origins of problems, common outlier conditions, which half a dozen or more things must all be true for the error to occur, and so forth. Observability is also ideal for swiftly identifying whether problems are restricted to a particular build ID, set of hosts, instance types, container versions, kernel patch versions, database secondaries, or any number of other architectural details.

However, a necessary component of observability is the creation of useful instrumentation. *Good instrumentation drives observability.* One way to think about how instrumentation is useful is to consider it in the context of pull requests. Pull requests should never be submitted or accepted without first asking yourself, "How will I know if this change is working as intended?"

A helpful goal when developing instrumentation is to create reinforcement mechanisms and shorter feedback loops. In other words, tighten the loop between shipping code and feeling the consequences of errors. This is also known as *putting the software engineers on call*.

One way to achieve this is to automatically page the person who just merged the code being shipped. For a brief period of time, maybe 30 minutes to 1 hour, if an alert is triggered in production, the alert gets routed to that person. When an engineer experiences their own code in production, their ability (and motivation) to instrument their code for faster isolation and resolution of issues naturally increases.

This feedback loop is not punishment; rather, it is *essential* to code ownership. You cannot develop the instincts and practices needed to ship quality code if you are insulated from the feedback of your errors. Every engineer should be expected to instrument their code such that they can answer these questions as soon as it's deployed:

- Is your code doing what you expected it to do?
- How does it compare to the previous version?
- Are users actively using your code?
- Are any abnormal conditions emerging?

A more advanced approach is to enable engineers to test their code against a small subset of production traffic. With sufficient instrumentation, the best way to understand how a proposed change will work in production is to measure how it will work by deploying it to production. That can be done in several controlled ways. For example, that can happen by deploying new features behind a feature flag and exposing it to only a subset of users. Alternatively, a feature could also be deployed directly to production and have only select requests from particular users routed to the new feature. These types of approaches shorten feedback loops to mere seconds or minutes, rather than what are usually substantially longer periods of time waiting for the release.

If you are capturing sufficient instrumentation detail in the context of your requests, you can systematically start at the edge of any problem and work your way to the correct answer every single time, with no guessing, intuition, or prior knowledge needed. This is one revolutionary advance that observability has over monitoring systems, and it does a lot to move operations engineering back into the realm of science, not magic and intuition.

Shifting Observability Left

While TDD ensures that developed software adheres to an isolated specification, *observability-driven development* ensures that software works in the messy reality that is a production environment. Now software is strewn across a complex infrastructure, at any particular point in time, experiencing fluctuating workloads, with certain users doing unpredictable things.

Building instrumentation into your software early in the development life cycle allows your engineers to more readily consider and more quickly see the impact that small changes truly have in production. By focusing on just adherence to an isolated specification, teams inadvertently create conditions that block their visibility into the chaotic playground where that software comes into contact with messy and unpredictable people problems. As you've seen in previous chapters, traditional monitoring approaches reveal only an aggregate view of measures that were developed in response to triggering alerts for known issues. Traditional tooling provides little ability to accurately reason about what happens in complex modern software systems.

Resulting from the inability to accurately reason about how production operates, teams will often approach production as a glass castle—a beautiful monument to their collective design over time, but one they're afraid to disturb because any unforeseen movement could shatter the entire structure. By developing the engineering skills to write, deploy, and use good telemetry and observability to understand behaviors in production, teams gain an ability to reason about what really happens in production. As a result, they become empowered to reach further and further into the development life cycle to consider the nuances of detecting unforeseen anomalies that could be roaming around their castles unseen.

Observability-driven development allows engineering teams to turn their glass castles into interactive playgrounds. Production environments aren't immutable but full of action, and engineers should be empowered to confidently walk into any game and score a win. But that happens only when observability isn't considered solely the domain of SREs, infrastructure engineers, or operations teams. Software engineers must adopt observability and work it into their development practices in order to unwind the cycle of fear they've developed over making any changes to production.

Using Observability to Speed Up Software Delivery

When software engineers bundle telemetry along with new features headed for production, they can shorten the time between the commit and a feature being released to end users. Patterns like using feature flags and progressive delivery (see Chapter 4) that decouple deployments from releases enable engineers to observe and understand the performance of their new feature as it is slowly released to production.

A common perception in the software industry is that a trade-off usually occurs between speed and quality: you can release software quickly or you can release high-quality software, but not both. A key finding of *Accelerate: Building and Scaling High Performing Technology Organizations* was that this inverse relationship is a myth.[1] For elite performers, speed and quality go up in tandem and reinforce each other. When speed gets faster, failures become smaller, happen less often, and—when they do happen—are easier to recover from. Conversely, for teams that move slowly, failures tend to happen more often and take substantially longer to recover.

When engineers treat production as a glass castle where they hesitate to tread, they will instinctively and comfortably roll back deployments at the slightest sign of any potential issues. Because they lack the controls to make small tweaks, tune settings, gracefully degrade services, or progressively deploy changes in response to problems they intimately understand, they will instead take their foot off the gas and halt any further deployments or further changes while they roll back the current change they don't fully understand. That's the opposite reaction to what would be most helpful in this situation.

The key metric for the health and effectiveness of an engineering team can be best captured by a single metric: the time elapsed from when code is written to when it is in production. Every team should be tracking this metric and working to improve it.

Observability-driven development in tandem with feature flags and progressive delivery patterns can equip engineering teams with the tools they need to stop instinctively rolling back deployments and instead dig in to further investigate what's really happening whenever issues occur during release of a new feature.

However, this all hinges on your team's ability to release code to production on a relatively speedy cadence. If that is not how your team currently operates, here are a few ways you can help speed up code delivery to production:

- Ship a single coherent bundle of changes one at a time, one merge by one engineer. The single greatest cause of deployments that break "something" and take hours or days to detangle and roll back is the batching of many changes by many people over many days.

- Spend real engineering effort on your deployment process and code. Assign experienced engineers to own it (not the intern). Make sure everyone can understand your deployment pipelines and that they feel empowered to continuously improve them. Don't let them be the sole province of a single engineer or team. Instead, get everyone's usage, buy-in, and contributions. For more tips on making your pipelines understandable for everyone, see Chapter 14.

---

1 Nicole Forsgren et al., *Accelerate: Building and Scaling High Performing Technology Organizations* (*https://oreil.ly/vgne4*) (Portland, OR: IT Revolution Press, 2018).

Conclusion

Observability can, and should, be used early in the software development life cycle. Test-driven development is a useful tool for examining how your code runs against a defined specification. Observability-driven development is a useful tool for examining how your code behaves in the chaotic and turbulent world of production.

For software engineers, a historical lack of being able to understand how production actually works has created a mindset that treats production like a glass castle. By properly observing the behavior of new features as they are released to production, you can change that mindset so that production instead becomes an interactive playground where you can connect with the way end users experience the software you write.

Observability-driven development is essential to being able to achieve a high-performing software engineering team. Rather than presuming that observability is the sole domain of SREs, infrastructure engineers, and ops teams, all software engineers should embrace observability as an essential part of their practices.

CHAPTER 12

Using Service-Level Objectives for Reliability

While observability and traditional monitoring can coexist, observability unlocks the potential to use more sophisticated and complementary approaches to monitoring. The next two chapters will show you how practicing observability and service-level objectives (SLOs) together can improve the reliability of your systems.

In this chapter, you will learn about the common problems that traditional threshold-based monitoring approaches create for your team, how distributed systems exacerbate those problems, and how using an SLO-based approach to monitoring instead solves those problems. We'll conclude with a real-world example of replacing traditional threshold-based alerting with SLOs. And in Chapter 13, we'll examine how observability makes your SLO-based alerts actionable and debuggable.

Let's begin with understanding the role of monitoring and alerting and the previous approaches to them.

Traditional Monitoring Approaches Create Dangerous Alert Fatigue

In monitoring-based approaches, alerts often measure the things that are easiest to measure. Metrics are used to track simplistic system states that might indicate a service's underlying process(es) may be running poorly or may be a leading indicator of troubles ahead. These states might, for example, trigger an alert if CPU is above 80%, or if available memory is below 10%, or if disk space is nearly full, or if more than x many threads are running, or any set of other simplistic measures of underlying system conditions.

While such simplistic "potential-cause" measures are easy to collect, they don't produce meaningful alerts for you to act upon. Deviations in CPU utilization may also be indicators that a backup process is running, or a garbage collector is doing its cleanup job, or that any other phenomenon may be happening on a system. In other words, those conditions may reflect any number of system factors, not just the problematic ones we really care about. Triggering alerts from these measures based on the underlying hardware creates a high percentage of false positives.

Experienced engineering teams that own the operation of their software in production will often learn to tune out, or even suppress, these types of alerts because they're so unreliable. Teams that do so regularly adopt phrases like "Don't worry about that alert; we know the process runs out of memory from time to time."

Becoming accustomed to alerts that are prone to false positives is a known problem and a dangerous practice. In other industries, that problem is known as *normalization of deviance*: a term coined during the investigation of the Challenger disaster (*https://pubmed.ncbi.nlm.nih.gov/25742063*). When individuals in an organization regularly shut off alarms or fail to take action when alarms occur, they eventually become so desensitized about the practice deviating from the expected response that it no longer feels wrong to them. Failures that are "normal" and disregarded are, at best, simply background noise. At worst, they lead to disastrous oversights from cascading system failures.

In the software industry, the poor signal-to-noise ratio of monitoring-based alerting often leads to *alert fatigue*—and to gradually paying less attention to all alerts, because so many of them are false alarms, not actionable, or simply not useful. Unfortunately, with monitoring-based alerting, that problem is often compounded when incidents occur. Post-incident reviews often generate action items that create new, more important alerts that, presumably, would have alerted in time to prevent the problem. That leads to an even larger set of alerts generated during the next incident. That pattern of alert escalation creates an ever-increasing flood of alerts and an ever-increasing cognitive load on responding engineers to determine which alerts matter and which don't.

That type of dysfunction is so common in the software industry that many monitoring and incident-response tool vendors proudly offer various solutions labeled "AIOps" to group, suppress, or otherwise try to process that alert load for you (see "This Misleading Promise of AIOps" on page 91 Engineering teams have become so accustomed to alert noise that this pattern is now seen as normal. If the future of running software in production is doomed to generate so much noise that it must be artificially processed, it's safe to say the situation has gone well beyond a normalization of deviance. Industry vendors have now productized that deviance and will happily sell you a solution for its management.

Again, we believe that type of dysfunction exists because of the limitations imposed by using metrics and monitoring tools that used to be the best choice we had to understand the state of production systems. As an industry, we now suffer a collective Stockholm Syndrome that is just the tip of the dysfunction iceberg when it comes to the many problems we encounter today as a result. The complexity of modern system architectures along with the higher demands for their resilience have pushed the state of these dysfunctional affairs away from tolerable and toward no longer acceptable.

Distributed systems today require an alternative approach. Let's examine why approaches to monitoring a monolith break down at scale and what we can do differently.

Threshold Alerting Is for Known-Unknowns Only

Anticipating failure modes is much easier in self-contained systems than in distributed systems. So, adding monitoring that expects each of those known failure modes to occur seems logical. Operations teams supporting self-contained production systems can write specific monitoring checks for each precise state.

However, as systems become more complex, they create a combinatorial explosion of potential failure modes. Ops teams accustomed to working with less complex systems will rely on their intuition, best guesses, and memories of past outages to predict any possible system failures they can imagine. While that approach with traditional monitoring may work at smaller scales, the explosion of complexity in modern systems requires teams to write and maintain hundreds, or even thousands, of precise state checks to look for every conceivable scenario.

That approach isn't sustainable. The checks aren't maintainable, often the knowledge isn't transferable, and past historical behavior doesn't necessarily predict failures likely to occur in the future. The traditional monitoring mindset is often about preventing failure. But in a distributed system with hundreds or thousands of components serving production traffic, *failure is inevitable*.

Today, engineering teams regularly distribute load across multiple disparate systems. They split up, shard, horizontally partition, and replicate data across geographically distributed systems. While these architectural decisions optimize for performance, resiliency, and scalability, they can also make systemic failures impossible to detect or predict. Emergent failure modes can impact your users long before the coarse synthetic probes traditionally used as indicators will tell you. Traditional measurements for service health suddenly have little value because they're so irrelevant to the behavior of the system as a whole.

Traditional system metrics often miss unexpected failure modes in distributed systems. An abnormal number of running threads on one component might indicate garbage collection is in progress, or it might also indicate slow response times might be imminent in an upstream service. It's also possible that the condition detected via system metrics might be entirely unrelated to service slowness. Still, that system operator receiving an alert about that abnormal number of threads in the middle of the night won't know which of those conditions is true, and it's up to them to divine that correlation.

Further, distributed systems design for resilience with loosely coupled components. With modern infrastructure tooling, it's possible to automatically remediate many common issues that used to require waking up an engineer. You probably already use some of the current and commonplace methods for building resilience into your systems: autoscaling, load balancing, failover, and so forth. Automation can pause further rollout of a bad release or roll it back. Running in an active-active configuration or automating the process of promoting passive to active ensures that an AZ failure will cause damage only transiently. Failures that get automatically remediated *should not trigger alarms*. (Anecdotally, some teams may do just that in an attempt to build valuable "intuition" about the inner workings of a service. On the contrary, that noise only serves to starve the team of time they could be building intuition about the inner workings of service components that don't have auto-remediation.)

That's not to say that you shouldn't debug auto-remediated failures. You should absolutely debug those failures *during normal business hours*. The entire point of alerts is to bring attention to an emergency situation that simply cannot wait. Triggering alerts that wake up engineers in the middle of the night to notify them of transient failures simply creates noise and leads to burnout. Thus, we need a strategy to define the urgency of problems.

In a time of complex and interdependent systems, teams can easily reach fatigue from the deluge of alerts that may, but probably don't, reliably indicate a problem with the way customers are currently using the services your business relies on. Alerts for conditions that aren't tied directly to customer experience will quickly become nothing more than background noise. Those alerts are no longer serving their intended purpose and, more nefariously, actually serve the opposite purpose: they distract your team from paying attention to the alerts that really do matter.

If you expect to run a reliable service, your teams must remove any unreliable or noisy alerts. Yet many teams fear removing those unnecessary distractions. Often the prevailing concern is that by removing alerts, teams will have no way of learning about service degradation. But it's important to realize that these types of traditional alerts are helping you detect only *known-unknowns*: problems you know could happen but are unsure may be happening at any given time. That alert coverage provides a false sense of security because it does nothing to prepare you for dealing with new and novel failures, or the *unknown-unknowns*.

Practitioners of observability are looking for these unknown-unknowns, having outgrown those systems in which only a fixed set of failures can ever occur. While reducing your unknowns to only known-unknowns might be closer to achievable for legacy self-contained software systems with few components, that's certainly not the case with modern systems. Yet, organizations hesitate to remove many of the old alerts associated with traditional monitoring.

Later in this chapter, we'll look at ways to feel confident when removing unhelpful alerts. For now, let's define the criteria for an alert to be considered helpful. The Google SRE book indicates that a good alert must reflect urgent user impact, must be actionable, must be novel, and must require investigation rather than rote action.[1]

We'll define our alerting criteria to be a two-part subset. First, it must be a reliable indicator that the user experience of your service is in a degraded state. Second, the alert must be solvable. There must be a systematic (but not pure rote automatable) way to debug and take action in response to the alert that does not require a responder to divine the right course of action. If those two conditions are not true, any alert you have configured is no longer serving its intended purpose.

User Experience Is a North Star

To echo the words of the Google SRE book again, potential-cause alerts have poor correlation to real problems, but symptom-of-user-pain alerts better allow you to understand user impacts and the state of the system as experienced by customers.

How, then, do you focus on setting up alerts to detect failures that impact user experience? This is where a departure from traditional monitoring approaches becomes necessary. The traditional metrics-based monitoring approach relies on using static thresholds to define optimal system conditions. Yet the performance of modern systems—even at the infrastructure level—often changes shape dynamically under different workloads. Static thresholds simply aren't up to the task of monitoring impact on user experience.

Setting up traditional alerting mechanisms to monitor user experience means that system engineers must choose arbitrary constants that predict when that experience is poor. For example, these alerts might be implemented to trigger when "10 users have experienced slow page-load times," or "the 95th percentile of requests have persisted above a certain number of milliseconds." In a metrics-based approach, system engineers are required to divine which exact static measures indicate that unacceptable problems are occurring.

Yet system performance varies significantly throughout the day as different users, in different time zones, interact with your services in different ways. During slow

---

1 Betsy Beyer et al., "Tying These Principles Together" (*https://oreil.ly/vRbQf*), in *Site Reliability Engineering* (Sebastopol, CA: O'Reilly, 2016), 63–64.

traffic times, when you may have hundreds of concurrent sessions, 10 users experiencing slow page-load times might be a significant metric. But that significance drops sharply at peak load times when you may have tens of thousands of concurrent sessions running.

Remember that in distributed systems, failure is inevitable. Small transient failures are always occurring without you necessarily noticing. Common examples include a failed request that later succeeds on a retry; a critical process that initially fails, but its completion is merely delayed until it gets routed to a newly provisioned host; or a service that becomes unresponsive until its requests are routed to a backup service. The additional latency introduced by these types of transient failures might blend into normal operations during peak traffic, but p95 response times would be more sensitive to individual data points during periods of low traffic.

In a similar vein, these examples also illustrate the coarseness of time-based metrics. Let's say p95 response time is being gauged in five-minute intervals. Every five minutes, performance over the trailing five-minute interval reports a value that triggers an alert if it exceeds a static threshold. If that value exceeds the threshold, the entire five-minute interval is considered bad (and conversely, any five-minute interval that didn't exceed the threshold is considered good). Alerting on that type of metric results in high rates of both false positives and false negatives. It also has a level of granularity that is insufficient to diagnose exactly when and where a problem may have occurred.

Static thresholds are too rigid and coarse to reliably indicate degraded user experience in a dynamic environment. They lack context. Reliable alerts need a finer level of both granularity and reliability. This is where SLOs can help.

What Is a Service-Level Objective?

Service-level objectives (SLOs) are internal goals for measurement of service health. Popularized by the Google SRE book (*https://landing.google.com/sre/sre-book/chapters/service-level-objectives*), SLOs are a key part of setting external service-level agreements between service providers and their customers. These internal measures are typically more stringent than externally facing agreements or availability commitments. With that added stringency, SLOs can provide a safety net that helps teams identify and remediate issues before external user experience reaches unacceptable levels.

We recommend Alex Hidalgo's book, *Implementing Service Level Objectives* (O'Reilly), for a deeper understanding of the subject.

Much has been written about the use of SLOs for service reliability, and they are not unique to the world of observability. However, using an SLO-based approach to monitoring service health requires having observability built into your applications. SLOs can be, and sometimes are, implemented in systems without observability. But the ramifications of doing so can have severe unintended consequences.

Reliable Alerting with SLOs

SLOs quantify an agreed-upon target for service availability, based on critical end-user journeys rather than system metrics. That target is measured using service-level indicators (SLIs), which categorize the system state as good or bad. Two kinds of SLIs exist: *time-based measures* (such as "99th percentile latency less than 300 ms over each 5-minute window"), and *event-based measures* (such as "proportion of events that took less than 300 ms during a given rolling time window").

Both attempt to express the impact to end users but differ on whether data about the incoming user traffic has been pre-aggregated by time bucket. We recommend setting SLIs that use event-based measures as opposed to time-based measures, because event-based measures provide a more reliable and more granular way to quantify the state of a service. We discuss the reasons for this in the next chapter.

Let's look at an example of how to define an event-based SLI. You might define a good customer experience as being a state when "a user should be able to successfully load your home page and see a result quickly." Expressing that with an SLI means qualifying events and then determining whether they meet our conditions. In this example, your SLI would do the following:

- Look for any event with a request path of */home*.
- Screen qualifying events for conditions in which the event duration < 100 ms.
- If the event duration < 100 ms *and* was served successfully, consider it OK.
- If the event duration > 100 ms, consider that event an error even if it returned a success code.

Any event that is an error would spend some of the error budget allowed in your SLO. We'll closely examine patterns for proactively managing SLO error budgets and triggering alerts in the next chapter. For now, we'll summarize by saying that given enough errors, your systems could alert you to a potential breach of the SLO.

SLOs narrow the scope of your alerts to consider only symptoms that impact what the users of our service experience. If an underlying condition is impacting "a user loading our home page and seeing it quickly," an alert should be triggered, because someone needs to investigate why. However, there is no correlation as to *why* and *how* the service might be degraded. We simply know that something is wrong.

In contrast, traditional monitoring relies on a cause-based approach: a previously known cause is detected (e.g., an abnormal number of threads), signaling that users might experience undesirable symptoms (slow page-load times). That approach fuses the "what" and "why" of a situation in an attempt to help pinpoint where investigation should begin. But, as you've seen, there's a lot more to your services than just the known states of up, down, or even slow. Emergent failure modes can impact your users long before coarse synthetic probes will tell you. Decoupling "what" from "why" is one of the most important distinctions in writing good monitoring with maximum signal and minimum noise.

The second criteria for an alert to be helpful is that it must be *actionable*. A system-level potential-cause alert that the CPU is high tells you nothing about whether users are impacted and whether you should take action. In contrast, SLO-based alerts are symptom based: they tell you that something is wrong. They are actionable because now it is up to the responder to determine why users are seeing an impact and to mitigate. However, if you cannot sufficiently debug your systems, resolving the problem will be challenging. That's where a shift to observability becomes essential: debugging in production must be safe and natural.

In an SLO-based world, you need observability: the ability to ask novel questions of your systems without having to add new instrumentation. As you've seen throughout this book, observability allows you to debug from first principles. With rich telemetry you can start wide and then filter to reduce the search space. That approach means you can respond to determine the source of any problem, regardless of how novel or emergent the failure may be.

In self-contained, unchanging systems with a long-lived alert set, it's possible to have a large collection of alerts that correspond to all known failures. Given the resources and time, it's also theoretically possible to mitigate and even prevent all of those known failures (so why haven't more teams done that already?). The reality is that no matter how many known failures you automatically fix, the emergent failure modes that come with modern distributed systems can't be predicted. There's no going back in time to add metrics around the parts of your system that happened to break unexpectedly. When anything can break at any time, you need data for everything. Note that's *data* for everything and not *alerts* for everything. Having alerts for everything is not feasible. As we've seen, the software industry as a whole is already drowning in the noise.

Observability is a requirement for responding to novel, emergent failure modes. With observability, you can methodically interrogate your systems by taking one step after another: ask one question and examine the result, then ask another, and so on. No longer are you limited by traditional monitoring alerts and dashboards. Instead, you can improvise and adapt solutions to find any problem in your system.

Instrumentation that provides rich and meaningful telemetry is the basis for that approach. Being able to quickly analyze that telemetry data to validate or falsify hypotheses is what empowers you to feel confidence in removing noisy, unhelpful alerts. Decoupling the "what" from the "why" in your alerting is possible when using SLO-based alerts in tandem with observability.

When most alerts are not actionable, that quickly leads to alert fatigue. To eliminate that problem, it's time to delete all of your unactionable alerts.

Still not sure you can convince your team to remove all of those unhelpful alerts? Let's look at a real example of what it takes to drive that sort of culture change.

Changing Culture Toward SLO-Based Alerts: A Case Study

Just having queryable telemetry with rich context, on its own, might not be enough for your team to feel confident deleting all of those existing unhelpful alerts. That was our experience at Honeycomb. We'd implemented SLOs, but our team didn't quite fully trust them yet. SLO alerts were being routed to a low-priority inbox, while the team continued to rely on traditional monitoring alerts. That trust wasn't established until we had a few incidents of SLO-based alerts flagging issues *long before* traditional alerts provided any useful signal.

To illustrate how this change occurred, let's examine an incident from the end of 2019. Liz had developed our SLO feature and was paying attention to SLO alerts while the rest of the team was focused on traditional alerts. In this outage, the Shepherd service that ingests all of our incoming customer data had its SLO begin to burn and sent an alert to the SLO test channel. The service recovered fairly quickly: a 1.5% brownout had occurred for 20 minutes. The SLO error budget had taken a ding because that burned most of the 30-day budget. However, the problem appeared to go away by itself.

Our on-call engineer was woken up by the SLO alert at 1:29 a.m. his time. Seeing that the service was working, he blearily decided it was probably just a blip. The SLO alert triggered, but traditional monitoring that required consecutive probes in a row to fail didn't detect a problem. When the SLO alert triggered a fourth time, at 9:55 a.m., this was undeniably not a coincidence. At that time, the engineering team was willing to declare an incident even though traditional monitoring had still not detected a problem.

While investigating the incident, another engineer thought to check the process uptime (Figure 12-1). In doing so, they discovered a process had a memory leak. Each machine in the cluster had been running out of memory, failing in synchrony, and restarting. Once that problem was identified, it was quickly correlated with a new deployment, and we were able to roll back the error. The incident was declared resolved at 10:32 a.m.

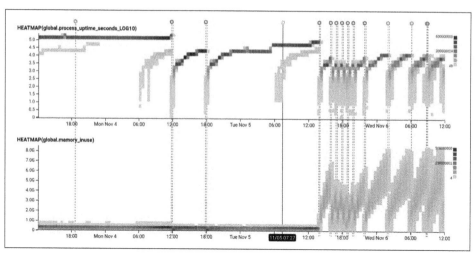

Figure 12-1. A heatmap showing uptime of a crashing fleet, restarting together around 18:30, and the memory profile showing leaking and triggering an out of memory condition

At this point, we have to acknowledge that many engineers who are reading this story might challenge that traditional cause-based alerting would have worked well enough in this case. Why not alert on memory and therefore get alerts when the system runs out of memory (OOM)? There are two points to consider when addressing that challenge.

First, at Honeycomb, our engineers had long since been trained out of tracking OOMs. Caching, garbage collection, and backup processes all opportunistically used—and occasionally used up—system memory. "Ran out of memory" turned out to be common for our applications. Given our architecture, even having a process crash from time to time turned out not to be fatal, so long as all didn't crash at once. For our purposes, tracking those individual failures had not been useful at all. We were more concerned with the availability of the cluster as a whole.

Given that scenario, traditional monitoring alerts did not—and never would have—noticed this gradual degradation at all. Those simple coarse synthetic probes could detect only a total outage, not one out of 50 probes failing and then recovering. In that state, machines were still available, so the service was up, and most data was making it through.

Second, even if it were somehow possible to introduce enough complicated logic to trigger alerts when only a certain notable number of specific types of OOMs were detected, we would have needed to predict this exact failure mode, well in advance of this one bespoke issue ever occurring, in order to devise the right incantation of conditions on which to trigger a useful alert. That theoretical incantation might have detected this one bespoke issue this one time, but would likely most often exist just to generate noise and propagate alert fatigue.

Although traditional monitoring never detected the gradual degradation, the SLO hadn't lied: users were seeing a real effect. Some incoming customer data had been dropped. It burned our SLO budget almost entirely from the start (Figure 12-2).

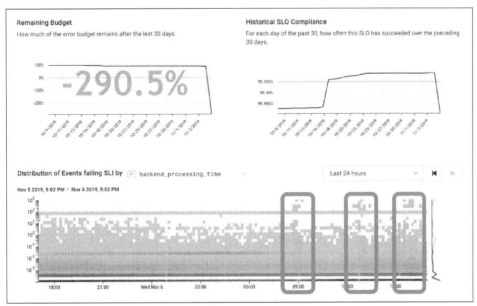

Figure 12-2. The SLO error budget burned –566% by the time the incident was over; compliance dropped to 99.97% (from the target of 99.995%). The boxed areas on the timeline show events marked as bad—and that they occurred fairly uniformly at fairly regular intervals until corrected.

By that stage, if the team had started treating SLO-based alerts as primary alerting, we would have been less likely to look for external and transient explanations. We would have instead moved to actually fix the issue, or at least roll back the latest deploy. SLOs proved their ability to detect brownouts and prompt the appropriate response.

That incident changed our culture. Once SLO burn alerts had proven their value, our engineering team had as much respect for SLO-based alerts as they did for traditional alerts. After a bit more time relying on SLO-based alerts, our team became increasingly comfortable with the reliability of alerting purely on SLO data.

At that point, we deleted all of our traditional monitoring alerts that were based on percentages of errors for traffic in the past five minutes, the absolute number of errors, or lower-level system behavior. We now rely on SLO-based alerts as our primary line of defense.

Conclusion

In this chapter, we provided a high-level overview of SLOs as a more effective alerting strategy than traditional threshold monitoring. Alert fatigue, prevalent in the software industry, is enabled by the potential-cause-based approach taken by traditional monitoring solutions.

Alert fatigue can be solved by focusing on creating only helpful alerts that meet two criteria. First, they must trigger as reliable indicators only that the user experience of your service is in a degraded state. Second, they must be actionable. Any alert that does not meet that criteria is no longer serving its purpose and should be deleted.

SLOs decouple the "what" and "why" behind incident alerting. Focusing on symptom-of-pain-based alerts means that SLOs can be reliable indicators of customer experience. When SLOs are driven by event-based measures, they have a far lesser degree of false positives and false negatives. Therefore, SLO-based alerts can be a productive way to make alerting less disruptive, more actionable, and more timely. They can help differentiate between systemic problems and occasional sporadic failures.

On their own, SLO-based alerts can tell you there is pain, but not why it is happening. For your SLO-based alerts to be actionable, your production systems must be sufficiently debuggable. Having observability in your systems is critical for success when using SLOs.

In the next chapter, we'll delve into the inner workings of SLO burn budgets and examine how they're used in more technical detail.

CHAPTER 13

Acting on and Debugging SLO-Based Alerts

In the preceding chapter, we introduced SLOs and an SLO-based approach to monitoring that makes for more effective alerting. This chapter closely examines how observability data is used to make those alerts both actionable and debuggable. SLOs that use traditional monitoring data—or metrics—create alerts that are not actionable since they don't provide guidance on fixing the underlying issue. Further, using observability data for SLOs makes them both more precise and more debuggable.

While independent from practicing observability, using SLOs to drive alerting can be a productive way to make alerting less noisy and more actionable. SLIs can be defined to measure customer experience of a service in ways that directly align with business objectives. Error budgets set clear expectations between business stakeholders and engineering teams. Error budget *burn alerts* enable teams to ensure a high degree of customer satisfaction, align with business goals, and initiate an appropriate response to production issues without the kind of cacophony that exists in the world of symptom-based alerting, where an excessive alert storm is the norm.

In this chapter, we will examine the role that error budgets play and the mechanisms available to trigger alerts when using SLOs. We'll look at what an SLO error budget is and how it works, which forecasting calculations are available to predict that your SLO error budget will be exhausted, and why it is necessary to use event-based observability data rather than time-based metrics to make reliable calculations.

Alerting Before Your Error Budget Is Empty

An *error budget* represents that maximum amount of system unavailability that your business is willing to tolerate. If your SLO is to ensure that 99.9% of requests are successful, a time-based calculation would state that your system could be unavailable for no more than 8 hours, 45 minutes, 57 seconds in one standard year (or 43 minutes, 50 seconds per month). As shown in the previous chapter, an event-based calculation considers each individual event against qualification criteria and keeps a running tally of "good" events versus "bad" (or errored) events.

Because availability targets are represented as percentages, the error budget corresponding to an SLO is based on the number of requests that came in during that time period. For any given period of time, only so many errors can be tolerated. A system is out of compliance with its SLO when its entire error budget has been spent. Subtract the number of failed (*burned*) requests from your total calculated error budget, and that is known colloquially as the *amount of error budget remaining*.

To proactively manage SLO compliance, you need to become aware of and resolve application and system issues long before your entire error budget is burned. Time is of the essence. To take corrective action that averts the burn, you need to know whether you are on a trajectory to consume that entire budget well before it happens. The higher your SLO target, the less time you have to react. Figure 13-1 shows an example graph indicating error budget burn.

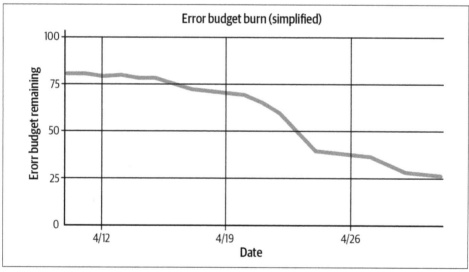

Figure 13-1. A simple graph showing error budget burn over approximately three weeks

For SLO targets up to about 99.95%—indicating that up to 21 minutes, 54 seconds of full downtime are tolerable per month—a reasonable enough time period exists for your team to be alerted to potential issues and still have enough time to act proactively before the entire error budget is burned.

Error budget burn alerts are designed to provide early warning about future SLO violations that would occur if the current burn rate continues. Therefore, effective burn alerts must forecast the amount of error budget that your system will have burned at some future point in time (anywhere from several minutes to days from now). Various methods are commonly used to make that calculation and decide when to trigger alerts on error budget burn rate.

Before proceeding, it's worth noting that these types of preemptive calculations work best to prevent violations for SLOs with targets up to 99.95% (as in the previous example). For SLOs with targets exceeding 99.95%, these calculations work less preventatively but can still be used to report on and warn about system degradation.

 For more information on mitigations for this situation, see "Alerting on SLOs" in Chapter 5 of *The Site Reliability Workbook*, edited by Betsy Beyer et al. (O'Reilly). In fact, we recommend reading that chapter in its entirety to those who have a deeper interest in alternative perspectives on this topic.

The rest of this chapter closely examines and contrasts various approaches to making effective calculations to trigger error budget burn alerts. Let's examine what it takes to get an error budget burn alert working. First, you must start by setting a frame for considering the all-too-relative dimension of time.

Framing Time as a Sliding Window

The first choice is whether to analyze your SLO across a fixed window or a sliding window. An example of a *fixed window* is one that follows the calendar—starting on the 1st day of the month and ending on the 30th. A counterexample is a *sliding window* that looks at any trailing 30-day period (see Figure 13-2).

Figure 13-2. A rolling three-day window (left) and a three-day resetting window (right)

For most SLOs, a 30-day window is the most pragmatic period to use. Shorter windows, like 7 or 14 days, won't align with customer memories of your reliability or with product-planning cycles. A window of 90 days tends to be too long; you could burn 90% of your budget in a single day and still technically fulfill your SLO even if your customers don't agree. Long periods also mean that incidents won't roll off quickly enough.

You might choose a fixed window to start with, but in practice, fixed window availability targets don't match the expectations of your customers. You might issue a customer a refund for a particular bad outage that happens on the 31st of the month, but that does not wave a magic wand that suddenly makes them tolerant of a subsequent outage on the 2nd of the next month—even if that second outage is legally within a different window.

As covered in Chapter 12, SLOs should be used as a way to measure customer experience and satisfaction, not legal constraints. The better SLO is one that accounts for human emotions, memories, and recency bias. Human emotions don't magically reset at the end of a calendar month.

If you use a fixed window to set error budgets, those budgets reset with dramatic results. Any error burns away a sliver of the budget, with a cumulative effect gradually counting down toward zero. That gradual degradation continually chips away at the amount of time your team has to proactively respond to issues. Then, suddenly, on the first day of a new month, everything is reset, and you start the cycle again.

In contrast, using a sliding window to track the amount of error budget you've burned over a trailing period offers a smoother experience that more closely resembles human behavior. At every interval, the error budget can be burned a little or restored a little. A constant and low level of burn never completely exhausts the error budget, and even a medium-sized drop will gradually be paid off after a sufficiently stable period of time.

The correct first choice to make when calculating burn trajectories is to frame time as a sliding window, rather than a static fixed window. Otherwise, there isn't enough data after a window reset to make meaningful decisions.

Forecasting to Create a Predictive Burn Alert

With a timeframe selected, you can now set up a trigger to alert you about error budget conditions you care about. The easiest alert to set is a *zero-level alert*—one that triggers when your entire error budget is exhausted.

What Happens When You Exhaust Your Error Budget

When you transition from having a positive error budget to a negative one, a necessary practice is to shift away from prioritizing work on new features and toward work on service stability. It's beyond the scope of this chapter to cover exactly what happens after your error budget is exhausted. But your team's goal should be to prevent the error budget from being entirely spent.

Error-budget overexpenditures translate into stringent actions such as long periods of feature freezes in production. The SLO model creates incentives to minimize actions that jeopardize service stability once the budget is exhausted. For an in-depth analysis of how engineering practices should change in these situations and how to set up appropriate policies, we recommend reading *Implementing Service Level Objectives*.

A trickier alert to configure is one that is preemptive. If you can foresee the emptying of your error budget, you have an opportunity to take action and introduce fixes that prevent it from happening. By fixing the most egregious sources of error sooner, you can forestall decisions to drop any new feature work in favor of reliability improvements. Planning and forecasting are better methods than heroism when it comes to sustainably ensuring team morale and stability.

Therefore, a solution is to track your error budget burn rate and watch for drastic changes that threaten to consume the entire budget. At least two models can be used to trigger burn alerts above the zero-level mark. The first is to pick a nonzero threshold on which to alert. For example, you could alert when your remaining error budget dips below 30%, as shown in Figure 13-3.

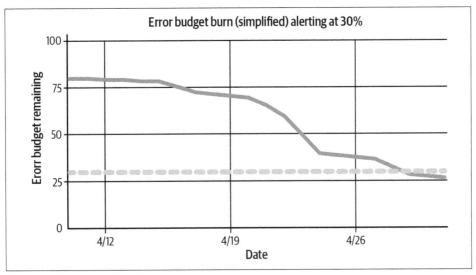

Figure 13-3. In this model, an alert triggers when the remaining error budget (solid line) dips below the selected threshold (dashed line)

A challenge with this model is that it effectively just moves the goalpost by setting a different empty threshold. This type of "early warning" system can be somewhat effective, but it is crude. In practice, after crossing the threshold, your team will act as if the entire error budget has been spent. This model optimizes to ensure a slight bit of headroom so that your team meets its objectives. But that comes at the cost of forfeiting additional time that you could have spent delivering new features. Instead, your team sits in a feature freeze while waiting for the remaining error budget to climb back up above the arbitrary threshold.

A second model for triggering alerts above the zero-level mark is to create *predictive* burn alerts (Figure 13-4). These forecast whether current conditions will result in burning your entire error budget.

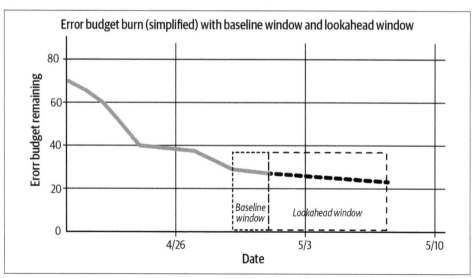

Figure 13-4. For predictive burn alerts, you need a baseline window of recent past data to use in your model and a lookahead window that determines how far into the future your forecast extends

When using predictive burn alerts, you need to consider the *lookahead window* and the *baseline* (or *lookback*) *window*: how far into the future are you modeling your forecast, and how much recent data should you be using to make that prediction? Let's start by considering the lookahead window since it is simpler to consider.

The Lookahead Window

In the predictive model, we can see that not every error that affects your error budget requires waking someone up. For example, let's say you have introduced a performance regression such that your service, with a 99.9% SLO target, is now on track to instead deliver 99.88% reliability one month from now. That is not an emergency situation requiring immediate attention. You could wait for the next business day for someone to investigate and correct the trajectory back above 99.9% reliability overall for the full month.

Conversely, if your service experiences a significant fraction of its requests failing such that you are on track to reach 98% within one hour, that should require paging the on-call engineer. If left uncorrected, such an outage could hemorrhage your error budget for the entire month, quarter, or year within a matter of hours.

Both of these examples illustrate that it's important to know whether your error budget will become exhausted at some point in the future, based on current trends. In the first example, that happens in days, and in the second, that happens in minutes or hours. But what exactly does "based on current trends" mean in this context?

The scope for current trends depends on how far into the future we want to forecast. On a macroscopic scale, most production traffic patterns exhibit both cyclical behavior and smoothed changes in their utilization curves. Patterns can occur in cycles of either minutes or hours. For example, a periodic cron job that runs a fixed number of transactions through your application without jitter can influence traffic in predictable ways that repeat every few minutes. Cyclical patterns can also occur by day, week, or year. For example, the retail industry experiences seasonal shopping patterns with notable spikes around major holidays.

In practice, that cyclical behavior means that some baseline windows are more appropriate to use than others. The past 30 minutes or hour are somewhat representative of the next few hours. But small minute-by-minute variations can be smoothed out when zooming out to consider daily views. Attempting to use the micro scale of past performance for the last 30 minutes or hour to extrapolate what could happen in the macro scale of performance for the next few days runs the risk of becoming flappy and bouncing in and out of alert conditions.

Similarly, the inverse situation is also dangerous. When a new error condition occurs, it would be impractical to wait for a full day of past performance data to become available before predicting what might happen in the next several minutes. Your error budget for the entire year could be blown by the time you make a prediction. Therefore, your baseline window should be about the same order of magnitude as your lookahead window.

In practice, we've found that a given baseline window can linearly predict forward by a factor of four at most without needing to add compensation for seasonality (e.g., peak/off-peak hours of day, weekday versus weekend, or end/beginning of month). Therefore, you can get an accurate enough prediction of whether you'll exhaust your error budget in four hours by extrapolating the past one hour of observed performance four times over. That extrapolation mechanism is discussed in more detail later in "Context-aware burn alerts" on page 148.

Extrapolating the future from current burn rate

Calculating what may happen in the lookahead window is a straightforward computation, at least for your first guess at burn rate. As you saw in the preceding section, the approach is to extrapolate future results based on the current burn rate: how long will it take before we exhaust our error budget?

Now that you know the approximate order of magnitude to use as a baseline, you can extrapolate results to predict the future. Figure 13-5 illustrates how a trajectory can be calculated from your selected baseline to determine when your entire error budget would be completely exhausted.

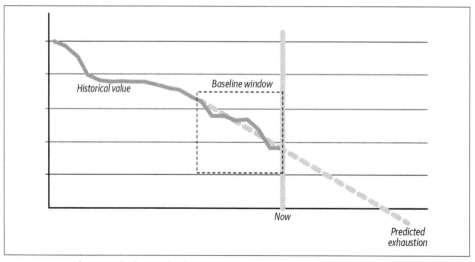

Figure 13-5. This graph shows the level of error budget (y-axis) remaining over time (x-axis). By extrapolating a baseline window, you can predict the moment when the error budget will empty.

This same technique of linear extrapolation often surfaces in areas such as capacity planning or project management. For example, if you use a weighted system to estimate task length in your ticketing system, you will have likely used this same approach to extrapolate when a feature might be delivered during your future sprint planning. With SLOs and error budget burn alerts, a similar logic is being applied to help prioritize production issues that require immediate attention.

Calculating a first guess is relatively straightforward. However, you must weigh additional nuances when forecasting predictive burn alerts that determine the quality and accuracy of those future predictions.

In practice, we can use two approaches to calculate the trajectory of predictive burn alerts. *Short-term burn alerts* extrapolate trajectories using only baseline data from the most recent time period and nothing else. *Context-aware burn alerts* take historical performance into account and use the total number of successful and failed events for the SLO's entire trailing window to make calculations.

The decision to use one method or the other typically hinges on two factors. The first is a trade-off between computational cost and sensitivity or specificity. Context-aware burn alerts are computationally more expensive than short-term burn alerts. However, the second factor is a philosophical stance on whether the total amount of error budget remaining should influence how responsive you are to service degradation. If resolving a significant error when only 10% of your burn budget remains carries more urgency than resolving a significant error when 90% of your burn budget remains, you may favor context-aware burn alerts.

In the next two sections, *unit* refers to the granular building block on which SLO burn alert calculations are made. These units can be composed of time-series data like metrics. Coarse measures like metrics have an aggregated granularity that marks a unit of time (like a minute or a second) as being either good or bad. These units can also be composed of event data, with each individual event corresponding to a user transaction that can be marked as either good or bad. In "Using Observability Data for SLOs Versus Time-Series Data" on page 154, we'll examine the ramifications of which type of data is used. For now, the examples will be agnostic to data types by using arbitrarily specific *units* that correspond to one data point per minute.

Let's look at examples of how decisions are made when using each of those approaches.

Short-term burn alerts

When using *short-term*, or *ahistorical*, burn alerts, you record the actual number of failed SLI units along with the total number of SLI-eligible units observed over the baseline window. You then use that data to extrapolate forward, and compute the number of minutes, hours, or weeks it would take to exhaust the error budget. For this calculation, you assume that no errors occurred prior to the events observed in the baseline window as well as the typical number of measurement units that the SLO typically sees.

Let's work an example. Say you have a service with an SLO target indicating 99% of units will succeed over a moving 30-day window. In a typical month, the service sees 43,800 units. In the past 24 hours, the service has seen 1,440 units, 50 of which failed. In the past 6 hours, the service has seen 360 units, 5 of which failed. To achieve the 99% target, only 1% of units are allowed to fail per month. Based on typical traffic volume (43,800 units), only 438 units are allowed to fail (your error budget). You want to know if, at this rate, you will burn your error budget in the next 24 hours.

A simple short-term burn alert calculates that in the past 6 hours, you burned only 5 units. Therefore, in the next 24 hours, you will burn another 20 units, totalling 25 units. You can reasonably project that you will not exhaust your error budget in 24 hours because 25 units is far less than your budget of 438 units.

A simple short-term burn alert calculation would also consider that in the past 1 day, you've burned 50 units. Therefore, in the next 8 days, you will burn another 400 units, totalling 450 units. You can reasonably project that you will exhaust your error budget in 8 days, because 450 units is more than your error budget of 438 units.

This simple math is used to illustrate projection mechanics. In practice, the situation is almost certainly more nuanced since your total amount of eligible traffic would typically fluctuate throughout the day, week, or month. In other words, you can't reliably estimate that 1 error over the past 6 hours forecasts 4 errors over the next 24 hours if that error happens overnight, over a weekend, or whenever your service is receiving one-tenth of its median traffic levels. If this error happened while you saw a tenth of the traffic, you might instead expect to see something closer to 30 errors over the next 24 hours, since that curve would smooth with rising traffic levels.

So far, in this example, we've been using linear extrapolation for simplicity. But proportional extrapolation is far more useful in production. Consider this next change to the preceding example.

Let's say you have a service with an SLO target indicating 99% of units will succeed over a moving 30-day window. In a typical month, the service sees 43,800 units. In the past 24 hours, the service has seen 1,440 units, 50 of which failed. *In the past 6 hours, the service has seen 50 units, 25 of which failed.* To achieve the 99% target, only 1% of units are allowed to fail per month. Based on typical traffic volume (43,800 units), only 438 units are allowed to fail (your error budget). You want to know if, at this rate, you will burn your error budget in the next 24 hours.

Extrapolating linearly, you would calculate that 25 failures in the past 6 hours mean 100 failures in the next 24 hours, totalling 105 failures, which is far less than 438.

Using *proportional extrapolation*, you would calculate that in any given 24-hour period, you would expect to see 43,800 units / 30 days, or 1,440 units. In the last 6 hours, 25 of 50 units (50%) failed. If that proportional failure rate of 50% continues for the next 24 hours, you will burn 50% of 1,440 units, or 720 units—far more than your budget of 438 units. With this proportional calculation, you can reasonably project that your error budget will be exhausted in about half a day. An alert should trigger to notify an on-call engineer to investigate immediately.

Context-aware burn alerts

When using *context-aware*, or *historical*, burn alerts, you keep a rolling total of the number of good and bad events that have happened over the entire window of the SLO, rather than just the baseline window. This section unpacks the various calculations you need to make for effective burn alerts. But you should tread carefully when practicing these techniques. The computational expense of calculating these values at each evaluation interval can quickly become financially expensive as well. At Honeycomb, we found this out the hard way when small SLO data sets suddenly started to rack up over $5,000 of AWS Lambda costs per day. :-)

To see how the considerations are different for context-aware burn alerts, let's work an example. Say you have a service with an SLO target indicating 99% of units will succeed over a moving 30-day window. In a typical month, the service sees 43,800 units. *In the previous 26 days, you have already failed 285 units out of 37,960. In the past 24 hours, the service has seen 1,460 units, 130 of which failed.* To achieve the 99%

target, only 1% of units are allowed to fail per month. Based on typical traffic volume (43,800 units), only 438 units are allowed to fail (your error budget). You want to know if, at this rate, you will burn your error budget in the next four days.

In this example, you want to project forward on a scale of days. Using the maximum practical extrapolation factor of 4, as noted previously, you set a baseline window that examines the last one day's worth of data to extrapolate forward four days from now.

You must also consider the impact that your chosen scale has on your sliding window. If your SLO is a sliding 30-day window, your adjusted lookback window would be 26 days: 26 lookback days + 4 extrapolated days = your 30-day sliding window, as shown in Figure 13-6.

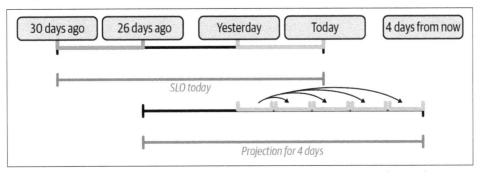

Figure 13-6. An adjusted SLO 30-day sliding window. When projecting forward 4 days, the lookback period to consider must be shortened to 26 days before today. The projection is made by replicating results from the baseline window for the next 4 days and adding those to the adjusted sliding window.

With those adjusted timeframes defined, you can now calculate how the future looks four days from now. For that calculation, you would do the following:

1. Examine every entry in the map of SLO events that has occurred in the past 26 days.

2. Store both the total number of events in the past 26 days and the total number of errors.

3. Reexamine map entries that occurred within that last 1 day to determine the baseline window failure rate.

4. Extrapolate the next 4 days of performance by presuming they will behave similarly to the 1-day baseline window.

5. Calculate the adjusted SLO 30-day sliding window as it would appear 4 days from now.

6. Trigger an alert if the error budget would be exhausted by then.

Using a Go-based code example, you could accomplish this task if you had a given time-series map containing the number of failures and successes in each window:

```go
func isBurnViolation(
    now time.Time, ba *BurnAlertConfig, slo *SLO, tm *timeseriesMap,
) bool {
    // For each entry in the map, if it's in our adjusted window, add its totals.
    // If it's in our projection use window, store the rate.
    // Then project forward and do the SLO calculation.
    // Then fire off alerts as appropriate.

    // Compute the window we will use to do the projection, with the projection
    // offset as the earliest bound.
    pOffset := time.Duration(ba.ExhaustionMinutes/lookbackRatio) * time.Minute
    pWindow := now.Add(-pOffset)

    // Set the end of the total window to the beginning of the SLO time period,
    // plus ExhaustionMinutes.
    tWindow := now.AddDate(0, 0, -slo.TimePeriodDays).Add(
        time.Duration(ba.ExhaustionMinutes) * time.Minute)

    var runningTotal, runningFails int64
    var projectedTotal, projectedFails int64
    for i := len(tm.Timestamps) - 1; i >= 0; i-- {
        t := tm.Timestamps[i]

        // We can stop scanning backward if we've run off the end.
        if t.Before(tWindow) {
            break
        }

        runningTotal += tm.Total[t]
        runningFails += tm.Fails[t]

        // If we're within the projection window, use this value to project forward,
        // counting it an extra lookbackRatio times.
        if t.After(pWindow) {
            projectedTotal += lookbackRatio * tm.Total[t]
            projectedFails += lookbackRatio * tm.Fails[t]
        }
    }

    projectedTotal = projectedTotal + runningTotal
    projectedFails = projectedFails + runningFails

    allowedFails := projectedTotal * int64(slo.BudgetPPM) / int64(1e6)
    return projectedFails != 0 && projectedFails >= allowedFails
}
```

To calculate an answer to the example problem, you note that in the past 26 days, there have already been 37,960 units, and 285 failed. The baseline window of 1 day will be used to project forward 4 days. At the start of the baseline window, you are at day 25 of the data set (1 day ago).

Visualizing results as a graph, as shown in Figure 13-7, you see that when the one-day baseline window started, you still had 65% of your error budget remaining. Right now, you have only 35% of your error budget remaining. In one day, you've burned 30% of your error budget. If you continue to burn your error budget at that rate, it will be exhausted in far less than four days. You should trigger an alarm.

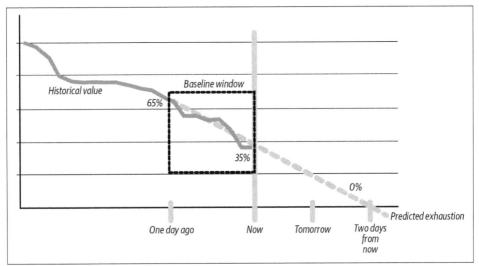

Figure 13-7. One day ago, 65% of the error budget remained. Now, only 35% of the error budget remains. At the current rate, the error budget will be exhausted in less than two days.

The Baseline Window

Having considered the lookahead window and the way it's used, let's now shift our attention back to the baseline window.

There's an interesting question of how *much* of a baseline to use when extrapolating forward. If the performance of a production service suddenly turns downhill, you want to be aware of that fairly quickly. At the same time, you also don't want to set such a small window that it creates noisy alerts. If you used a baseline of 15 minutes to extrapolate three days of performance, a small blip in errors could trigger a false alarm. Conversely, if you used a baseline of three days to extrapolate forward an hour, you'd be unlikely to notice a critical failure until it's too late.

We previously described a practical choice as a factor of four for the timeline being considered. You may find that other more sophisticated algorithms can be used, but our experience has indicated that the factor of four is generally reliable. The baseline multiplier of 4 also gives us a handy heuristic: a 24-hour alarm is based on the last 6 hours of data, a 4-hour alarm is based on the last 1 hour of data, and so forth. It's a good place to start when first approaching SLO burn alerts.

An odd implication when setting baseline windows proportionally is also worth mentioning. Setting multiple burn alerts on an SLO by using different lookahead window sizes is common. Therefore, it becomes possible for alarms to trigger in seemingly illogical order. For example, a system issue might trigger a burn alert that says you'll exhaust your budget within two hours, but it won't trigger a burn alert that says you'll exhaust it within a day. That's because the extrapolation for those two alerts comes from different baselines. In other words, if you keep burning at the rate from the last 30 minutes, you'll exhaust in two hours—but if you keep burning at the rate from the last day, you'll be fine for the next four days.

For these reasons, you should measure both, and you should act whenever either projection triggers an alert. Otherwise, you risk potentially waiting hours to surface a problem on the burn-down timescale of one day—when a burn alert with hour-level granularity means you could find out sooner. Launching corrective action at that point could also avert triggering the one-day projection alert. Conversely, while an hourly window allows teams to respond to sudden changes in burn rate, it's far too noisy to facilitate task prioritization on a longer timescale, like sprint planning.

That last point is worth dwelling on for a moment. To understand why both time-scales should be considered, let's look at the actions that should be taken when an SLO burn alert is triggered.

Acting on SLO Burn Alerts

In general, when a burn alert is triggered, teams should initiate an investigative response. For a more in-depth look at various ways to respond, refer to Hidalgo's *Implementing Service Level Objectives*. For this section, we'll examine a few broader questions you should ask when considering response to a burn alert.

First, you should diagnose the type of burn alert you received. Is a new and unexpected type of burn happening? Or is it a more gradual and expected burn? Let's first look at various patterns for consuming error budgets.

Figures 13-8, 13-9, and 13-10 display *error budget remaining* over *time*, for the duration of the SLO window. Gradual error budget burns, which occur at a slow but steady pace, are a characteristic of most modern production systems. You expect a certain threshold of performance, and a small number of exceptions fall out of that. In some situations, disturbances during a particular period may cause exceptions to occur in bursts.

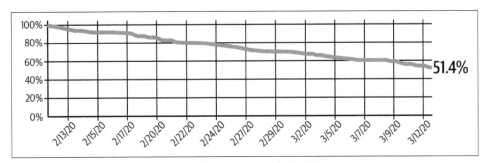

Figure 13-8. A gradual error budget burn rate, with 51.4% remaining

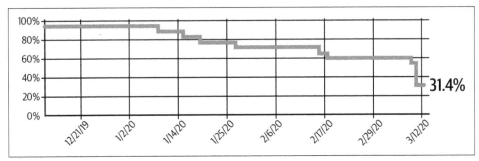

Figure 13-9. An error budget of 31.4% remaining, which is burned in bursts

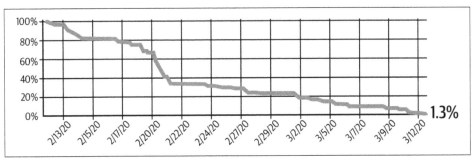

Figure 13-10. A system that usually burns slowly but had an incident that burned a significant portion of the error budget all at once, with only 1.3% remaining

When a burn alert is triggered, you should assess whether it is part of a burst condition or is an incident that could burn a significant portion of your error budget all at once. Comparing the current situation to historical rates can add helpful context for triaging its importance.

Instead of showing the instantaneous 31.4% remaining and how we got there over the trailing 30 days as we did in Figure 13-9, Figure 13-11 zooms out to examine the 30-day-cumulative state of the SLO for each day in the past 90 days. Around the beginning of February, this SLO started to recover above its target threshold. This likely occurs, in part, because a large dip in performance aged out of the 90-day window.

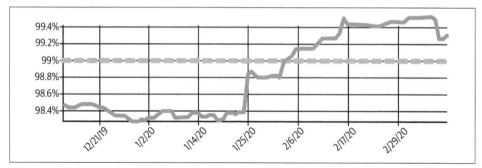

Figure 13-11. A 90-day sliding window for an SLO performs below a 99% target before recovering toward the start of February

Understanding the general trend of the SLO can also answer questions about how urgent the incident feels—and can give a hint for solving it. Burning budget all at once suggests a different sort of failure than burning budget slowly over time.

Using Observability Data for SLOs Versus Time-Series Data

Using time-series data for SLOs introduces a few complications. In the examples in earlier sections, we used a generic unit to consider success or failure. In an event-based world, that unit is an *individual user request*: did this request succeed or fail? In a time-series world, that unit is a *particular slice of time*: did the entire system succeed or fail during this time? When using time-series data, an aggregate view of system performance gets measured.

The problem with time-series data becomes particularly pronounced in the case of *stringent SLOs*—those with 99.99% availability targets and higher. With these SLOs, error budgets can be exhausted within minutes or seconds. In that scenario, every second especially matters, and several mitigation steps (for example, automated remediations) must be enacted to achieve that target. The difference between finding out about critical error budget burn in one second versus one minute won't matter much if a responding human needs three minutes to acknowledge the alert, unlock their laptop, log in, and manually run the first remediation they conjure (or even more time if the issue is complex and requires further debugging).

Another mitigation can come by way of using event data for SLOs rather than time-series data. Consider the way time-series evaluation functions in the context of stringent SLOs. For example, let's say you have an SLI specifying that requests must have a p95 less than 300 milliseconds. The error budget calculation then needs to classify short time periods as either good or bad. When evaluating on a per minute basis, the calculation must wait until the end of the elapsed minute to declare it either good or bad. If the minute is declared bad, you've already lost that minute's worth of response time. This is a nonstarter for initiating a fast alerting workflow when error budgets can be depleted within seconds or minutes.

The granularity of "good minute" or "bad minute" is simply not enough to measure a four-9s SLO. In the preceding example, if only 94% of requests were less than 300 ms, the entire minute is declared bad. That one evaluation is sufficient enough to burn 25% of your 4.32-minute monthly error budget in one shot. And if your monitoring data is collected in only 5-minute windows (as is the fee-free default in Amazon CloudWatch), using such 5-minute windows for good/bad evaluation can fail only one single evaluation window before you are in breach of your SLO target.

In systems that use time-series data for SLO calculation, a mitigation approach might look something like setting up a system in which once three synthetic probes fail, automatic remediations are deployed and humans are then expected to double-check the results afterward. Another approach can be measuring with metrics the instantaneous percentage of requests that are failing in a shorter window of time, given a sufficiently high volume of traffic.

Rather than making aggregate decisions in the good minute / bad minute scenario, using event data to calculate SLOs gives you request-level granularity to evaluate system health. Using the same previous example SLI scenario, any single request with duration lower than 300 ms is considered good, and any with duration greater than 300 ms is considered bad. In a scenario with 94% of requests that were less than 300 ms, only 6% of those requests are subtracted from your SLO error budget, rather than the 100% that would be subtracted using an aggregate time-series measure like p95.

In modern distributed systems, 100% total failure blackouts are less common than partial failure brownouts, so event-based calculations are much more useful. Consider that a 1% brownout of a 99.99% reliability system is similar to measuring a 100% outage of a 99% reliability system. Measuring partial outages buys you more time to respond, as if it were a full outage of a system with a much less stringent SLO. In both cases, you have more than seven hours to remediate before the monthly error budget is exhausted.

Observability data that traces actual user experience with your services is a more accurate representation of system state than coarsely aggregated time-series data. When deciding which data to use for actionable alerting, using observability data enables teams to focus on conditions that are much closer to the truth of what the business cares about: the overall customer experience that is occurring at this moment.

It's important to align your reliability goals with what's feasible for your team. For very stringent SLOs—such as a five-9s system—you must deploy every mitigation strategy available, such as automatic remediation, based on extremely granular and accurate measurements that bypass traditional human-involved fixes requiring minutes or hours. However, even for teams with less stringent SLOs, using granular event-based measures can create more response time buffers than are typically available with time-series-based measures. That additional buffer ensures that reliability goals are much more feasible, regardless of your team's SLO targets.

Conclusion

We've examined the role that error budgets play and the mechanisms available to trigger alerts when using SLOs. Several forecasting methods are available that can be used to predict when your error budget will be burned. Each method has its own considerations and trade-offs, and the hope is that this chapter shows you which method to use to best meet the needs of your specific organization.

SLOs are a modern form of monitoring that solve many of the problems with noisy monitoring we outlined before. SLOs are not specific to observability. What is specific to observability is the additional power that event data adds to the SLO model. When calculating error budget burn rates, events provide a more accurate assessment of the actual state of production services. Additionally, merely knowing that an SLO is in danger of a breach does not necessarily provide the insight you need to determine which users are impacted, which dependent services are affected, or which combinations of user behavior are triggering errors in your service. Coupling observability data to SLOs helps you see where and when failures happened after a burn budget alert is triggered.

Using SLOs with observability data is an important component of both the SRE approach and the observability-driven-development approach. As seen in previous chapters, analyzing events that fail can give rich and detailed information about what is going wrong and why. It can help differentiate systemic problems and occasional sporadic failures. In the next chapter, we'll examine how observability can be used to monitor another critical component of a production application: the software supply chain.

CHAPTER 14

Observability and the Software Supply Chain

This chapter is contributed by Frank Chen,
senior staff software engineer at Slack

A Note from Charity, Liz, and George

So far in this book, we've examined observability as it relates to the code you write and how that code operates in production. But running in production is only one stage in your code's life cycle. Prior to running in production, automatically testing and deploying your code with build pipelines is common practice. Delving into specific continuous integration (CI) / continuous deployment (CD) architectures and practices is beyond the scope of this book, except for how observability can be used to debug pipeline issues.

Production is not the only ever-changing environment your code encounters. The systems you use to run your build pipelines can also change in unexpected and often unpredictable ways. Like applications we've discussed in this book, build system architectures can vary widely—from monolithic single nodes to vast build farms running parallel processes at scale. Systems with simpler architectures may be easier to debug by reasoning your way through potential failures. But once a system reaches a certain degree of complexity, observability can be an indispensable—and sometimes required—debugging tool to understand what's happening in your CI/CD pipelines. Just as in production, issues such as poor integration, invisible bottlenecks, and an inability to detect issues or debug their causes can also plague your build systems.

This chapter, written by Frank Chen, details how Slack uses observability to manage its software supply chain. We are so pleased to include Chen's work in this book, because it's a great example of using observability to build systems running at scale. You'll learn about how and where to use traces and observability to debug issues in your build pipelines, and the types of instrumentation that are particularly useful in this context.

Slack's story is framed from the point of view of an organization with large-scale software supply chains, though we believe it has lessons applicable at any scale. In Part IV, we'll specifically look at challenges that present themselves when implementing observability at scale.

I'm delighted to share this chapter on practices and use cases for integrating observability into your software supply chain. A *software supply chain* comprises "anything that goes into or affects your software from development, through your CI/CD pipeline, until it gets deployed into production."[1]

For the past three years, I have spent time building and learning about systems and human processes to deliver frequent, reliable, and high-quality releases that provide a simpler, more pleasant, and productive experience for Slack customers. For teams working on the software supply chain, the pipelines and tools to support CI/CD used by our wider organization are our production workload.

Slack invested early in CI development for collaboration and in CD for releasing software into the hands of customers. CI is a development methodology that requires engineers to build, test, and integrate new code as frequently as possible to a shared codebase. Integration and verification of new code in a shared codebase increases confidence that new code does not introduce expected faults to customers. Systems for CI enable developers to automatically trigger builds, test, and receive feedback when they commit new code.

> For a deeper dive into continuous integration, see "Continuous Architecture and Continuous Delivery" (*https://oreil.ly/ewm0i*) by Murat Erder and Pierre Pureur on the ScienceDirect website. In addition, "How to Get Started with Continuous Integration" (*https://oreil.ly/Dv4Zm*) by Sten Pittet on the Atlassian website is a particularly good guide.

Slack evolved from a single web app PHP monorepo (now mostly in Hack (*https://hacklang.org*)) to a topology of many languages, services, and clients to serve various needs. Slack's core business logic still lives in the web app and routes to downstream services like Flannel (*https://slack.engineering/flannel-an-application-level-edge-cache-to-make-slack-scale*). CI workflows at Slack include unit tests, integration tests, and end-to-end functional tests for a variety of codebases.

---

1 Maya Kaczorowski, "Secure at Every Step: What is Software Supply Chain Security and Why Does It Matter?" (*https://oreil.ly/3UZm4*), GitHub Blog, September 2, 2020.

For the purposes of this chapter, I focus on observability into our CI/CD systems and web app's CI, as this is where many engineers at Slack spend the majority of their time. The web app CI ecosystem spans Checkpoint, Jenkins builder/test executors, and QA environments (each capable of running Slack's web app codebase that routes to supporting dependent services). Checkpoint is an internally developed service that orchestrates CI/CD workflows. It provides an API and frontend for orchestrating stages of complex workflows like test execution and deployments. It also shares updates in Slack to users for events like test failures and pull request (PR) reviews.

Figure 14-1 shows an example workflow of an end-to-end web app test. A user pushes a commit to GitHub, Checkpoint receives webhooks from GitHub for codebase-related events, like a new commit. Checkpoint then sends requests to Jenkins for build and test workflows to be performed by Jenkins executors. Inside Jenkins builder and test executors, we use a codebase called CIBot that executes build and test scripts with a merge against the main branch (and then communicates with Checkpoint for orchestration and test result posting).

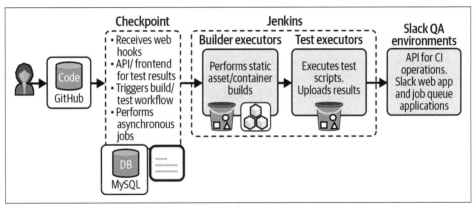

Figure 14-1. An example end-to-end workflow for testing the web app

Why Slack Needed Observability

Throughout its life cycle, Slack has grown tremendously in both customer count and codebases. While this is exciting for us, growth has a shadow side that can lead to increased complexity, fuzzy boundaries, and systems stretched to their limits. Test suite executions that were once measured in low thousands per day grew to high hundreds of thousands. Those workloads have a changing, diverse nature across codebases and many teams. At that scale, it's necessary to control costs and compute resources with strategies like adaptive capacity and oversubscription.

More details about Slack's CI systems and cost-control strategies can be found in Slack Engineering's blog article "Infrastructure Observability for Changing the Spend Curve" (*https://slack.engineering/infrastructure-observability-for-changing-the-spend-curve*).

As a result, our workflows to test and deploy code in a development environment could often have more complexity than some production services. Underlying dependencies in infrastructure types or runtime versions could unexpectedly change and introduce unintended failures. For example, Slack relies on Git for version control. Different versions of Git can have radically different performance characteristics when merging code. Anomaly detection on CI surfaces can involve debugging issues that might be in your code, test logic, dependent services, underlying infrastructure, or any permutation therein. When something goes wrong, issues could be hidden in any number of unpredictable places. Slack quickly realized we needed observability in our software supply chain.

Instrumenting the software supply chain is a competitive advantage, both for Slack and for your own business. Faster development + faster release cycles = better service for your customers. Observability played a large role in Slack's understanding of problems and in framing investments in CI/CD. In the following sections, you'll read about Slack instrumenting Checkpoint with improved distributed traces in 2019, and then case studies from 2020 and 2021 for specific problem solutions.

Internal tooling typically goes through the same multiple critical systems as production systems except with additional complexity to execute against development systems, and code merges for builds and tests. Internal tooling presents a different perspective than production services: the cardinality is significantly lower, but the criticality of any single event and span are significantly higher. A failure at any dependent system represents a slowdown in developer velocity and frustration by teams, and ultimately a slowdown to delivering software to your customers. In other words, if the first part of your software supply chain is slow or failure-prone, the remainder of your software supply chain—that relies on this critical part—will be bottlenecked.

"It is slow" is the hardest problem to debug in distributed systems. "It is flaky" is the most heard problem by teams supporting internal tools. The common challenge for both is how to correlate problems in high-complexity systems that interact. For example, when infrastructure or tests are flaky, developers experience a decrease in their ability to write code, and their trust in tooling is eroded, leading to frustration. This type of complexity led Slack to invest in building shared observability pipelines. You'll see more details about observability pipelines in Chapter 18, written by Slack's Suman Karumuri and Ryan Katkov. In the next section, you'll learn how dimensionality helps solve this problem.

Instrumentation: Shared Client Libraries and Dimensions

A primary challenge in Slack's CI has been complexity. A failure in an end-to-end test might be the result of multiple interacting codebases that require views across codebase changes, infrastructure changes, and platform runtimes. For a single commit from a web app developer in 2020, our CI pipeline would execute 30+ test suites that rely on GitHub, build pipelines by three platform teams (performance, backend, and frontend), across 20 teams/services with different requirements and areas of expertise. By mid-2020, our CI infrastructure started to be stretched to its limit, as a 10% month-over-month growth in test execution led to multiple downstream services having challenges scaling to meet the additional demand from test executions.

Slack attempted to solve this series of bottlenecks with distributed tracing. Slack's CI infrastructure in 2019 was mostly written by the CTO and early employees, and it remained mostly functional for years. But this infrastructure showed growing pains and lack of observability into many workflows.

By applying tracing to a multihop build system, our team was able to solve multiple challenges in CI workflows within hours of adding instrumentation:

- In 2019 Q2, we instrumented our CI runner with an afternoon prototype. Similarly to other trace use cases, within minutes of having trace data, we discovered anomalous runtimes for Git checkout. By looking at the underlying hosts, we found they were not being updated in the Auto Scaling group (ASG) like others and were quickly deprovisioned. This unlocked a simple solution to workflows that were not resulting in errors or failures but were nonetheless presenting a slow—and therefore bad—user experience.

- In 2019 Q3, our teams were in the midst of a multiday/multiteam incident. We implemented our first cross-service trace between our CI runner and test environments, and discovered a Git Large File Storage (LFS) issue that slowed system throughput. Initially, teams scrambled to bring multiple overloaded systems under control as one portion of our system cascaded failures to other systems. We added simple instrumentation, borrowed from our CI runner, and were able to resolve the incident in less than two hours by discovering a set of hosts that were failing to retrieve artifacts from Git LFS.

In Figure 14-2, you can see a simplified view of a test run after a user pushes a commit to GitHub. This test run is orchestrated by Checkpoint and subsequently passed onto a build step and then test step, each performed by Jenkins executors. In each stage, you see additional dimensions that contextualize execution in CI. Slack engineers then use single, or combinations of, dimensions as breadcrumbs to explore executions when performance or reliability issues arise in production. Each additional dimension is a direction and clue during issue investigation. You can combine clues to iteratively drill down for specific issues in deployed code.

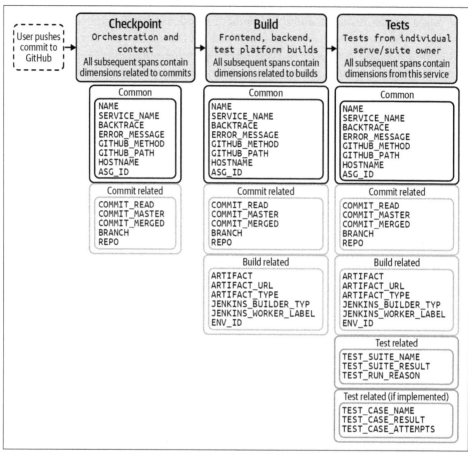

Figure 14-2. A simplified view of a single end-to-end test run orchestrated by our CI orchestration layer, highlighting the common dimensions shared across our workflow

Client dimensions are configured within each trace. (Figure 14-3 shows example dimensions.) Slack uses a TraceContext singleton that sets up these dimensions. Each TraceContext builds an initial trace with common dimensions and a new trace. Each trace contains multiple spans and an array of specific dimensions at each span. An individual span (e.g., in Figure 14-4 from runner.test_execution) can contain context on the original request and add dimensions of interest to the root span. As you add more dimensions, you add more context and richness to power issue investigations.

You can learn more about wide spans at "CircleCI: The Unreasonable Effectiveness of a Single Wide Event" (*https://hny.co/resources/the-unreasonable-effectiveness-of-a-single-wide-event*), by Glen Mailer, a video posted on the Honeycomb website.

```
enum ServiceName: string as string (
    CHECKPOINT_BG = 'ci_checkpoint_bg';
    CHECKPOINT_APP = 'ci_checkpoint_aa';
    CHECKPOINT_ENV_CONTROL = 'ci_checkpoint_env';
    CIBOT_RUNNER = 'ci_cibot_runner';
    CIBOT_BUILDER = 'ci_cibot_builder';
    DB_CLIENT = 'ci_db';
    DEFAULT = 'ci_defaut';
    ROOT = 'ci_root';
)

enum ServiceName: string as string (
// Global
    NAME = 'name';
    SERVICE_NAME = 'service_name';
    BACKTRACE = 'backtrace';
    ERROR_MESSAGE = 'error';
    IS_SYNTHETIC_SPAN = 'is_Synthetic_span';
    METHOD = 'method';
    STATUS_CODE = 'status';
)

// Commit related
    COMMIT_HEAD = 'commit_head';
    COMMIT_MASTER = 'commit_master';
    COMMIT_MERGED = 'commit_merged';
    BRANCH = 'branch';
    REPO = 'repo';
)

// Host related
    EVN_ID = 'env_id';
    HOSTNAME = 'hostname';
    ASG_ID = 'asg_id';
)
```

```
/ /Build
    ARTIFACT = 'artifact_id';
    ARTIFACT_URL = 'artifact_url';
    ARTIFACT_TYPE = 'artifact_type';
    JENKINS_BUILDER_TYPE = 'jenkins_builder_type';
    JENKINS_WORKER_LABEL = 'jenkins_worker_label';

// Test run
    TEST_SUITE_NAME = 'test_suite';
    TEST_SUITE_RESULT = 'test_suite_result';
    TEST_RUN_REASON = 'run_reason';

// Test case
    TEST_CASE_NAME = 'test_case_name';
    TEST_CASE_RESULT = 'test_case_result';
    TEST_CASE_ATTEMPTS = 'test_case_attempts';

// Orchestration
    ENTRYPOINT = 'entrypoint';
    REQUEST_ID = 'request_id';
    PATH = 'path';
    AUTH_METHOD = 'auth_method';

// Clients
    DB_QUERY = 'query';
    DB_TABLE = 'query_table';
    GITHUB_METHOD = 'github_method';
    GITHUB_PATH = 'github_path';
    /* [... Other dimensions ...] */
)
```

Figure 14-3. Common dimensions in our Hack codebase. You can use these as examples for structuring dimensions across spans and services in CI.

For example, Slack engineers might want to identify concurrency issues along common dimensions (like hostnames or groups of Jenkins workers). The TraceContext already provides a hostname tag. The CI runner client then appends a tag for the Jenkins worker label. Using a combination of these two dimensions, Slack engineers can then group individual hosts or groups of Jenkins workers that have runtime issues.

Similarly, Slack engineers might want to identify common build failures. The CI runner client appends a tag for the commit head or commit main branch. This combination allows for identifying which commits a broken build might come from.

The dimensions in Figure 14-3 are then used in various script and service calls as they communicate with one another to complete a test run (Figure 14-4).

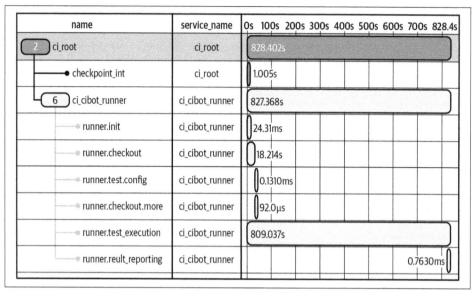

name	service_name	0s 100s 200s 300s 400s 500s 600s 700s 828.4s
2 ci_root	ci_root	828.402s
checkpoint_int	ci_root	1.005s
6 ci_cibot_runner	ci_cibot_runner	827.368s
runner.init	ci_cibot_runner	24.31ms
runner.checkout	ci_cibot_runner	18.214s
runner.test.config	ci_cibot_runner	0.1310ms
runner.checkout.more	ci_cibot_runner	92.0µs
runner.test_execution	ci_cibot_runner	809.037s
runner.reult_reporting	ci_cibot_runner	0.7630ms

Figure 14-4. A trace for the CI execution of a backend test suite called backend-php-unit

In the following sections, I'll share how Slack uses trace tooling and queries to make sense of the supply chain and how provenance can result in actionable alerting to resolve issues.

Case Studies: Operationalizing the Supply Chain

Observability through analyzing telemetry data consisting of metrics, events, logs, and traces is a key component to modeling internal customer experiences. The key for Slack infrastructure tooling and people is to consistently learn and embed observability into our tooling. This section presents case studies that bring observability into Slack developers' workflows. I hope by sharing Slack's approach to these problems, you can reuse these patterns for your own internal development.

Understanding Context Through Tooling

CI operates in a complex, distributed system; multiple small changes can be additive in their effect on the CI user experience. Multiple teams traditionally operated in silos to debug performance and resiliency issues in order to better serve their customers (e.g., backend, frontend, and middleware). However, for customers of CI who are doing development and then running tests, the user experience is best represented by the worst-performing or flakiest tests. A test is considered *flaky* when running the same code has a different result. Understanding context is critical for identifying bottlenecks.

For the rest of this section, I will walk through a case study of Slack teams working together to understand context from the problem of flaky tests. Slack teams were able to significantly reduce this problem for their internal customers by focusing on a few key tenets:

- Instrumenting the test platform with traces to capture previously underexplored runtime variables
- Shipping small, observability-driven feedback loops to explore interesting dimensionality
- Running reversible experiments on dimensions that correlated with flaky test configurations

Developer frustration across Slack engineering was increasing because of flaky end-to-end test runs in 2020. Test turnaround time (p95) was consistently above 30 minutes for a single commit (the time between an engineer pushing a commit to GitHub and all test executions returning). During this period, most of Slack's code testing was driven by end-to-end tests before an engineer merged their code to the mainline. Many end-to-end test suites had an average suite execution flake rate of nearly 15%. Cumulatively, these flaky test executions peaked at 100,000 weekly hours of compute time on discarded test executions.

By mid-2020, the combination of these metrics led to automation teams across Slack sharing a daily 30-minute triage session to dig into specific test issues. Automation team leads hesitated to introduce any additional variance to the way Slack used Cypress, an end-to-end testing platform. The belief was that flakiness was from the test code itself. Yet no great progress was made in verifying or ruling out that belief.

In late 2020, observability through tracing had shown great promise and impact in identifying infrastructure bottlenecks in other internal tooling. Internal tooling and automation teams worked to add tracing for a few runtime parameters and spans in Cypress.

Within days of instrumentation, multiple dimensions appeared very correlated with test suites that had higher flake rates. Engineers from these teams looked at this instrumentation and discovered that users and test suite owners of the test platform had drastically different configurations. During this discovery process, additional telemetry was added to the Docker runtime to add additional color to some flakes. Empowered with data, these engineers experimented to place better defaults for the platform and to place guardrails for flaky configurations. After these initial adjustments, test suite flake rates decreased significantly for many users (suites went from 15% to under 0.5% flake rates), as shown in Figure 14-5.

Because of the disparate nature of the runtime between end-to-end test suites that no central team had visibility into, context gathering became a critical piece between suites to identify specific dimensions that caused flakiness.

> For more on how Slack evolved its testing strategy and culture of safety, see the Slack blog post "Balancing Safety and Velocity in CI/CD at Slack" (*https://slack.engineering/balancing-safety-and-velocity-in-ci-cd-at-slack*). Slack describes how engineers initiated a project to transform testing pipelines and de-emphasize end-to-end testing for code safety. This drastically reduced user-facing flakiness and increased developer velocity in 2021.

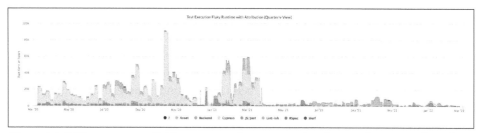

Figure 14-5. Time spent on flaking test runs between major classes of test runs for web app. The light colored bar shows flaky test executions from the Cypress platform tests.

With this shared understanding of context through tooling, Slack's next step was to embed actionable workflows through alerting.

Embedding Actionable Alerting

Slack integrates its own product into how engineers handle their development and triage issues in the infrastructure. Observability through tracing plays a critical role in helping engineers do their job by directing people in Slack messages and configured dashboards.

Let's examine a case study around test execution. A single test suite execution might be understood in different ways depending on code, infrastructure, or features in the product. Each team or platform might have multiple SLOs for various parts of a test execution. Here are a few examples:

- Test suite owner or platform teams might care about flakiness, reliability, or memory usage.
- Test infrastructure teams might care about performance and reliability of specific operations (like Docker ops or cost per test).
- Deployment owners might care about what was tested or upcoming hotfixes coming through CI.

- Internal tooling teams might care about throughput of test result processing through CI.

The prompt for identifying an issue might be anomaly detection alerts for a high-level business metric or a specific issue that's suite based (e.g., in Figure 14-6). The link to our observability tool might direct the user to a collection of views available based on the `test_suite` dimension.

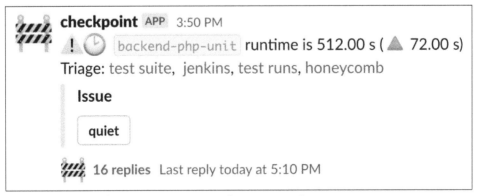

Figure 14-6. Identifying runtime increase for test suite above p50

At Slack, we've encouraged teams to make dashboards based on specific use cases. The Honeycomb link brings up a query from our CI Service Traces dashboard (Figure 14-7) that has parameters set for a potential issue for a test suite. This message helps inform responders of a specific issue—for example, a test suite called *backend-php-integration* is showing signs of a longer runtime—and responders might use Honeycomb to look at associated traces for potential issues.

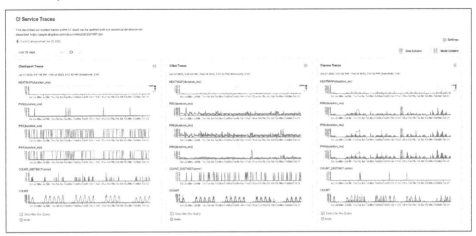

Figure 14-7. Slack's CI Service Traces dashboard displaying queries available to view different pieces of CI interactions

In Figure 14-8, you can see an example of a query looking at a high level at a rate, error, and duration query that responding teams might use.

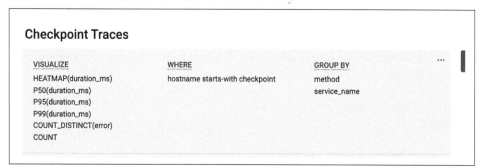

Figure 14-8. This sample drill-down query approximates a rate, error, and duration (RED) dashboard with visualizations by grouping individual methods between services in Checkpoint

With actionable alerting embedded, now we can understand what changed.

Understanding What Changed

Let's explore another case study of an August 2021 incident that combines a few of the preceding ideas. At Slack, we use the incident command system (*https:// response.pagerduty.com*) to handle incidents when an outage or service degradation is detected. The incident response begins with a new public Slack channel, and an incident commander adds responders from multiple teams to coordinate response and remediation of an outage.

In this situation, multiple users noted being blocked after seeing high rates of failures due to out-of-memory errors (OOMs) on test suite execution for backend unit and integration test suites. Each of these backend unit test suites may run tens of thousands of tests, and individually, test suite executions were occasionally passing.

Early in the incident, a responder found an anomaly from the previous day noting a higher flake rate (see Figure 14-9 for types of anomalies), potentially pointing to something that changed around that time. During the incident, responders looked at test case traces from backend tests to look at jumps in memory footprint for test cases. We were able to see multiple jumps in memory usage at p50, p95, and p99 over the last months, with fidelity down to the hour on what had changed.

Using this data, experts were able to identify potential PRs from the previous day and more from the previous months that appeared correlated with jumps in memory usage. Causation for degradations in large codebases or test suites are often challenging because of a high velocity of change and many variables both in the codebase and infrastructure that might lead to changes.

Conditions

- Backend (Hack) unit/integration tests are failing at a fairly high rate due to OOM conditions on hosts.
- Theory is that memory usage in tests has increased to a point where it's no longer feasible to run so many tests in parallel on the same host.
- We've identified a couple of inflection points over the past month where memory usage rose significantly.

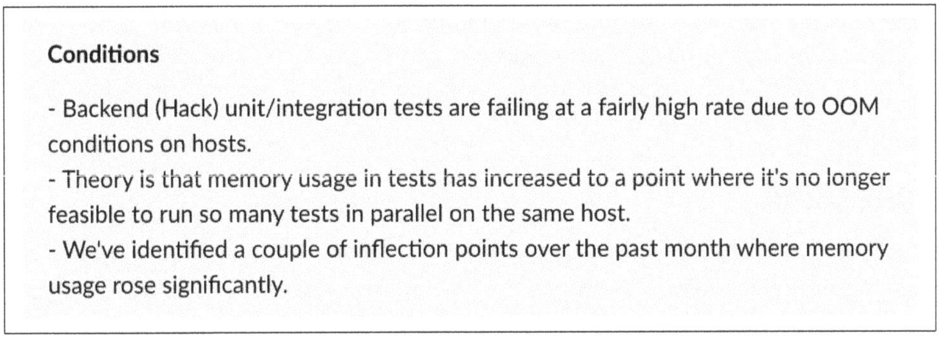

Figure 14-9. The Conditions section of a Conditions/Actions/Needs (CAN) process from that incident. There is a symptom of the outage that multiple test suites are failing due to OOM, and an ongoing theory that's being investigated.

A few potential culprit commits were reverted. Because of the potential large number of variables during an incident investigation, a holding pattern frequently occurs after a change, before telemetry can report healthiness. Figure 14-10 shows a long thread by subject-matter experts who were quickly able to test the hypothesis and see system health using distributed tracing in near-real time.

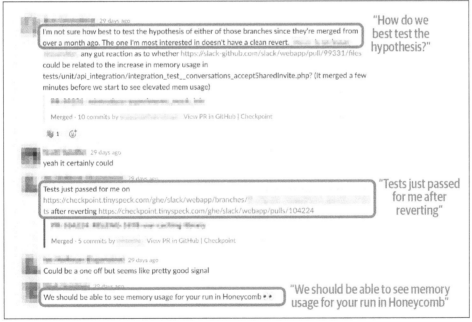

Figure 14-10. A Slack thread of questions during incident investigation that starts with testing a hypothesis, taking action, and using observability to validate the hypothesis (responder names blurred for privacy)

This data allowed Slack to look at telemetry with context over time. This is one of many examples of using observability in day-to-day operations at Slack. You can adopt a similar approach to identify changes and breaks by embedding observability into your own investigations.

Conclusion

This chapter illustrates how observability can be useful in the software supply chain. I shared how Slack instrumented the CI pipeline and recent examples of debugging distributed systems. The intricacies of debugging distributed systems are generally top of mind for application developers trying to understand how their code behaves in production environments. But, prior to production, other distributed systems may be equally challenging to properly understand and debug.

With the right tools and dimensionality in the software supply chain, Slack engineers were able to solve complex problems throughout the CI workflow that were previously invisible or undetected. Whether debugging complaints that an application is slow or that CI tests are flaky, observability can help developers correlate problems in high-complexity systems that interact.

PART IV

Observability at Scale

In Part III, we focused on overcoming barriers to getting started and new workflows that help change social and cultural practices in order to put some momentum behind your observability adoption initiatives. In this part, we examine considerations on the other end of the adoption spectrum: what happens when observability adoption is successful and practiced at scale?

When it comes to observability, "at scale" is probably larger than most people think. As a rough ballpark measure, when measuring telemetry events generated per day in the high hundreds of millions or low billions, you might have a scale issue. The concepts explored in this chapter are most acutely felt when operating observability solutions at scale. However, these lessons are generally useful to anyone going down the path of observability.

Chapter 15 explores the decision of whether to buy or build an observability solution. At a large enough scale, as the bill for commercial solutions grows, teams will start to consider whether they can save more by simply building an observability solution themselves. This chapter provides guidance on how best to approach that decision.

Chapter 16 explores how a data store must be configured in order to serve the needs of an observability workload. To achieve the functional requirements of iterative and open-ended investigations, several technical criteria must be met. This chapter presents a case study of Honeycomb's Retriever engine as a model for meeting these requirements.

Chapter 17 looks at how to reduce the overhead of managing large volumes of telemetry data at scale. This chapter presents several techniques to ensure high-fidelity observability data, while reducing the overall number of events that must be captured and stored in your backend data store.

Chapter 18 takes a look at another technique for managing large volumes of telemetry data at scale, or management via pipelines. This is a guest chapter by Suman Karumuri, senior staff software engineer, and Ryan Katkov, director of engineering, at Slack. It presents an in-depth look at how Slack uses telemetry management pipelines to route observability data at scale.

This part of the book focuses on observability concepts that are useful to understand at any scale but that become critical in large-scale use cases. In Part V, we'll look at techniques for spreading observability culture at any scale.

CHAPTER 15

Build Versus Buy and Return on Investment

So far in this book, we've examined both the technical fundamentals of observability and the social steps necessary to initiate the practice. In this part of the book, we will examine the considerations necessary when implementing observability at scale. We'll focus on the functional requirements that are necessary to achieve the observability workflows described in earlier parts.

At a large enough scale, the question many teams will grapple with is whether they should build or buy an observability solution. Observability can seem relatively inexpensive on the surface, especially for smaller deployments. As user traffic grows, so too does the infrastructure footprint and volume of events your application generates. When dealing with substantially more observability data and seeing a much larger bill from a vendor, teams will start to consider whether they can save more by simply building an observability solution themselves.

Alternatively, some organizations consider building an observability solution when they perceive that a vendor's ability to meet their specific needs is inadequate. Why settle for less than you need when software engineers can build the exact thing you want? As such, we see a variety of considerations play into arguments on whether the right move for any given team is to build a solution or buy one.

This chapter unpacks those considerations for teams determining whether they should build or buy an observability solution. It also looks at both quantifiable and unquantifiable factors when considering return on investment (ROI). The build-versus-buy choice is also not binary; in some situations, you may want to both buy *and* build.

We'll start by examining the true costs for buying and building. Then we'll consider circumstances that may necessitate one or the other. We'll also look at ways to potentially strike a balance between building everything yourself or just using a vendor solution. The recommendations in this chapter are most applicable to larger organizations, but the advice applies to teams weighing this decision at any scale.

How to Analyze the ROI of Observability

First, let's acknowledge that this book is written by employees of an observability software vendor. Clearly, we have our own sets of biases. That said, we can still unpack this problem methodically and start by quantifying costs.

No one-size-fits-all answer can indicate how much observability will cost you. But some broad generalizations can be made. The easiest place to start is with the factor that is most visible: the bill that you get from a commercial observability vendor. In a vendor relationship, it's easier to see the financial costs because they're right there in a line item.

When you first begin investigating observability vendor solutions (especially those from incumbent monitoring and APM solutions that simply apply an observability label onto their decades-old traditional tools), the total price can give you sticker shock. The sticker is shocking in part because new users compare that price to open source and "free" alternatives that they presumably could just build themselves. However, people are generally not accustomed to considering the price of their own time. When it takes an hour to spin up some infrastructure and configure software, it feels like a DIY solution is essentially free.

In reality, the costs of ongoing maintenance—the time burned for context switching, the opportunity cost of all those engineers devoting time to something of no core business value, all those hours being siphoned away by that free solution—are almost always underestimated. In practice, even when you think you've accounted for the underestimation, you'll likely still underestimate. As humans, our gut feelings are wildly, even charmingly, optimistic on the matter of maintenance costs. As a starting point, this is both understandable and forgivable.

Even when you do proceed beyond that starting point, sometimes the urge to build a solution yourself is a matter of encountering a budgetary mismatch. Getting approval to spend money on buying software may be harder than getting engineers you already employ to spend time building and supporting an in-house alternative. However, organizations that fall into this category are often reluctant to admit just how much that free effort is truly costing their business. Overcoming a budgetary mismatch may prompt an initial decision to build, but over the long term, that decision will present substantial costs to an organization that aren't usually being tracked after the initial decision to build is made.

To analyze the ROI of building or buying observability tools, first you must start by truly understanding the costs of both decisions. Calculating total cost of ownership

(TCO) requires factoring in many considerations to be exact, but you can use general guidelines to get started.

The Real Costs of Building Your Own

Let's start with opportunity costs. Resources are finite, and every choice to spend dollars or time impacts what your business will be able to accomplish. *Opportunity cost* is the value of the next-best alternative when a decision is made. By choosing to go the route you did, what did you give up in return?

Are you in the business of building observability solutions? If the answer to that question is no, building a bespoke observability tool is likely a distraction from your company's core objectives. Therefore, the opportunity cost of choosing to build one yourself is big.

The rarest naturally occurring element on Earth is astatine (atomic number 85 on the periodic table), with less than 1 gram present deep within the Earth's crust at any given time. The second rarest element is unallocated engineering time. We kid, of course. But if you're a product or an engineering manager, you're probably "lolsobbing" at that joke (sorry, managers!). In any given company, endless competing demands clamor for engineering cycles. As leaders and engineers, it's your job to filter out the noise and prioritize the most impactful needs requiring solutions that will move the business forward.

As software engineers, it's your job to write code. The opportunity cost problem comes into play whenever that talent is applied toward every arbitrary challenge that you might encounter. When you see a problem, if your first and foremost inclination is to just write some code to fix it, you may not be considering opportunity costs. While coding is fast and cheap, maintaining that code is extremely time-consuming and costly. As fellow engineers, we know that often we are so preoccupied with whether we *can* do something that we don't stop to think about whether we *should*.

To calculate opportunity costs, you must first calculate the financial costs of each option, quantify the benefits received with each, and compare the two. Let's start with an example of calculating the costs of building your own.

The Hidden Costs of Using "Free" Software

You could choose to build your own observability stack using open source components that you then assemble yourself. For simplicity, we'll presume this is the case. (An alternative build option of creating every stack component from scratch would carry costs at least an order of magnitude higher.) To illustrate actual operating costs, we'll use a real example.

We spoke to an engineering team manager who was considering investing in a commercial observability stack after having built an in-house ELK stack. We'd given him a quote that was about $80,000/month to provide observability for his organization. He immediately balked at the sticker shock of a nearly $1 million annual solution and pointed to the free ELK stack his team was running internally.

However, he wasn't counting the cost of the dedicated hardware used to run that ELK cluster ($80,000/month). He also wasn't counting the three extra engineers he had to recruit to help run it ($250,000 to $300,000 each, per year), plus all of the one-time costs necessary to get there, including recruiter fees (15% to 25% of annual earnings, or about $75,000 each), plus the less tangible (though still quantifiable) organizational time spent hiring and training them to become effective in their roles.

The seemingly free solution had been costing his company over $2 million each year, more than twice the cost of the commercial option. But he'd been spending that in ways that were less visible to the organization. Engineers are expensive, and recruiting them is hard. It seems especially wasteful to devote their talent to bespoke solutions in the name of saving a few dollars, when the reality is often much further from the truth.

Heidi Waterhouse, principal developer advocate at LaunchDarkly, muses that open source software is "free as in puppies, not free as in beer." Indeed, in the preceding example, this engineering manager was spending twice as much to do non-mission-critical work that did not advance his company's core competencies.

The first step to understanding ROI is to truly flesh out the hidden and less visible costs of running supposedly free software. This isn't to say that you shouldn't run open source software. It's to say that, when you do, you should be fully aware of what it is really costing you.

The Benefits of Building Your Own

In many organizations, the deciding factor comes down to justifying visible spending. When budgets and expectations are mismatched, justifying spending time and hiring additional developers to build and support an in-house solution is often easier than creating a new line item to pay to acquire software externally. While the true estimation of costs in those cases is misguided, building your own software provides an additional benefit that may balance the equation a bit.

Building your own software also builds in-house expertise. The very act of deciding to build your own custom approach means that it becomes someone's job to deeply understand your organizational needs and turn those into a set of functional requirements. As you work with internal stakeholders to support their needs, you will learn how to bridge the gap between technology and your business.

When building your own observability solution, you will inherently need to internalize and implement many of the solutions detailed in this book—from the necessary data granularity provided by events, to automating the core analysis loop, to optimizing your data store to performantly return results against large quantities of unpredictable high-cardinality data. But you will deeply internalize those solutions as they're implemented specifically to meet your organizational needs.

You'll learn how to make distributed tracing valuable for the needs of your own particular applications through numerous trials and many useful errors working with your own developer teams. You'll learn exactly where metrics are serving your business and where they're not by slamming headfirst into the limitations of their coarseness in the debugging loop. You'll learn how to adjust error budget burn alert calculations for your implementation SLOs as you miss timely responses to production outages.

Over time, you will so deeply understand your own organizational challenges that you will build a team whose job it is to write instrumentation libraries and useful abstractions for your software engineering teams. This observability team will standardize on naming conventions across the organization, handle updates and upgrades gracefully, and consult with other engineering teams on how to instrument their code for maximum effectiveness. Over the years, as the observability team grows and your custom implementation becomes a battle-tested and mature application, the team may even be able to shift its focus away from new feature development and ongoing support to instead look for ways to simplify and reduce friction.

Observability is a competitive advantage for organizations.[1] By building your own observability solution, you can develop a solution that is deeply ingrained in your own practices and culture and that leverages existing institutional knowledge. Rather than using generic prebuilt software designed to work with many workflows and implementations, you can customize your solution for deep integration with bespoke parts of your business, according to your own rules.

The Risks of Building Your Own

The deep in-house expertise developed by building your own observability solution does not come without risks. The first and most obvious risk centers around product management expertise and bandwidth. Does the observability team have a product manager—whether by title or by function—whose job it is to interview users, determine use cases, manage feature development by the team, deliver a minimum viable product, gather feedback for iteration, and balance constraints against business needs to deliver against a roadmap of functionality the business needs?

---

1 Dustin Smith, "2021 Accelerate State of DevOps Report Addresses Burnout, Team Performance" (*https://oreil.ly/h958I*), Google Cloud Blog, September 21, 2021.

Product-led organizations will have in-house product expertise that can make their in-house development of a custom observability product successful. Whether that product management expertise will be allocated away from core business objectives and toward building in-house tooling is another question. The biggest risk in building your own observability solution is whether the delivered product will meet the needs of your internal users very well.

This risk is somewhat mitigated when assembling a solution by piecing together various open source components. However, each of those components has its own designed user-experience and inherent workflow assumptions. As an engineering team building your own observability stack, your job will be to ease the friction among those components with integration libraries that enable the workflows needed by your own teams. Your job is to build a user interface that's easy to use, or you run the risk of having low adoption.

When deciding to build your own observability solution, it's critical to be realistic about both your organizational ability and your chances of developing something better than commercially available systems. Do you have the organizational expertise to deliver a system with the user interface, workflow flexibility, and speed required to encourage organizational-wide adoption? If you don't, it's entirely likely that you will have invested time, money, and lost business opportunities into a solution that never sees widespread adoption beyond those who are intimately familiar with its rough edges and workarounds.

Presuming your organization has the ability to deliver a better solution, another factor in considering your chances is time. Building out your own solutions and custom integrations takes time, which will delay your observability adoption initiatives. Can your business afford to wait several months to get a functional solution in place instead of getting started immediately with an already built commercial solution? This is like asking whether your business should wait to get operations underway while you first construct an office building. In some cases, considering longer-term impacts may require that approach. But often in business, reduced time to value is preferable.

Building your own observability product is not a one-and-done solution either. It requires ongoing support, and your custom-built software also needs to be maintained. Underlying third-party components in your stack will get software updates and patches. Organizational workflows and systems are constantly evolving. Introducing updates or enhancements in underlying components will require internal development efforts that must be accounted for. Unless those components and integrations stay current, custom solutions run the risk of becoming obsolete. You must also factor in the risks presented by ongoing support and maintenance.

An unfortunately common implementation pattern in many enterprises is to devote development effort toward building an initial version of internal tools and then moving on to the next project. As a result, it's also common to see enterprises abandon their custom-built solutions once development has stalled, adoption is low, and the time and effort required to make it meet current requirements is not a high-enough priority when compared against competing interests.

The Real Costs of Buying Software

Let's start with the most obvious cost of buying software: financial costs. In a vendor relationship, this cost is the most tangible. You see the exact financial costs whenever your software vendor sends you a bill.

A reality is that software vendors must make money to survive, and their pricing scheme will factor in a certain level of profit margin. In other words, you will pay a vendor more to use their software than it costs them to build and operate it for you.

The Hidden Financial Costs of Commercial Software

While it may be fair (and necessary) for vendors to set prices that help them recoup their cost to deliver a market-ready solution, what is considerably less fair is obscuring the real costs, avoiding transparency, or stacking in so many pricing dimensions that consumers cannot reasonably predict what their usage patterns will cost them in the future.

A common pattern to be on the lookout for uses pricing strategies that obscure TCO, such as per seat, per host, per service, per query, or per any other impossible-to-predict metering mechanism. Pay-as-you-go pricing may seem approachable at first—that is, until your usage of a particular tool explodes at a rate disproportionately more expensive than the revenue it helps you generate.

That's not to say that pay-as-you-go pricing is unfair. It's simply harder to project into the future. As a consumer, it's up to you to avoid pricing schemes that disproportionately cost you more when using an observability tool for its intended purpose. You may initially opt for pricing that presents a lower barrier to entry, but inadvertently lock yourself into a ballooning budget with a tool you've learned to successfully use. You can avoid this by learning how to forecast hidden costs.

Will the size of your team change as your start-up becomes a more successful business? More than likely, yes. So it may seem reasonable to you to adopt a tool with a per seat licensing strategy: when your company is more profitable, you'll be willing to pay more. Will your start-up significantly grow its number of hosts in the future? Possibly? Likely yes, but instance resizing may also be a factor. Will there be more services? Very few, perhaps. Maybe you'll launch a few new products or features that necessitate more, but that's difficult to say. What about the number of queries you run? Almost certainly yes, if this tool is successfully used. Will that growth be linear or exponential? What happens if you decide to decompose your monoliths into microservices? What happens if an adjacent team you didn't account for also finds this tool useful?

The future is unpredictable. But when it comes to observability—regardless of how your production services change—you can (and should) predict how your usage will take shape when you're adopting it successfully. Given the same set of observability data, the recommended practice is to analyze it with increasing curiosity. You should see exponential growth in data queries as a culture of observability spreads in your organization.

For example, observability is useful in your CI/CD build pipelines (see Chapter 14). As you'll see in the next couple of chapters, analyzing observability data is also useful to product, support, finance, executive, or any number of business teams that stretch well beyond engineering. You will want to slice and dice your observability data in many ways, across many dimensions, to coax out any performance outliers that may be hiding in your application systems.

Therefore, you should avoid observability tools with pricing schemes that penalize adoption and curiosity. You will want to ensure that as many people in your company as possible have the ability to understand how your customers use your software, in as many ways as possible.

As a consumer, you should demand your vendors be transparent and help you calculate hidden costs and forecast usage patterns. Ask them to walk you through detailed cost estimates of both your starting point today and your likely usage patterns in the future. Be wary of any vendor unwilling to provide an exceptional level of detail about how their pricing will change as your business needs grow.

To factor in the hidden financial costs of commercial observability solutions, start with the real costs of using it as you do today. Then apply a logical rubric to that price: how much will that tool cost you if you want to ensure that as many people as possible have the ability to understand how your customers use your software, in as many arbitrary ways as possible? That will help you quantify the cost in terms of dollars spent.

The Hidden Nonfinancial Costs of Commercial Software

A secondary hidden cost of commercial solutions is time. Yes, you will lower your time to value by buying a ready-made solution. But you should be aware of a hidden trap when going this route: vendor lock-in. Once you've made the choice to use this commercial solution, how much time and effort would be required from you to migrate to a different solution?

When it comes to observability, the most labor-intensive part of adoption comes by way of instrumenting your applications to emit telemetry data. Many vendors shortcut this time to adoption by creating proprietary agents or instrumentation libraries that are prebuilt to generate telemetry in proprietary ways their tools expect to see data. While some of those proprietary agents may be quicker to get started with, any time and effort devoted to making them work must be repeated when even considering evaluating a possible alternative observability solution.

The open source OpenTelemetry project (see Chapter 7) solves this problem by providing an open standard that many observability tools support. OTel allows you to also shortcut time to value with proprietary tools by enabling the use of OTel distributions (or *distros*). OTel distros allow product vendors to layer boilerplate configurations and functionality on top of standard OTel libraries.

As a consumer, your strategy to avoid vendor lock-in should be to use native OTel functionality by default in your applications and rely on distros to handle vendor configuration. Should you wish to evaluate or migrate to a different tool, you can replace configurations with different distros or configure OTel exporters to send your data to multiple backends. Getting started with OTel will have an initial time cost (as would any instrumentation approach), but most of that time investment should be reusable should you wish to use other solutions in the future.

The Benefits of Buying Commercial Software

The most obvious benefit of buying an observability solution is time to value. You don't need to custom build a solution; you're purchasing one that's ready to go. In most cases, you can get started within minutes or hours and be well on your way to understanding production differently than you did without observability.

Part of the reason that fast on-ramping is possible with commercial solutions is that they generally have more streamlined user experience than open source solutions. Open source solutions are generally designed as building blocks that can be assembled as part of a toolchain you design yourself. Commercial software is often more opinionated: it tends to be a finished product with a specific workflow. Product designers work to streamline ease of use and maximize time to value. Commercial software *needs to be* incredibly faster and easier to learn and use than free alternatives. Otherwise, why would you pay for them?

Perhaps you'd also pay for commercial software because you offload maintenance and support to your vendor. You save time and effort. Rather than burning your own engineering cycles, you pay someone else to take on that burden for you. And you'll enjoy better economies of scale. Often the choice to go commercial is all about increasing speed and lowering organizational risk, at the trade-off of cost.

But buying a commercial solution has one other, mostly overlooked, benefit. By purchasing tooling from a company whose core competency is focusing on a particular problem, you potentially gain a partner with years of expertise in solving that problem in a variety of ways. You can leverage this commercial relationship to tap into invaluable expertise in the observability domain that would otherwise take you years to build on your own.

The Risks of Buying Commercial Software

That last benefit is also one of the bigger risks in buying commercial software. By shoving off responsibility to your vendor, you potentially risk not developing your own in-house observability expertise. By simply consuming a ready-made solution, your organization may not have the need to dive into your problem domain to understand how exactly observability applies to your particular business needs.

Commercial products are built for a wide audience. While they have opinionated designs, they're also generally built to adapt to a variety of use cases. A commercial product is, by definition, not specifically built to accommodate your special needs. Features that are important to you may not be as important to your vendor. They may be slow to prioritize those features on their roadmap, and you may be left waiting for functionality that is critical for your business.

But there is a way to mitigate these risks and still develop in-house expertise when it comes to adopting observability tools.

Buy Versus Build Is Not a Binary Choice

The choice to build or to buy is a false dichotomy when it comes to observability tools. Your choice is not limited to simply building or buying. A third option is to buy *and* to build. In fact, we authors recommend that approach for most organizations. You can minimize internal opportunity costs and build solutions that are specific to your organization's unique needs. Let's see what that looks like in practice by examining how an *observability team* should work in most organizations.

Buying a vendor solution doesn't necessarily mean your company won't need an observability team. Rather than having that team build your observability tooling from scratch or assemble open source components, the team can act as an intermediary integration point between the vendor and your engineering organization, with the explicit goal of making that interface seamless and friendly.

We already know from industry research that the key to success when outsourcing work is to carefully curate how that work makes its way back into the organization.[2] Outsourced contributions should be embedded within cross-functional teams that manage integrating that work back into the broader organization. That research specifically looks at contractual deliverables, but the same type of model applies to interacting with your vendors.

---

2 Nicole Forsgren et al., *Accelerate State of DevOps* (*https://oreil.ly/2Gqjz*), DORA, 2019.

High-performing organizations use great tools. They know engineering cycles are scarce and valuable. So they train their maximum firepower on solving core business problems, and they equip engineers with best-of-breed tools that help them be radically more effective and efficient. They invest in solving bespoke problems (or building bespoke tools) only to the extent that they have become an obstacle to delivering that core business value.

Lower-performing engineering organizations settle for using mediocre tools, or they copy the old tools without questioning. They lack discipline and consistency around adoption and deprecation of tools meant to solve core business problems. Because they attempt to solve most problems themselves, they leak lost engineering cycles throughout the organization. They lack the focus to make strong impacts that deliver core business value.

Your observability team should write libraries and useful abstractions, standardize on naming schemes across the organization, handle updates and upgrades gracefully, and consult with other engineering teams on how to instrument their code for maximum effectiveness (see "Use Case: Telemetry Management at Slack" on page 235). They should manage vendor relationships, make decisions about when to adopt new technologies, and look for ways to simplify and reduce friction and costs.

For organizations that consider building their own observability stack because they can suit it to their specific needs, this is an especially effective approach. Using an observability team to build on top of an extensible vendor solution can minimize sunken costs that distract from delivering core business value. Rather than reinventing the wheel, your observability team can build integrations that mount that wheel to the fast-moving car you've already built.

The key to enabling that balance is to ensure that your team uses a product that has a well-developed API that lets them configure, manage, and run queries against your observability data. You should be able to get results programmatically and use those in your own customized workflows. Last-mile problem-solving requires substantially less investment and lets you build just the components you need while buying a vast majority of things your company doesn't need to build. When seeking a commercial tool, you should look for products that give you the flexibility to manipulate and adapt your observability data as you see fit.

Conclusion

This chapter presents general advice, and your own situation may, of course, be different. When making your own calculations around building or buying, you must first start by determining the real TCO of both options. Start with the more visibly quantifiable costs of both (time when considering building, and money when considering buying). Then be mindful of the hidden costs of each (opportunity costs and less visibly spent money when considering building, and future usage patterns and vendor lock-in when considering buying).

When considering building with open source tools, ensure that you weigh the full impact of hidden costs like recruiting, hiring, and training the engineers necessary to develop and maintain bespoke solutions (including their salaries and your infrastructure costs) in addition to the opportunity costs of devoting those engineers to running tools that are not delivering against core business value. When purchasing an observability solution, ensure that vendors give you the transparency to understand their complicated pricing schemes and apply logical rubrics when factoring in both system architecture and organizational adoption patterns to determine your likely future costs.

When adding up these less visible costs, the TCO for free solutions can be more adequately weighed against commercial solutions. Then you can also factor in the less quantifiable benefits of each approach to determine what's right for you. Also remember that you can buy *and* build to reap the benefits of either approach.

Remember that, as employees for a software vendor, we authors have some implicit bias in this conversation. Even so, we believe the advice in this chapter is fair and methodical, and in alignment with our past experience as consumers of observability tooling rather than producers. Most of the time, the best answer for any given team focused on delivering business value is to buy an observability solution rather than building one themselves. However, that advice comes with the caveat that your team should be building an integration point enabling that commercial solution to be adapted to the needs of your business.

In the next chapter, should you decide to build your own observability solution, we will look at what it takes to optimize a data store for the needs of delivering against an observability workload.

CHAPTER 16

Efficient Data Storage

In this chapter, we'll look at the challenges that must be addressed to effectively store and retrieve your observability data when you need it most. Speed is a common concern with data storage and retrieval, but other functional constraints impose key challenges that must be addressed at the data layer. At scale, the challenges inherent to observability become especially pronounced. We will lay out the functional requirements necessary to enable observability workflows. Then we will examine real-life trade-offs and possible solutions by using the implementation of Honeycomb's proprietary Retriever data store as inspiration.

You will learn about the various considerations required at the storage and retrieval layers to ensure speed, scalability, and durability for your observability data. You will learn about a columnar data store and why it is particularly well suited for observability data, how querying workloads must be handled, and considerations for making data storage durable and performant. The solutions presented in this chapter are not the only possible solutions to the various trade-offs you may encounter. However, they're presented as real-world examples of achieving the necessary results when building an observability solution.

The Functional Requirements for Observability

When you're experiencing an outage in production, every second counts. Queries against your observability data must return results as quickly as possible. If you submit a query and can get a cup of coffee while you wait for results to return, you're fighting a losing battle with a tool unfit for production (see "Debugging from First Principles" on page 85). Getting results within seconds is what makes observability a useful investigative practice that lets you iterate quickly until you find meaningful results.

As covered in Part II, events are the building blocks of observability, and traces are a collection of interrelated events (or trace spans). Finding meaningful patterns within those events requires an ability to analyze high-cardinality and high-dimensionality data. Any field within any event (or within any trace span) must be queryable. Those events cannot be pre-aggregated since, in any given investigation, you won't know in advance which fields may be relevant. All telemetry data must be available to query in pre-aggregate resolution, regardless of its complexity, or you risk hitting investigative dead ends.

Further, because you don't know which dimensions in an event may be relevant, you cannot privilege the data-retrieval performance of any particular dimension over others (they must all be equally fast). Therefore, all possible data needed must be indexed (which is typically prohibitively expensive), or data retrieval must always be fast without indexes in place.

Typically, in observability workflows, users are looking to retrieve data in specific time ranges. That means the only exception to privileged data is the dimension of time. It is imperative that queries return all data recorded within specific time intervals, so you must ensure that it is indexed appropriately. A TSDB would seem to be the obvious choice here, but as you'll see later in this chapter, using one for observability presents its own set of incompatible constraints.

Because your observability data is used to debug production issues, it's imperative to know whether the specific actions you've taken have resolved the problem. Stale data can cause engineers to waste time on red herrings or make false conclusions about the current state of their systems. Therefore, an efficient observability system should include not just historical data but also fresh data that reflects the current state in close to real time. No more than seconds should elapse between when data is received into the system and when it becomes available to query.

Lastly, that data store must also be durable and reliable. You cannot lose the observability data needed during your critical investigations. Nor can you afford to delay your critical investigations because any given component within your data store failed. Any mechanisms you employ to retrieve data must be fault-tolerant and designed to return fast query results despite the failure of any underlying workers. The durability of your data store must also be able to withstand failures that occur within your own infrastructure. Otherwise, your observability solution may also be inoperable while you're attempting to debug why the production services it tracks are inoperable.

Given these functional requirements necessary to enable real-time debugging workflows, traditional data storage solutions are often inadequate for observability. At a small enough scale, data performance within these parameters can be more easily achieved. In this chapter, we'll examine how these problems manifest when you go beyond single-node storage solutions.

Time-Series Databases Are Inadequate for Observability

At its core, observability data consists of structured events representing information about a program's execution. As seen in Chapter 5, these structured events are essentially collections of key-value pairs. In the case of tracing, the structured events can be related to one another in order to visualize parent-child relationships between trace spans. Some of those fields may be "known" (or predictable), given the auto-instrumentation use case seen in Chapter 7. However, the most valuable data will be custom to your particular application. That custom data is often generated ad hoc, meaning that the schema used to store it is often dynamic or flexible.

As discussed in Chapter 9, time-series data (metrics) aggregates system performance into simple measures. Metrics aggregate all underlying events over a particular time window into one simple and decomposable number with an associated set of tags. This allows for a reduction in the volume of data sent to a telemetry backend data store and improves query performance but limits the number of answers that can later be derived from that data. While some metrics data structures (like those used to generate histograms) may be slightly more sophisticated, they still essentially bucket similar value ranges together and record counts of events sharing similar values (see Figure 16-1).

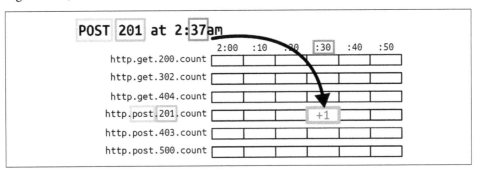

Figure 16-1. A prototypical TSDB showing a limited amount of cardinality and dimensionality: tags for HTTP method and status code, bucketed by timestamp

Traditionally, a *time-series database* (TSDB) is used to store aggregated metrics. Time-series data storage mechanisms aim to amortize the cost of additional traffic by ensuring that new combinations of aggregations and tags are rare; a high overhead is associated with creating a record (or database row) for each unique time series, but appending a numeric measurement to a time series that already exists has a low cost. On the query side, the predominant resource cost in a TSDB is finding which time series matches a particular expression; scanning the set of results is inexpensive since millions of events can be reduced into a small number of time-windowed counts.

In an ideal world, you could simply switch to recording structured events utilizing the same TSDB. However, the functional observability requirement to surface meaningful patterns within high-cardinality and high-dimensionality data makes using a TSDB prohibitive. Although you could convert each dimension to a tag name, and each value to the tag's value, this will create a new time series for each unique combination of tag values (see Figure 16-2).

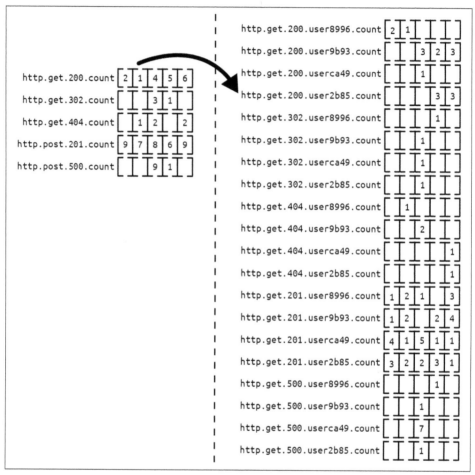

Figure 16-2. The explosion of that same TSDB when a high-cardinality index, userid, is added

The cost of creating new time series amortizes to 0 across measurements only if the same tags are reused and incremented often. But each structured event is often *unique* and will cause the overhead of row creation to be linear with the number of events received. This problem of *cardinality explosion* thus makes TSDBs unsuitable for storing structured events. We need a different solution.

Other Possible Data Stores

At first pass, storing structured sets of key-value pairs may appear similar to other workloads that can be addressed by general-purpose storage NoSQL databases, like MongoDB or Snowflake. However, while the ingress of event telemetry data (or event ingestion) is well suited to those databases, the egress patterns for that data (or event querying) are dramatically different from traditional workloads because of the functional requirements for observability.

That iterative analysis approach (described in Chapter 8) requires the ability to understand more than one dimension at a time, regardless of the number of possible values each of those dimensions contains. In other words, you must be able to query on data with arbitrary dimensionality and cardinality. A NoSQL database is likely to be slow for these kinds of arbitrary queries, unless the query utilizes only specific fields that are already indexed. But pre-indexing doesn't allow you to arbitrarily slice and dice; you're limited to slicing and dicing along one dimension at a time, and only the dimensions you remembered to index or pre-aggregate up front. And if each value is unique, it will take up as much space in the index as in the original table, resulting in a collection of indices larger than the original data if we index every column. So trying to tune a NoSQL database to optimize its queries won't work. What if instead of trying to make a subset of queries fast, we tried to make *all* queries possible to complete within a reasonable amount of time?

At Facebook, the Scuba system effectively solved the problem of real-time observability querying through consumption of huge amounts of RAM in order to allow full table accesses.[1] However, it made the performance trade-off of using system memory for storage to speed up querying. That implementation decision made Scuba economically infeasible for mass adoption beyond the walls of Facebook. As of the time of this writing, 1 terabyte of RAM costs approximately $4,000, whereas 1 TB of SSD costs approximately $100. If attempting to use Scuba as a data store, an organization would be limited to querying only the amount of data available in RAM. For most large organizations with a reasonably sized infrastructure, that constraint would limit the time window for queryable telemetry data to minutes rather than hours or days.

---

1 Lior Abraham et al., "Scuba: Diving into Data at Facebook" (*https://oreil.ly/j2OZy*), Proceedings of the VLDB Endowment 6.11 (2013): 1057–1067.

Perhaps we can look to other data stores that are used to store event-like data—namely, telemetry backends for tracing solutions. At the time of this writing, a few open source implementations of large-scale storage engines exist, mostly interoperable with the Jaeger tracing frontend (*https://www.jaegertracing.io/docs/1.17/features/ #multiple-storage-backends*): Apache Cassandra, Elasticsearch/OpenSearch, ScyllaDB, and InfluxDB. These allow ingestion and durable storage of tracing data using a schema, but they are not necessarily purpose-built for tracing specifically. Grafana Tempo is an example of a newer implementation purpose-built for tracing, but it is not necessarily built for the functional querying requirements of observability, as we will see throughout this chapter. Perhaps the best open source approach in the long term is to adopt a columnar store such as ClickHouse (*https://clickhouse.com*) or Apache Druid (*https://druid.apache.org*) with extensions to optimize for tracing, as SigNoz (*https://signoz.io/docs/architecture*) has done. At the time of writing, Polar Signals just announced ArcticDB (*https://www.polarsignals.com/blog/posts/2022/05/04/ introducing-arcticdb*), an open source columnar store for profiling and other observability data.

In the next section, we will examine the technical requirement to both store and query trace data so that it meets the functional requirements of observability. While anything is technically possible, the chapter will look at implementations that are financially feasible at scale so that you can store your event data and derive insights beyond what is possible from just examining individual traces.

Data Storage Strategies

Conceptually, wide events and the trace spans they represent can be thought of as a table with rows and columns. Two strategies can be used to store a table: row-based storage and column-based storage. For the observability domain, *rows* pertain to individual telemetry events, and *columns* pertain to the fields or attributes of those events.

In *row-based storage*, each row of data is kept together (as in Figure 16-3), with the assumption that the entire row will be fetched at once. In *column-based storage*, columns of data are kept together, disaggregated from their rows. Each approach has trade-offs. To illustrate these trade-offs, we will use the time-tested Dremel (*https://oreil.ly/TtCUa*), ColumnIO, and Google's Bigtable (*https://oreil.ly/uILVW*) as exemplars of the broader computational and storage models, rather than focus on specific open source telemetry stores used in practice today. In fact, the Dapper tracing system (*https://oreil.ly/cW1Px*) was originally built on the Bigtable data store.

idx	Col1	Col2	Col3	Col4	Col5	Col6	Col7	Col8	Col9	Cola	Colb	Colc	Cold	...
1														
2														
3														
4														
5														
6														
7														
8														
9														
10														

Figure 16-3. A row store, indicating sharding of contiguous rows kept together as a single unit (a tablet) for lookup and retrieval

Bigtable uses a row-based approach, meaning that the retrieval of individual traces and spans is fast because the data is serialized and the primary key is indexed (e.g., by time). To obtain one row (or scan a few contiguous rows), a Bigtable server needs to retrieve only one set of files with their metadata (a *tablet*). To function efficiently for tracing, this approach requires Bigtable to maintain a list of rows sorted by a primary row key such as trace ID or time. Row keys that arrive out of strict order require the server to insert them at the appropriate position, causing additional sorting work at write time that is not required for the nonsequential read workload.

As a mutable data store, Bigtable supports update and deletion semantics and dynamic repartitioning. In other words, data in Bigtable has flexibility in data processing at the cost of complexity and performance. Bigtable temporarily manages updates to data as an in-memory mutation log plus an ongoing stack of overlaid files containing key-value pairs that override values set lower in the stack. Periodically, once enough of these updates exist, the overlay files must be "compacted" back into a base immutable layer with a process that rewrites records according to their precedence order. That compaction process is expensive in terms of disk I/O operations.

For observability workloads, which are effectively write-once read-many, the compaction process presents a performance quandary. Because newly ingested observability data must be available to query within seconds, with Bigtable the compaction process would either need to run constantly, or you would need to read through each of the stacked immutable key-value pairs whenever a query is submitted. It's impractical to perform analysis of arbitrary fields without performing a read of all columns for the row's tablet to reproduce the relevant fields and values. It's similarly impractical to have compaction occur after each write.

Bigtable optionally allows you to configure *locality groups* per set of columns in a column family that can be stored separately from other column families. But examining data from even a single column from within a locality group still reads the entire locality group, while discarding most of the data, slowing the query and wasting CPU and I/O resources. You can add indices on selected columns or break out locality groups by predicted access patterns, but this workaround contradicts the observability requirement of arbitrary access. Sparse data within a locality group's columns is inexpensive within Bigtable since columns exist only within the locality group, but locality groups as a whole should not be empty because of their overhead.

Taken to the extreme limit of adding an index on each column or storing each column in a separate locality group, the cost adds up.[2] Notably, the Google Dapper backend paper notes that attempts to generate indexes in Bigtable on just three fields (service, host, and timestamp) for the Dapper Depots produced data that was 76% the size of the trace data itself.[3] Therefore, if you could entirely eliminate the need for indexing, you'd have a more practical approach to storing distributed traces.

Independent of strategies like Bigtable, when using a column-based approach, it is possible to quickly examine only the desired subset of data. Incoming data is partitioned into columns (as in Figure 16-4), with a synthetic id column providing a primary key for each row. Each column file with a mapping from primary key to the value for that column is stored separately. Thus, you can independently query and access the data from each column.

However, the column-based approach does not guarantee that any given row's data is stored in any particular order. To access the data for one row, you may need to scan an arbitrary quantity of data, up to the entire table. The Dremel and ColumnIO storage models attempt to solve this problem by breaking tables down with manual, coarse sharding (e.g., having separate tables for tablename.20200820, tablename.20200821, etc.) and leaving it to you, the user, to identify and join together tables at query time. This becomes immensely painful to manage at large data volume; the shards either become too large to efficiently query, or are broken into such numerous small shards (tablename.20200820-000123) that a human being has trouble constructing the query with the right shards.

---

2 Google, "Schema Design Best Practices" (*https://oreil.ly/8cFn6*), Google Cloud Bigtable website.

3 Benjamin H. Sigelman et al., "Dapper, a Large-Scale Distributed Systems Tracing Infrastructure," Google Technical Report (April 2010).

---

idx	Col1	Col2	Col3	Col4	Col5	Col6	Col7	Col8	Col9	Cola	Colb	Colc	Cold	...
1														
2														
3														
4														
5														
6														
7														
8														
9														
10														

Figure 16-4. Column store showing data broken down by column rather than by row, with each set of columns able to be independently accessed, but with a full row scan necessitating pulling each column file

Neither the row-based or column-based approach is entirely adequate to meet the functional needs for observability. To address the trade-offs of both row and columnar storage, a hybrid approach—utilizing the best of both worlds—can meet the types of tracing workloads needed for observability. A hybrid approach would allow you to efficiently perform partial scans of both rows and columns. Remember that, for observability workloads, it is more important for query results to return fast than it is for them to be perfect.

To illustrate how you might practically achieve such a balance, we will examine the architecture of Honeycomb's storage engine that represents one way to achieve those functional requirements.

Case Study: The Implementation of Honeycomb's Retriever

In this section, we explain the implementation of Honeycomb's columnar data store (aka Retriever) to show how you can meet the functional requirements for observability with a similar design. This reference architecture is not the only way to achieve these functional requirements; as stated earlier, you could build an observability backend using ClickHouse or Druid as a foundation. However, we hope to illustrate concrete implementation and operational trade-offs that you would not otherwise see in an abstract discussion of a theoretical model.

Partitioning Data by Time

Earlier, when we discussed the challenges of row-based versus column-based storage, we suggested a hybrid approach of partitioning the search space by timestamp to reduce the search space. However, time in a distributed system is never perfectly consistent, and the timestamp of a trace span could be the *start* rather than end time of a span, meaning data could arrive seconds or minutes behind the current time. It would not make sense to reach back into already saved bytes on disk to insert records in the middle, as that would incur costs to rewrite the data. How exactly should you perform that partitioning instead to make it efficient and viable in the face of out-of-order data arrival?

One optimization you can make is assuming that events are likely to arrive in close proximity to the timestamps at which they were actually generated, and that you can correct out-of-order arrival at read time. By doing this, you can continue to treat files storing incoming data as append-only, significantly simplifying the overhead at write time.

With Retriever, newly arriving trace spans for a particular tenant are inserted at the end of the currently active set of storage files (*segment*) for that tenant. To be able to query the right segments at read time, Retriever tracks the oldest and newest event timestamp for the current segment (creating a window that can potentially overlap with other segments' windows). Segments eventually do need to end and be finalized, so you should pick appropriate thresholds. For instance, when one hour has elapsed, more than 250,000 records have been written, or when it has written more than 1 GB, Retriever finalizes the current segment as read-only and records the final oldest and newest timestamps of that segment in the metadata.

If you have adopted this windowed segment pattern, at read time you can utilize the metadata with timestamp windows of each segment to fetch only the segments containing the relevant timestamps and tenant data sets for the query you wish to perform (as shown in Figure 16-5). Typically, an observability workload is looking for data in a specific time range when queries are performed (e.g., "now to two hours ago," or "2021-08-20 00:01 UTC to 2021-09-20 23:59 UTC"). Any other time range is extraneous to the query and, with this implementation, you don't need to examine data for irrelevant segments that lack an overlap with the query time.

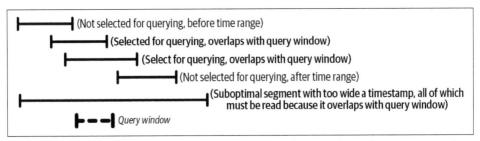

Figure 16-5. Segments selected for querying are those that overlap at least in part with the query window; segments that start and end before or after the query window are excluded from analysis.

The advantage of this segment partitioning by time is twofold:

- Individual events do not need to be sorted and put into a strict order by event timestamp, as long as the start and end timestamp of each segment is stored as metadata and events arrive with a consistent lag.
- The contents of each segment are append-only artifacts that can be frozen as is once finished rather than needing to be built as mutable overlays/layers and compacted periodically.

The segment-partitioning approach has one potential weakness: when backfilled data is intermingled with current data (for instance, if a batch job finishes and reports timestamps from hours or days ago), each segment written will have metadata indicating it spans a broad time window covering not just minutes, but potentially hours' or days' worth of time. In this case, segments will need to be scanned for any query in that wide window, rather than being scanned for data in only the two narrower windows of time—the current time, and the time around when the backfilled events happened. Although the Retriever workload has not necessitated this to date, you could layer on more sophisticated segment partitioning mechanisms if it became a significant problem.

Storing Data by Column Within Segments

As with the pure Dremel-like column-based approach outlined earlier, the next logical way to break down data after time has been taken out of the equation is by decomposing events into their constituent fields, and storing the contents of each field together with the same field across multiple events. This leads to a layout on disk of one append-only file per field per segment, plus a special timestamp index field (since every event must have a timestamp). As events arrive, you can append an entry to each corresponding file in the currently active segment for the columns they reference.

Once you have performed the filtering by segment timestamp described in the pre-ceding section, you can restrict the amount of data that you access upon query to only the relevant columns specified in the query by accessing the appropriate columns' own files. To be able to reconstruct the source rows, each row is assigned a timestamp and relative sequence within the segment. Each column file exists on disk as an array holding, alternately, sequence numbers for each row and the column's value for each row (according to the sequence).

For instance, this source collection of rows (which we've supposed is ordered by time of arrival) might be transformed as follows:

```
Row 0: { "timestamp": "2020-08-20 01:31:20.123456",
  "trace.trace_id": "efb8d934-c099-426e-b160-1145a87147e2", "field1": null, ... }
Row 1: { "timestamp": "2020-08-20 01:30:32.123456",
  "trace.trace_id": "562eb967-9171-424f-9d89-046f019b4324", "field1": "foo", ... }
Row 2: { "timestamp": "2020-08-20 01:31:21.456789",
  "trace.trace_id": "178cdf06-dbc5-4c0d-b6b7-5383218e1f6d", "field1": "foo", ... }
Row 3: { "timestamp": "2020-08-20 01:31:21.901234",
  "trace.trace_id": "178cdf06-dbc5-4c0d-b6b7-5383218e1f6d", "field1": "bar", ... }

Timestamp index file
idx value
0 "2020-08-20 01:31:20.123456"
1 "2020-08-20 01:30:32.123456" (note: timestamps do not need to be chronological)
2 "2020-08-20 01:31:21.456789"
3 "2020-08-20 01:31:21.901234"
[...]

Raw segment column file for column `field1`
(note there is neither a row index nor value for missing/null values of a column)
idx value
1 "foo"
2 "foo"
3 "bar"
[...]
```

Given the tendency of columns to either be null or to contain repeated values that may have been seen before, you could use dictionary-based compression, sparse encoding, and/or run-length encoding to reduce the amount of space that each value takes when serializing the entire column.[4] This benefits your backend in terms of the amount of data that must be tiered across your backend storage, as well as the amount of time that it takes to retrieve and scan that data:

```
compacted timestamp index file:
["2020-08-20 01:31:20.123456",
 "2020-08-20 01:30:32.123456",
 "2020-08-20 01:31:21.456789",
```

---

4 Terry Welch et. al., "A Technique for High-Performance Data Compression," *Computer* 17, no. 6 (1984): 8–19.

```
  "2020-08-20 01:31:21.901234",
  ...]

compacted segment column file, with dictionary, for column `example`
dictionary: {
  1: "foo",
  2: "bar",
  ...
}

presence:
[Bitmask indicating which rows have non-null values]

data from non-null row indices:
[1, 1, 2, ...]
```

Once a column is compacted, it (or the segment as a whole, consisting of a collection of column files) is then compressed with a standard algorithm such as LZ4 in order to further reduce the space it takes when archived.

In a column store, the cost of creating and tracking a column gets amortized against all of the values written to it; its analogue in the metrics world is the row/set of tags whose cost is amortized across all values. So, it is performant to create new columns whenever you might occasionally have non-null values, but it is not performant to create one-time-use columns that have only a single row with a non-null value.

In practice, this means that you don't need to worry about manually adding new attributes/key names to your spans/events when writing your code, but you don't want to programmatically create a column named timestamp_2021061712345 that gets used once to write true and is never written to again; instead, use timestamp as the column value and 2021061712345 as the key.

Performing Query Workloads

Performing a query by using a column store designed similarly to Retriever consists of six steps:

1. Identify all segments that potentially overlap with the time range of the query, using the start/end time of the query and start/end time of each eligible segment.

2. Independently, for each matching segment: for the columns used for the filters of the query (e.g., WHERE) or used for the output (e.g., used as a SELECT or GROUP), scan the relevant column files. To perform a scan, track the current offset you are working on. Evaluate the timestamp of the row at the current offset first to validate whether the row falls within the time range of the query. If not, advance to the next offset and try again.

---

3. For rows that fall within the time bound, scan the value at that offset for each column used as an input or output, emitting output values into the reconstructed row where the input filters match. Increment all offsets for all open column files to the next row once the row is processed. Individual rows can be processed and then discarded, minimizing the amount of data held in RAM to just a single value rather than the entire file for the column's values in the segment.

Note that an implicit GROUP is performed on timestamp where there's the need for subwindows within the original time range (e.g., reporting 24 five-minute windows for the past two hours of data).

4. Aggregate within the segment. For each GROUP, merge SELECTed values from step 3. For instance, COUNT simply collects the number of matching rows for each GROUP value, while SUM(example) might add all identified values for a column example for each GROUP value. After each segment is analyzed, its file handle can be unloaded.

5. Aggregate across segments by sending results to a single worker for each GROUP. Merge the aggregated values for each GROUP for each segment, and aggregate them into a single value (or set of values per time granularity bucket) for the time range.

6. Sort the groups and pick the top K groups to include in the graph. A default value of K should be used to avoid transmitting thousands of matching groups as a complete result set, unless the user requests it.

We can work through here in pseudocode, calculating SUM, COUNT, AVG, MAX, etc. based on keeping a cumulative sum or highest value seen to date—for instance, on the value of the field x grouped by fields a and b, where y is greater than zero:

```
groups := make(map[Key]Aggregation)
for _, s := range segments {
  for _, row := range fieldSubset(s, []string{"a", "b", "x", "y"})) 
    if row["y"] > 0 {
      continue
    }
    Key := Key{A: row["a"], B: row["b"]}
    aggr := groups[Key]
    aggr.Count++
    aggr.Sum += row["x"]
    if aggr.Max < row["x"] {
      aggr.Max = row["x"]
    }
    groups[Key] = aggr
  }
}
for k := range groups {
  groups[k].Avg = groups[k].Sum / groups[k].Count
}
```

For production use, this code would need to be generalized to support encoding arbitrarily many groups, arbitrary filters, and computing aggregations across multiple values, but it gives an idea as to how to compute aggregations in an efficiently parallelizable way. Algorithms such as quantile estimation with *t*-digest (*https://arxiv.org/abs/1902.04023*) and HyperLogLog (*https://hal.archives-ouvertes.fr/hal-00406166*) are required for calculating more complex aggregations such as p99 (for the 99th percentile of a set of numerical values) and COUNT DISTINCT (for the number of unique values in a column). You can further explore these sophisticated algorithms by referring to the academic literature.

In this fashion, you are able to performantly solve the problems of high cardinality and high dimensionality. No dimension (aside from timestamp) is privileged over any other dimension. It is possible to filter by an arbitrarily complex combination of one or more fields, because the filter is processed ad hoc at read time across all relevant data. Only the relevant columns are read for the filter and processing steps, and only the relevant values corresponding to a matching row ID are plucked out of each column's data stream for emitting values.

There is no need for pre-aggregation or artificial limits on the complexity of data. Any field on any trace span can be queried. A finite cost is associated with ingesting and unpacking each record into constituent columns at write time, and the computational cost of reading remains reasonable.

Querying for Traces

Retrieving traces is a specific, degenerate kind of query against this columnar store. To look for root spans, you query for spans WHERE trace.parent_id is null. And looking for all spans with a given trace_id to assemble a trace waterfall is a query for SELECT timestamp, duration, name, trace.parent_id, trace.span_id WHERE trace.trace_id = "guid".

With the column storage design, it is possible to get insights on traces and to decompose traces into individual spans that can be queried across multiple traces. This design makes it feasible for Retriever to query for the duration of a span relative to other similar spans in other traces.

In other solutions that are more limited in cardinality, trace.trace_id might be special-cased and used as an index/lookup, with all spans associated with a given trace stored together. While this does give higher performance for visualizing individual traces, and creates a special case path to avoid the cardinality explosion of every trace_id being unique, it suffers in terms of inflexibility to decompose traces into their constituent spans for analysis.

Querying Data in Real Time

As established in functional requirements for observability, data must be accessible in real time. Stale data can cause operators to waste time on red herrings, or make false conclusions about the current state of their systems. Because a good observability system should include not just historical data but also blend in fresh-off-the-presses data, you cannot wait for segments to be finalized, flushed, and compressed before making them eligible for querying.

In the implementation of Retriever, we ensure that open column files are always queryable and that the query process can force a flush of partial files for reading, even if they have not yet been finalized and compressed. In a different implementation, another possible solution could be to allow querying data structures in RAM for segment files that have not yet been finalized and compressed. Another possible solution (with significantly higher overhead) could be to forcibly flush data every few seconds, regardless of the amount of data that has arrived. This last solution could be the most problematic at scale.

The first solution allows for separation of concerns between the ingestion and query processes. The query processor can operate entirely via files on disk. The ingestion process can focus only on creating the files on disk without having to also maintain shared state. We found this to be an elegant approach appropriate to the needs of our Retriever.

Making It Affordable with Tiering

Depending on the volume of data managed, using different tiers of data storage can result in pretty significant cost savings. Not all data is queried equally often. Typically, observability workflows are biased toward querying newer data, especially in the case of incident investigation. As you've seen, data must be available for querying within seconds of ingestion.

The most recent minutes of data may need to live on the local SSD of a query node while it is being serialized. But older data can and should be offloaded to a more economical and elastic data store. In the implementation of Retriever, closed segment directories older than a certain age are compacted (e.g., by rewriting with a bitmask of present/absent entries and/or being compressed) and uploaded to a longer-term durable network file store. Retriever uses Amazon S3, but you could use a different solution like Google Cloud Storage. Later, when that older data is needed again for querying, it can be fetched back from S3 into memory of the process doing computation, unpacked in memory if it was a collection of sparse files, and the column scan performed upon each matching column and segment.

Making It Fast with Parallelism

Speed is another functional requirement for observability workflows: query results must return within seconds to drive iterative investigation. And this should hold true regardless of whether queries are retrieving 30 minutes of data or an entire week of data. Users must often compare current state to historical baselines to have an accurate idea of whether behavior is anomalous.

When performing queries against data in a cloud file storage system in a map-reduce-style pattern with serverless computation, we have found that performance can be faster than executing that same query against serial data in local SSDs with a single query engine worker. What matters to end users is the speed at which query results return, not where the data is stored.

Fortunately, using the approaches seen in earlier sections, you can independently compute the result of a query for each segment. There's no need to process segments serially, as long as a reduction step takes the output of the query for each segment and merges the results together.

If you have already tiered data onto a durable network file store—S3 in our case—there is no contention upon a single query worker holding the bytes on disk. Your cloud provider has already taken on the burden of storing files in a distributed manner that is unlikely to have single points of congestion.

Therefore, a combination of a mapper-reducer-style approach (*https://oreil.ly/ivNPL*) and serverless technology enables us to get distributed, parallelized, and fast query results for Retriever without having to write our own job management system. Our cloud provider manages a pool of serverless workers, and we simply need to provide a list of inputs to map. Each Lambda (or serverless) function is a mapper that processes one or more segment directories independently, and feeds its results through a collection of intermediate merges to a central reduce worker to compute the final results.

But serverless functions and cloud object storage aren't 100% reliable. In practice, the latency at the tails of the distribution of invocation time can be significant orders of magnitude higher than the median time. That last 5% to 10% of results may take tens of seconds to return, or may *never* complete. In the Retriever implementation, we use impatience to return results in a timely manner. Once 90% of the requests to process segments have completed, the remaining 10% are re-requested, without canceling the still-pending requests. The parallel attempts race each other, with whichever returns first being used to populate the query result. Even if it is 10% more expensive to always retry the slowest 10% of subqueries, a different read attempt against the cloud provider's backend will likely perform faster than a "stuck" query blocked on S3, or network I/O that may never finish before it times out.

For Retriever, we've figured out this method to mitigate blocked distributed performance so that we always return query results within seconds. For your own implementation, you will need to experiment with alternative methods in order to meet the need of observability workloads.

Dealing with High Cardinality

What happens if someone attempts to group results by a high-cardinality field? How can you still return accurate values without running out of memory? The simplest solution is to fan out the reduce step by assigning reduce workers to handle only a proportional subset of the possible groups. For instance, you could follow the pattern Chord does (*https://doi.org/10.1145/964723.383071*) by creating a hash of the group and looking up the hash correspondence in a ring covering the keyspace.

But in the worst case of hundreds of thousands of distinct groups, you may need to limit the number of returned groups by the total amount of memory available across all your reducers, estimate which groups are most likely to survive the ORDER BY/LIMIT criterion supplied by the user, or simply abort a query that returns too many groups. After all, a graph that is 2,000 pixels tall will not be very useful with a hundred thousand unique lines smudged into a blur across it!

Scaling and Durability Strategies

For small volumes of data, querying a single small-throughput data stream across arbitrarily long time windows is more easily achievable. But larger data sets require scaling out horizontally, and they must be kept durable against data loss or temporary node unavailability. Fundamental limits exist on how fast any one worker, no matter how powerful, can process incoming trace spans and wide events. And your system must be able to tolerate individual workers being restarted (e.g., either for hardware failure or maintenance reasons).

In the Retriever implementation, we use streaming data patterns for scalability and durability. We've opted not to reinvent the wheel and leverage existing solutions where they make sense. Apache Kafka has a streaming approach that enables us to keep an ordered and durable data buffer that is resilient to producers restarting, consumers restarting, or intermediary brokers restarting.

See *Kafka: The Definitive Guide* by Gwen Shapira et al. (O'Reilly) for more information on Kafka.

For example, a row stored at index 1234567 in a given topic and partition will always precede the row stored at index 1234568 in Kafka. That means two consumers that must read data starting at index 1234567 will always receive the same records in the same order. And two producers will never conflict over the same index—each producer's committed rows will be written in a fixed order.

When receiving incoming telemetry, you should use a lightweight, stateless receiver process to validate the incoming rows and produce each row to one selected Kafka topic and partition. Stateful indexing workers then can consume the data in order from each Kafka partition. By separating the concerns of receipt and serialization, you'll be able to restart receiver workers or storage workers at will without dropping or corrupting data. The Kafka cluster needs to retain data only as long as the maximum duration that would be needed for replay in a disaster-recovery scenario—hours to days, but not weeks.

To ensure scalability, you should create as many Kafka partitions as necessary for your write workload. Each partition produces its own set of segments for each set of data. When querying, it is necessary to query all matching segments (based on time and data set) regardless of which partition produced them, since a given incoming trace span could have gone through any eligible partition. Maintaining a list of which partitions are eligible destinations for each tenant data set will enable you to query only the relevant workers; however, you will need to combine the results from workers performing the query on different partitions by performing a final result-merging step on a leader node for each query.

To ensure redundancy, more than one ingestion worker can consume from any given Kafka partition. Since Kafka ensures consistent ordering and the ingestion process is deterministic, parallel ingestion workers consuming a single partition must produce identical output in the form of serialized segment files and directories. Therefore, you can select one ingestion worker from each set of consumers to upload finalized segments to S3 (and spot-check that the output is identical on its peer).

If a given ingestion worker process needs to be restarted, it can checkpoint its current Kafka partition index and resume serializing segment files from that point once it is restarted. If an ingestion node needs to be entirely replaced, it can be started with a data snapshot and Kafka offset taken from an earlier healthy node and replay forward from that point.

In Retriever, we've separated the concerns of ingesting and serializing data from those of querying data. If you split the observability data workloads into separate processes that share only the filesystem, they no longer need to maintain shared data structures in RAM and can have greater fault tolerance. That means whenever you encounter a problem with the serialization process, it can only delay ingestion, rather than prevent querying of older data. This has the added benefit of also meaning that a spike in queries against the query engine will not hold up ingestion and serialization of data.

In this fashion, you can create a horizontally scalable version of the column storage system that allows for fast and durable querying across arbitrary cardinality and dimensionality. As of November 2021, Retriever operates as a multitenant cluster consisting of approximately 1,000 vCPU of receiver workers, 100 vCPU of Kafka brokers, and 1,000 vCPU of Retriever ingest + query engine workers, plus 30,000 peak concurrent Lambda executions. This cluster serves queries against approximately 700 TB of columnar data in 500 million compressed segment archives spanning two months of historical data. It ingests over 1.5 million trace spans per second with a maximum lag of milliseconds until they are queryable. It does this while delivering tens of read queries per second with a median latency of 50 ms and a p99 of 5 seconds.[5]

Notes on Building Your Own Efficient Data Store

Observability workloads require a unique set of performance characteristics to ingest telemetry data and make it queryable in useful ways throughout the course of investigating any particular issue. A challenge for any organization seeking to build its own observability solution will be to set up an appropriate data abstraction that enables the type of iterative investigative work for open-ended exploration, to identify any possible problem. You must address the functional requirements necessary for observability in order to use your telemetry data to solve hard problems.

If your problems are too hard to solve, you probably have the wrong data abstraction (*https://sandimetz.com/blog/2016/1/20/the-wrong-abstraction*). Building on the correct data abstraction allows for making the best trade-offs for solving a given data domain. For the problem of observability and tracing, a distributed hybrid columnar store segmented by time is one approach that meets all of the critical requirements of speed, cost, and reliability. While previous generation data stores struggle to meet the demands of arbitrary cardinality and dimensionality and of tracing, the Retriever data store at Honeycomb exemplifies one approach that can solve the problem.

We hope the lessons we have learned serve you well in understanding the underlying architecture of a modern observability backend, or in solving your own observability problems should you need an in-house solution. We also urge you to not suffer through the headaches of maintaining an Elasticsearch or Cassandra cluster that is not as suitable for this purpose as a dedicated column store.

---

5 This may not seem impressive, until you realize routine queries scan hundreds of millions of records!

Conclusion

Numerous challenges exist when it comes to effectively storing and performantly retrieving your observability data in ways that support real-time debugging workflows. The functional requirements for observability necessitate queries that return results as quickly as possible, which is no small feat when you have billions of rows of ultrawide events, each containing thousands of dimensions, all of which must be searchable, many of which may be high-cardinality data, and when none of those fields are indexed or have privileged data retrieval over others. You must be able to get results within seconds, and traditional storage systems are simply not up to performing this task. In addition to being performant, your data store must also be fault-tolerant and production worthy.

We hope that the case study of Honeycomb's Retriever implementation helps you better understand the various trade-offs that must be made at the data layer and possible solutions for managing them. Retriever is not the only way to implement solutions to these challenges, but it does present a thorough example of how they can be addressed. Other publicly available data stores we're aware of that could properly handle an observability workload include Google Cloud BigQuery, ClickHouse, and Druid. However, these data stores are less operationally tested for observability-specific workloads and may require custom work to support the automated sharding required. At scale, the challenges inherent to managing observability become especially pronounced. For smaller, single-node storage solutions, you may be less likely to struggle with some of the trade-offs outlined.

Now that we've looked at how very large volumes of telemetry data are stored and retrieved, the next chapter examines how the network transmission of very large volumes of telemetry data can be managed via telemetry pipelines.

CHAPTER 17

Cheap and Accurate Enough: Sampling

In the preceding chapter, we covered how a data store must be configured in order to efficiently store and retrieve large quantities of observability data. In this chapter, we'll look at techniques for reducing the amount of observability data you may need to store. At a large enough scale, the resources necessary to retain and process every single event can become prohibitive and impractical. Sampling events can mitigate the trade-offs between resource consumption and data fidelity.

This chapter examines why sampling is useful (even at a smaller scale), the various strategies typically used to sample data, and trade-offs between those strategies. We use code-based examples to illustrate how these strategies are implemented and progressively introduce concepts that build upon previous examples. The chapter starts with simpler sampling schemes applied to single events as a conceptual introduction to using a statistical representation of data when sampling. We then build toward more complex sampling strategies as they are applied to a series of related events (trace spans) and propagate the information needed to reconstruct your data after sampling.

Sampling to Refine Your Data Collection

Past a certain scale, the cost to collect, process, and save every log entry, every event, and every trace that your systems generate dramatically outweighs the benefits. At a large enough scale, it is simply not feasible to run an observability infrastructure that is the same size as your production infrastructure. When observability events quickly become a flood of data, the challenge pivots to a trade-off between scaling back the amount of data that's kept and potentially losing the crucial information your engineering team needs to troubleshoot and understand your system's production behaviors.

The reality of most applications is that many of their events are virtually identical and successful. The core function of debugging is searching for emergent patterns or examining failed events during an outage. Through that lens, it is then wasteful to transmit 100% of all events to your observability data backend. Certain events can be selected as representative examples of what occurred, and those sample events can be transmitted along with metadata your observability backend needs to reconstruct what actually occurred among the events that weren't sampled.

To debug effectively, what's needed is a representative sample of successful, or "good," events, against which to compare the "bad" events. Using representative events to reconstruct your observability data enables you to reduce the overhead of transmitting every single event, while also faithfully recovering the original shape of that data. Sampling events can help you accomplish your observability goals at a fraction of the resource cost. It is a way to refine the observability process at scale.

Historically in the software industry, when facing resource constraints in reporting high-volume system state, the standard approach to surfacing the signal from the noise has been to generate aggregated metrics containing a limited number of tags. As covered in Chapter 2, aggregated views of system state that cannot be decomposed are far too coarse to troubleshoot the needs of modern distributed systems. Pre-aggregating data before it arrives in your debugging tool means that you can't dig further past the granularity of the aggregated values.

With observability, you can sample events by using the strategies outlined in this chapter and still provide granular visibility into system state. Sampling gives you the ability to decide which events are useful to transmit and which ones are not. Unlike pre-aggregated metrics that collapse all events into one coarse representation of system state over a given period of time, sampling allows you to make informed decisions about which events can help you surface unusual behavior, while still optimizing for resource constraints. The difference between sampled events and aggregated metrics is that full cardinality is preserved on each dimension included in the representative event.

At scale, the need to refine your data set to optimize for resource costs becomes critical. But even at a smaller scale, where the need to shave resources is less pressing, refining the data you decide to keep can still provide valuable cost savings. First, let's start by looking at the strategies that can be used to decide which data is worth sampling. Then, we'll look at when and how that decision can be made when handling trace events.

Using Different Approaches to Sampling

Sampling is a common approach when solving for resource constraints. Unfortunately, the term *sampling* is used broadly as a one-size-fits-all label for the many types of approaches that might be implemented. Many concepts and implementations of sampling exist, some less effective for observability than others. We need to disambiguate the term by naming each sampling technique that is appropriate for observability and distinguishing how they are different, and similar, to one another.

Constant-Probability Sampling

Because of its understandable and easy-to-implement approach, *constant-probability sampling* is what most people think of when they think of sampling: a constant percentage of data is kept rather than discarded (e.g., keep 1 out of every 10 requests).

When performing analysis of sampled data, you will need to transform the data to reconstruct the original distribution of requests. Suppose that your service is instrumented with both events and metrics, and receives 100,000 requests. It is misleading for your telemetry systems to report receiving only 100 events if each received event represents approximately 1,000 similar events. Other telemetry systems such as metrics will record increment a counter for each of the 100,000 requests that your service has received. Only a fraction of those requests will have been sampled, so your system will need to adjust the aggregation of events to return data that is approximately correct. For a fixed sampling rate system, you can multiply each event by the sampling rate in effect to get the estimated count of total requests and sum of their latency. Scalar distribution properties such as the p99 and median do not need to be adjusted for a constant probability sampling, as they are not distorted by the sampling process.

The basic idea of constant sampling is that, if you have enough volume, any error that comes up will happen again. If that error is happening enough to matter, you'll see it. However, if you have a moderate volume of data, constant sampling does not maintain the statistical likelihood that you still see what you need to see. Constant sampling is not effective in the following circumstances:

- You care a lot about error cases and not very much about success cases.
- Some customers send orders of magnitude more traffic than others, and you want all customers to have a good experience.
- You want to ensure that a huge increase in traffic on your servers can't overwhelm your analytics backend.

For an observable system, a more sophisticated approach ensures that enough telemetry data is captured and retained so that you can see into the true state of any given service at any given time.

Sampling on Recent Traffic Volume

Instead of using a fixed probability, you can dynamically adjust the rate at which your system samples events. Sampling probability can be adjusted upward if less total traffic was received recently, or decreased if a traffic surge is likely to overwhelm the backend of your observability tool. However, this approach adds a new layer of complexity: without a constant sampling rate, you can no longer multiply out each event by a constant factor when reconstructing the distribution of your data.

Instead, your telemetry system will need to use a weighted algorithm that accounts for the sampling probability in effect at the time the event was collected. If one event represents 1,000 similar events, it should not be directly averaged with another event that represents 100 similar events. Thus, for calculating a count, your system must add together the number of *represented* events, not just the number of collected events. For aggregating distribution properties such as the median or p99, your system must expand each event into many when calculating the total number of events and where the percentile values lie.

For example, suppose you have pairs of values and sample rates: [{1,5}, {3,2}, {7,9}]. If you took the median of the values without taking the sample rate into account, you would naively get the value of 3 as a result—because it's at the center of [1,3,7]. However, you must take the sample rate into account. Using the sample rate to reconstruct the entire set of values can be illustrated by writing out the entire set of values in long form: [1,1,1,1,1,3,3,7,7,7,7,7,7,7,7,7]. In that view, it becomes clear that the median of the values is 7 after accounting for sampling.

Sampling Based on Event Content (Keys)

This dynamic sampling approach involves tuning the sample rate based on event payload. At a high level, that means choosing one or more fields in the set of events and designating a sample rate when a certain combination of values is seen. For example, you could partition events based on HTTP response codes and then assign sample rates to each response code. Doing that allows you to specify sampling conditions such as these:

- Events with *errors* are more important than those with *successes*.
- Events for *newly placed orders* are more important than those checking on *order status.*
- Events affecting *paying customers* are more important to keep than those for customers using the *free tier.*

With this approach, you can make the keys as simple (e.g., HTTP method) or complicated (e.g., concatenating the HTTP method, request size, and user-agent) as needed to select samples that can provide the most useful view into service traffic.

Sampling at a constant percentage rate based on event content alone works well when the key space is small (e.g., there are a finite number of HTTP methods: GET, POST, HEAD, etc.) *and* when the relative rates of given keys stay consistent (e.g., when you can assume errors are less frequent than successes). It's worth noting that sometimes that assumption can be wrong, or it can be reversed in bad cases. For those situations, you should validate your assumptions and have a plan for dealing with event traffic spikes if the assumed conditions reverse.

Combining per Key and Historical Methods

When the content of traffic is harder to predict, you can instead continue to identify a key (or combination of keys) for each incoming event, and then *also* dynamically adjust the sample rate for each key based on the volume of traffic recently seen for that key. For example, base the sample rate on the number of times a given key combination (such as [customer ID, dataset ID, error code]) is seen in the last 30 seconds. If a specific combination is seen many times in that time, it's less interesting than combinations that are seen less often. A configuration like that allows proportionally fewer of the events to be propagated verbatim until that rate of traffic changes and it adjusts the sample rate again.

Choosing Dynamic Sampling Options

To decide which sampling strategy to use, it helps to look at the traffic flowing through a service, as well as the variety of queries hitting that service. Are you dealing with a front-page app, and 90% of the requests hitting it are nearly indistinguishable from one another? The needs of that situation will differ substantially from dealing with a proxy fronting a database, where many query patterns are repeated.

A backend behind a read-through cache, where each request is mostly unique (with the cache already having stripped all the boring ones away) will have different needs from those two. Each of these situations benefits from a slightly different sampling strategy that optimizes for their needs.

When to Make a Sampling Decision for Traces

So far, each of the preceding strategies has considered *what* criteria to use when selecting samples. For events involving an individual service, that decision solely depends on the preceding criteria. For trace events, *when* a sampling decision gets made is also important.

Trace spans are collected across multiple services—with each service potentially employing its own unique sample strategy and rate. The probability that every span necessary to complete a trace will be the event that each service chooses to sample is relatively low. To ensure that every span in a trace is captured, special care must be taken depending on when the decision about whether to sample is made.

As covered earlier, one strategy is to use a property of the event itself—the return status, latency, endpoint, or a high-cardinality field like customer ID—to decide if it is worth sampling. Some properties within the event, such as endpoint or customer ID, are static and known at the start of the event. In *head-based sampling* (or *up-front sampling*), a sampling decision is made when the trace event is initiated. That decision is then propagated further downstream (e.g., by inserting a "require sampling" header bit) to ensure that every span necessary to complete the trace is sampled.

Some fields, like return status or latency, are known only in retrospect after event execution has completed. If a sampling decision relies on dynamic fields, by the time those are determined, each underlying service will have already independently chosen whether to sample other span events. At best, you may end up keeping the downstream spans deemed interesting outliers, but none of the other context. Properly making a decision on values known only at the end of a request requires *tail-based sampling*.

To collect full traces in the tail-based approach, all spans must first be collected in a buffer and then, retrospectively, a sampling decision can be made. That buffered sampling technique is computationally expensive and not feasible in practice entirely from within the instrumented code. Buffered sampling techniques typically require external collector-side logic.

Additional nuances exist for determining the *what* and *when* of sampling decisions. But at this point, those are best explained using code-based examples.

Translating Sampling Strategies into Code

So far, we've covered sampling strategies on a conceptual level. Let's look at how these strategies are implemented in code. This pedagogical example uses Go to illustrate implementation details, but the examples would be straightforward to port into any language that supports hashes/dicts/maps, pseudorandom number generation, and concurrency/timers.

The Base Case

Let's suppose you would like to instrument a high-volume handler that calls a downstream service, performs some internal work, and then returns a result and unconditionally records an event to your instrumentation sink:

```
func handler(resp http.ResponseWriter, req *http.Request) {
    start := time.Now()
    i, err := callAnotherService()
    resp.Write(i)
    RecordEvent(req, start, err)
}
```

At scale, this instrumentation approach is unnecessarily noisy and would result in sky-high resource consumption. Let's look at alternate ways of sampling the events this handler would send.

Fixed-Rate Sampling

A naive approach might be probabilistic sampling using a fixed rate, by randomly choosing to send 1 in 1,000 events:

```
var sampleRate = flag.Int("sampleRate", 1000, "Static sample rate")

func handler(resp http.ResponseWriter, req *http.Request) {
    start := time.Now()
    i, err := callAnotherService()
    resp.Write(i)

    r := rand.Float64()
    if r < 1.0 / *sampleRate {
        RecordEvent(req, start, err)
    }
}
```

Every 1,000th event would be kept, regardless of its relevance, as representative of the other 999 events discarded. To reconstruct your data on the backend, you would need to remember that each event stood for `sampleRate` events and multiply out all counter values accordingly on the receiving end at the instrumentation collector. Otherwise, your tooling would misreport the total number of events actually encountered during that time period.

Recording the Sample Rate

In the preceding clunky example, you would need to manually remember and set the sample rate at the receiving end. What if you need to change the sample rate value at some point in the future? The instrumentation collector wouldn't know exactly when the value changed. A better practice is to explicitly pass the current `sampleRate` when sending a sampled event (see Figure 17-1)—indicating that the event statistically represents `sampleRate` similar events. Note that sample rates can vary not only between services but also within a single service.

Status code	Time	Sample rate
ok	1:00	100
ok	1:00	100
err	1:00	1
ok	1:01	80
err	1:01	1
ok	1:01	80
ok	1:01	80

Figure 17-1. Different events may be sampled at different rates

Recording the sample rate within an event can look like this:

```
var sampleRate = flag.Int("sampleRate", 1000, "Service's sample rate")

func handler(resp http.ResponseWriter, req *http.Request) {
    start := time.Now()
    i, err := callAnotherService()
    resp.Write(i)

    r := rand.Float64()
    if r < 1.0 / *sampleRate {
        RecordEvent(req, *sampleRate, start, err)
    }
}
```

With this approach, you can keep track of the sampling rate in effect when each sampled event was recorded. That gives you the data necessary to accurately calculate values when reconstructing your data, even if the sampling rate dynamically changes. For example, if you were trying to calculate the total number of events meeting a filter such as "err != nil", you would multiply the count of seen events with "err != nil" by each one's sampleRate (see Figure 17-2). And, if you were trying to calculate the sum of durationMs, you would need to weight each sampled event's durationMs and multiply it by sampleRate before adding up the weighted figures.

Status code	Time	Count (reweighted)
ok	1:00	200
err	1:00	1
ok	1:01	240
err	1:01	1

Figure 17-2. Total events can be calculated using weighted numbers

This example is simplistic and contrived. Already, you may be seeing flaws in this approach when it comes to handling trace events. In the next section, we will look at additional considerations for making dynamic sampling rates and tracing work well together.

Consistent Sampling

So far in our code, we've looked at *how* a sampling decision is made. But we have yet to consider *when* a sampling decision gets made in the case of sampling trace events. The strategy of using head-based, tail-based, or buffered sampling matters when considering how sampling interacts with tracing. We'll cover how those decisions get implemented toward the end of the chapter. For now, let's examine how to propagate context to downstream handlers in order to (later) make that decision.

To properly manage trace events, you should use a centrally generated *sampling/tracing ID* propagated to all downstream handlers instead of independently generating a sampling decision inside each one. Doing so lets you make consistent sampling decisions for different manifestations of the same end user's request (see Figure 17-3). In other words, this ensures that you capture a full end-to-end trace for any given sampled request. It would be unfortunate to discover that you have sampled an error far downstream for which the upstream context is missing because it was dropped because of how your sampling strategy was implemented.

HASH (traceid)	Sampled?
8464143	
9976727	
2046000	YES
8697994	
1983000	YES
3427217	
6152331	
4919000	YES
6122453	

Figure 17-3. Sampled events containing a `TraceId`

Consistent sampling ensures that when the sample rate is held constant, traces are either kept or sampled away in their entirety. And if children are sampled at a higher sample rate—for instance, noisy Redis calls being sampled 1 for 1,000, while their parents are kept 1 for 10—it will never be the case that a broken trace is created from a Redis child being kept while its parent is discarded.

Let's modify the previous code sample to read a value for sampling probability from the `TraceID/Sampling-ID`, instead of generating a random value at each step:

```go
var sampleRate = flag.Int("sampleRate", 1000, "Service's sample rate")

func handler(resp http.ResponseWriter, req *http.Request) {
    // Use an upstream-generated random sampling ID if it exists.
    // otherwise we're a root span. generate & pass down a random ID.
    var r float64
    if r, err := floatFromHexBytes(req.Header.Get("Sampling-ID")); err != nil {
        r = rand.Float64()
    }

    start := time.Now()
    // Propagate the Sampling-ID when creating a child span
    i, err := callAnotherService(r)
    resp.Write(i)

    if r < 1.0 / *sampleRate {
        RecordEvent(req, *sampleRate, start, err)
    }
}
```

Now, by changing the `sampleRate` feature flag to cause a different proportion of traces to be sampled, you have support for adjusting the sample rate without recompiling, including at runtime. However, if you adopt the technique we'll discuss next, target rate sampling, you won't need to manually adjust the rate.

Target Rate Sampling

You don't need to manually flag-adjust the sampling rates for each of your services as traffic swells and sags. Instead, you can automate this process by tracking the incoming request rate that you're receiving (see Figure 17-4).

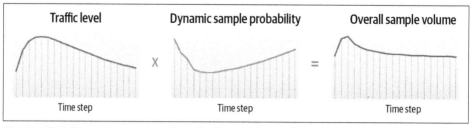

Figure 17-4. You can automate the calculation of overall sample volume

Let's see how that is done in our code example:

```go
var targetEventsPerSec = flag.Int("targetEventsPerSec", 5,
    "The target number of requests per second to sample from this service.")

// Note: sampleRate can be a float! doesn't have to be an integer.
var sampleRate float64 = 1.0
// Track requests from previous minute to decide sampling rate for the next
// minute.
var requestsInPastMinute *int

func main() {
    // Initialize counters.
    rc := 0
    requestsInPastMinute = &rc

    go func() {
        for {
            time.Sleep(time.Minute)
            newSampleRate = *requestsInPastMinute / (60 * *targetEventsPerSec)
            if newSampleRate < 1 {
                sampleRate = 1.0
            } else {
                sampleRate = newSampleRate
            }
            newRequestCounter := 0
            // Real production code would do something less prone to race
            // conditions
            requestsInPastMinute = &newRequestCounter
        }
    }()
    http.Handle("/", handler)
    [...]
}

func handler(resp http.ResponseWriter, req *http.Request) {
    var r float64
    if r, err := floatFromHexBytes(req.Header.Get("Sampling-ID")); err != nil {
        r = rand.Float64()
    }

    start := time.Now()
    *requestsInPastMinute++
    i, err := callAnotherService(r)
    resp.Write(i)

    if r < 1.0 / sampleRate {
        RecordEvent(req, sampleRate, start, err)
    }
}
```

This example provides predictable experience in terms of resource cost. However, the technique still lacks flexibility for sampling at variable rates depending on the volume of each key.

Having More Than One Static Sample Rate

If the sampling rate is high, whether due to being dynamically or statically set high, you need to consider that you could miss long-tail events—for instance, errors or high-latency events—because the chance that a 99.9th percentile outlier event will be chosen for random sampling is slim. Likewise, you may want to have at least some data for each of your distinct sources, rather than have the high-volume sources drown out the low-volume ones.

A remedy for that scenario is to set more than one sample rate. Let's start by varying the sample rates by key. Here, the example code samples any baseline (non-outlier) events at a rate of 1 in 1,000 and chooses to tail-sample any errors or slow queries at a rate of 1 in 1 and 1 in 5, respectively:

```go
var sampleRate = flag.Int("sampleRate", 1000, "Service's sample rate")
var outlierSampleRate = flag.Int("outlierSampleRate", 5, "Outlier sample rate")

func handler(resp http.ResponseWriter, req *http.Request) {
    start := time.Now()
    i, err := callAnotherService(r)
    resp.Write(i)

    r := rand.Float64()
    if err != nil || time.Since(start) > 500*time.Millisecond {
        if r < 1.0 / *outlierSampleRate {
            RecordEvent(req, *outlierSampleRate, start, err)
        }
    } else {
        if r < 1.0 / *sampleRate {
            RecordEvent(req, *sampleRate, start, err)
        }
    }
}
```

Although this is a good example of using multiple static sample rates, the approach is still susceptible to spikes of instrumentation traffic. If the application experiences a spike in the rate of errors, every single error gets sampled. Next, we will address that shortcoming with target rate sampling.

Sampling by Key and Target Rate

Putting two previous techniques together, let's extend what we've already done to target specific rates of instrumentation. If a request is anomalous (for example, has latency above 500ms or is an error), it can be designated for tail sampling at its own guaranteed rate, while rate-limiting the other requests to fit within a budget of sampled requests per second:

```
var targetEventsPerSec = flag.Int("targetEventsPerSec", 4,
    "The target number of ordinary requests/sec to sample from this service.")
var outlierEventsPerSec = flag.Int("outlierEventsPerSec", 1,
    "The target number of outlier requests/sec to sample from this service.")

var sampleRate float64 = 1.0
var requestsInPastMinute *int

var outlierSampleRate float64 = 1.0
var outliersInPastMinute *int

func main() {
    // Initialize counters.
    rc := 0
    requestsInPastMinute = &rc
    oc := 0
    outliersInPastMinute = &oc

    go func() {
        for {
            time.Sleep(time.Minute)
            newSampleRate = *requestsInPastMinute / (60 * *targetEventsPerSec)
            if newSampleRate < 1 {
                sampleRate = 1.0
            } else {
                sampleRate = newSampleRate
            }
            newRequestCounter := 0
            requestsInPastMinute = &newRequestCounter

            newOutlierRate = outliersInPastMinute / (60 * *outlierEventsPerSec)
            if newOutlierRate < 1 {
                outlierSampleRate = 1.0
            } else {
                outlierSampleRate = newOutlierRate
            }
            newOutlierCounter := 0
            outliersInPastMinute = &newOutlierCounter
        }
    }()
    http.Handle("/", handler)
    [...]
}

func handler(resp http.ResponseWriter, req *http.Request) {
    var r float64
    if r, err := floatFromHexBytes(req.Header.Get("Sampling-ID")); err != nil {
        r = rand.Float64()
    }
```

```
start := time.Now()
i, err := callAnotherService(r)
resp.Write(i)
if err != nil || time.Since(start) > 500*time.Millisecond {
    *outliersInPastMinute++
    if r < 1.0 / outlierSampleRate {
        RecordEvent(req, outlierSampleRate, start, err)
    }
} else {
    *requestsInPastMinute++
    if r < 1.0 / sampleRate {
        RecordEvent(req, sampleRate, start, err)
    }
}
}
```

That extremely verbose example uses chunks of duplicate code, but is presented in that manner for clarity. If this example were to support a third category of request, it would make more sense to refactor the code to allow setting sampling rates across an arbitrary number of keys.

Sampling with Dynamic Rates on Arbitrarily Many Keys

In practice, you likely will not be able to predict a finite set of request quotas that you may want to set. In the preceding example, our code had many duplicate blocks, and we were designating target rates manually for each case (error/latency versus normal).

A more realistic approach is to refactor the code to use a map for each key's target rate and the number of seen events. The code would then look up each key to make sampling decisions. Doing so modifies our example code like so:

```
var counts map[SampleKey]int
var sampleRates map[SampleKey]float64
var targetRates map[SampleKey]int

func neverSample(k SampleKey) bool {
    // Left to your imagination. Could be a situation where we know request is a
    // keepalive we never want to record, etc.
    return false
}

// Boilerplate main() and goroutine init to overwrite maps and roll them over
// every interval goes here.

type SampleKey struct {
    ErrMsg         string
    BackendShard   int
    LatencyBucket  int
}

// This might compute for each k: newRate[k] = counts[k] / (interval *
```

```
// targetRates[k]), for instance.

func checkSampleRate(resp http.ResponseWriter, start time.Time, err error,
        sampleRates map[any]float64, counts map[any]int) float64 {
    msg := ""
    if err != nil {
        msg = err.Error()
    }
    roundedLatency := 100 *(time.Since(start) / (100*time.Millisecond))
    k := SampleKey {
        ErrMsg:        msg,
        BackendShard: resp.Header().Get("Backend-Shard"),
        LatencyBucket: roundedLatency,
    }
    if neverSample(k) {
        return -1.0
    }

    counts[k]++
    if r, ok := sampleRates[k]; ok {
        return r
    } else {
        return 1.0
    }
}

func handler(resp http.ResponseWriter, req *http.Request) {
    var r float64
    if r, err := floatFromHexBytes(req.Header.Get("Sampling-ID")); err != nil {
        r = rand.Float64()
    }

    start := time.Now()
    i, err := callAnotherService(r)
    resp.Write(i)

    sampleRate := checkSampleRate(resp, start, err, sampleRates, counts)
    if sampleRate > 0 && r < 1.0 / sampleRate {
        RecordEvent(req, sampleRate, start, err)
    }
}
```

At this point, our code example is becoming quite large, and it still lacks more-sophisticated techniques. Our example has been used to illustrate how sampling concepts are implemented.

Luckily, existing code libraries can handle this type of complex sampling logic. For Go, the *dynsampler-go* library (*https://github.com/honeycombio/dynsampler-go*) maintains a map over any number of sampling keys, allocating a fair share of sampling to each key as long as it is novel. That library also contains more-advanced techniques of computing sample rates, either based on target rates or without explicit target rates at all.

For this chapter, we're close to having put together a complete introductory tour of applying sampling concepts. Before concluding, let's make one last improvement by combining the tail-based sampling you've done so far with head-based sampling that can request tracing be sampled by all downstream services.

Putting It All Together: Head and Tail per Key Target Rate Sampling

Earlier in this chapter, we noted that head-based sampling requires setting a header to propagating a sampling decision downstream. For the code example we've been iterating, that means the parent span must pass both the head-sampling decision and its corresponding rate to all child spans. Doing so forces sampling to occur for all child spans, even if the dynamic sampling rate at that level would not have chosen to sample the request:

```go
var headCounts, tailCounts map[interface{}]int
var headSampleRates, tailSampleRates map[interface{}]float64

// Boilerplate main() and goroutine init to overwrite maps and roll them over
// every interval goes here. checkSampleRate() etc. from above as well

func handler(resp http.ResponseWriter, req *http.Request) {
    var r, upstreamSampleRate, headSampleRate float64
    if r, err := floatFromHexBytes(req.Header.Get("Sampling-ID")); err != nil {
        r = rand.Float64()
    }

    // Check if we have a non-negative upstream sample rate; if so, use it.
    if upstreamSampleRate, err := floatFromHexBytes(
        req.Header.Get("Upstream-Sample-Rate")
    ); err == nil && upstreamSampleRate > 1.0 {
        headSampleRate = upstreamSampleRate
    } else {
        headSampleRate := checkHeadSampleRate(req, headSampleRates, headCounts)
        if headSampleRate > 0 && r < 1.0 / headSampleRate {
            // We'll sample this when recording event below; propagate the
            // decision downstream though.
        } else {
            // Clear out headSampleRate as this event didn't qualify for
            // sampling. This is a sentinel value.
            headSampleRate = -1.0
        }
    }

    start := time.Now()
    i, err := callAnotherService(r, headSampleRate)
    resp.Write(i)
```

```
    if headSampleRate > 0 {
        RecordEvent(req, headSampleRate, start, err)
    } else {
        // Same as for head sampling, except here we make a tail sampling
        // decision we can't propagate downstream.
        tailSampleRate := checkTailSampleRate(
            resp, start, err, tailSampleRates, tailCounts,
        )
        if tailSampleRate > 0 && r < 1.0 / tailSampleRate {
            RecordEvent(req, tailSampleRate, start, err)
        }
    }
}
```

At this point, our code example is rather complicated. However, even at this level, it illustrates a powerful example of the flexibility that sampling can provide to capture all the necessary context needed to debug your code. In high-throughput modern distributed systems, it may be necessary to get even more granular and employ more sophisticated sampling techniques.

For example, you may want to change the sampleRate of head-based samples for increased probability whenever a downstream tail-based heuristic captures an error in the response. In that example, collector-side buffered sampling is a mechanism that would allow deferring a sampling decision until after an entire trace has been buffered—bringing together the advantages of head-based sampling to properties only known at the tail.

Conclusion

Sampling is a useful technique for refining your observability data. While sampling is necessary when running at scale, it can be useful in a variety of circumstances even at smaller scales. The code-based examples illustrate how various sampling strategies are implemented. It's becoming increasingly common for open source instrumentation libraries—such as OTel—to implement that type of sampling logic for you. As those libraries become the standard for generating application telemetry data, it should become less likely that you would need to reimplement these sampling strategies in your own code.

However, even if you rely on third-party libraries to manage that strategy for you, it is essential that you understand the mechanics behind how sampling is implemented so you can understand which method is right for your particular situation. Understanding how the strategies (static versus dynamic, head versus tail, or a combination thereof) work in practice enables you to use them wisely to achieve data fidelity while also optimizing for resource constraints.

Similar to deciding what and how to instrument your code, deciding *what, when,* and *how* to sample is best defined by your unique organizational needs. The fields in your events that influence how interesting they are to sample largely depend on how useful they are to understanding the state of your environment and their impact on achieving your business goals.

In the next chapter, we'll examine an approach to routing large volumes of telemetry data: telemetry management with pipelines.

CHAPTER 18

Telemetry Management with Pipelines

This chapter is contributed by Suman Karumuri, senior staff software engineer at Slack, and Ryan Katkov, director of engineering at Slack

A Note from Charity, Liz, and George

In this part of the book, we've unpacked observability concepts that are most acutely felt at scale but that can be helpful at any scale for a variety of reasons. In the previous chapter, we looked at what happens when the typical trickle of observability data instead becomes a flood and how to reduce that volume with sampling. In this chapter, we'll look at a different way to manage large volumes of telemetry data: with pipelines.

Beyond data volume, *telemetry pipelines* can help manage application complexity. In simpler systems, the telemetry data from an application can be directly sent to the appropriate data backend. In more-complex systems, you may need to route telemetry data to many backend systems in order to isolate workloads, meet security and compliance needs, satisfy different retention requirements, or for a variety of other reasons. When you add data volume on top of that, managing the many-to-many relationship between telemetry producers and consumers of that data can be extraordinarily complex. Telemetry pipelines help you abstract away that complexity.

This chapter, written by Suman Karumuri and Ryan Katkov, details Slack's use of telemetry pipelines to manage its observability data. Similar to the other guest-contributed chapter in this book, Chapter 14, Slack's application infrastructure is a wonderful example of elegantly tackling issues of complexity and scale in ways that surface helpful concepts to engineers using observability at any scale. We're delighted to be able to share these lessons with you in the context of this book.

The rest of this chapter is told from the perspective of Suman and Ryan.

In this chapter, we will go over how telemetry pipelines can benefit your organization's observability capabilities, describe the basic structure and components of a telemetry pipeline, and show concrete examples of how Slack uses a telemetry pipeline, using mainly open source software components. Slack has been using this pattern in production for the past three years, scaling up to millions of events per second.

Establishing a telemetry management practice is key for organizations that want to focus on observability adoption and decrease the amount of work a developer needs to do to make their service sufficiently observable. A strong telemetry management practice lays the foundation for a consolidated instrumentation framework and creates a consistent developer experience, reducing complexity and churn, especially when it comes to introducing new telemetry from new software.

At Slack, we generally look for these characteristics when we envision an ideal telemetry system: we want the pipeline to be able to collect, route, and enrich data streams coming from applications and services. We are also opinionated about the components that operate as part of a stream, and we make available a consistent set of endpoints or libraries. Finally, we use a prescribed common event format that applications can leverage quickly to realize value.

As an organization grows, observability systems tend to evolve from a simple system in which applications and services produce events directly to the appropriate backend, to more-complex use cases. If you find yourself needing greater security, workload isolation, retention requirement enforcement, or a greater degree of control over the quality of your data, then telemetry management via pipelines can help you address those needs. At a high level, a pipeline consists of components between the application and the backend in order to process and route your observability data.

By the end of this chapter, you'll understand how and when to design a telemetry pipeline as well as the fundamental building blocks necessary to manage your growing observability data needs.

Attributes of Telemetry Pipelines

Building telemetry pipelines can help you in several ways. In this section, you will learn about the attributes commonly found in telemetry pipelines and how they can help you.

Routing

At its simplest, the primary purpose of a telemetry pipeline is to *route* data from where it is generated to different backends, while centrally controlling the configuration of what telemetry goes where. Statically configuring these routes at the source to directly send the data to the data store is often not desirable because often you want to route the data to different backends without needing application changes, which are often burdensome in larger-scale systems.

For example, in a telemetry pipeline, you might like to route a trace data stream to a tracing backend, and a log data stream to a logging backend. In addition, you may also want to tee a portion of the same trace data stream to an Elasticsearch cluster so you can do real-time analytics on it. Having flexibility through routing and translation helps increase the value of the data stream because different tools may provide different insights on a data set.

Security and Compliance

You may also want to route the telemetry data to different backends for *security* reasons. You may want only certain teams to access the telemetry data. Some applications may log data containing sensitive personally identifiable information (PII), and allowing broad access to this data may lead to compliance violations.

Your telemetry pipeline may need features to help enforce legal compliance for entities such as the General Data Protection Regulation (GDPR) and the Federal Risk and Authorization Management Program (FedRAMP). Such features may limit where the telemetry data is stored and who has access to the telemetry data, as well as enforce retention or deletion life cycles.

Slack is no stranger to compliance requirements, and we enforce those requirements through a combination of pattern matching and redaction, and a service that detects and alerts on the existence of sensitive information or PII. In addition to those components, we provide tooling to allow self-service deletion of data that is out of compliance.

Workload Isolation

Workload isolation allows you to protect the reliability and availability of data sets in critical scenarios. Partitioning your telemetry data across multiple clusters allows you to isolate workloads from one another. For example, you may wish to separate an application that produces a high volume of logs from an application that produces a very low volume of log data. By putting the logs of these applications in the same cluster, an expensive query against the high-volume log can frequently slow cluster performance, negatively affecting the experience for other users on the same cluster. For lower-volume logs such as host logs, having a higher retention period for this data may be desirable, as it may provide historical context. By isolating workloads, you gain flexibility and reliability.

Data Buffering

Observability backends will not be perfectly reliable and can experience outages. Such outages are not typically measured in the SLOs of a service that relies on that observability backend. It is entirely possible for a service to be available but your observability backend to be unavailable for unrelated reasons, impairing visibility into the service itself. In those cases, to prevent a gap in your telemetry data, you may want to temporarily *buffer* the data onto a local disk on a node, or leverage a message queue system such as Kafka or RabbitMQ, which will allow messages to be buffered and replayed.

Telemetry data can have large spikes in volume. Natural patterns like users using the service more or an outage on a critical database component failure often lead to errors in all infrastructure components, leading to a higher volume of emitted events and a cascading failure. Adding a buffer would smooth the data ingestion to the backend. This also improves the reliability of data ingestion into the backend since it is not being saturated by those spikes in volume.

A buffer also acts as an intermediate step to hold data, especially when further processing is desired before sending the data to the backend. Multiple buffers can be used—for example, combining a local disk buffer on the application with a dead-letter queue to protect timeliness of data during volume spikes.

We use Kafka extensively at Slack to achieve this goal of buffering data, and our clusters retain up to three days of events to ensure data consistency after a backend recovers from an outage. In addition to Kafka, we use a limited on-disk buffer in our producer component, allowing our ingestion agents to buffer events if a Kafka cluster becomes unavailable or saturated. End to end, the pipeline is designed to be resilient during service disruptions, minimizing data loss.

Capacity Management

Often for capacity planning or cost-control reasons, you may want to assign quotas for categories of telemetry and enforce with rate limiting, sampling, or queuing.

Rate limiting

Since the telemetry data is often produced in relationship to natural user requests, the telemetry data from applications tend to follow unpredictable patterns. A telemetry pipeline can smooth these data spikes for the backend by sending the telemetry to the backend at only a constant rate. If there is more data than this rate, the pipeline can often hold data in memory until the backend can consume it.

If your systems consistently produce data at a higher rate than the backend can consume, your telemetry pipeline can use *rate limits* to mitigate impacts. For instance, you could employ a hard rate limit and drop data that is over the rate limit, or ingest the data under a soft rate limit but aggressively sample the data until a hard rate limit is hit, allowing you to protect availability. It can be considered acceptable to make this trade-off in cases where the event data is redundant, so while you drop events, you will not experience a loss of signal.

Sampling

As discussed in Chapter 17, your ingestion component can utilize moving average *sampling*, progressively increasing sample rates as volume increases to preserve signal and avoid saturating backends downstream in the pipeline.

Queuing

You can prioritize ingesting recent data over older data to maximize utility to developers. This feature is especially useful during log storms in logging systems. *Log storms* happen when the system gets more logs than its designed capacity.

For instance, a large-scale incident like a critical service being down would cause clients to report a higher volume of errors and would overwhelm the backend. In this case, prioritizing fresh logs is more important than catching up with old logs, since fresh logs indicate the current state of the system, whereas older logs tell you the state of the system at a past time, which becomes less relevant the further you are from the incident. A backfill operation can tidy up the historical data afterward, when the system has spare capacity.

Data Filtering and Augmentation

In the case of metrics (e.g., Prometheus), an engineer may accidentally add a high-cardinality field like user ID or an IP address, leading to *cardinality explosion*. Typically, metrics systems are not designed to handle high-cardinality fields, and a pipeline can provide a mechanism to handle them. This could be something as simple as dropping the time series containing high-cardinality fields. To reduce impact of a cardinality explosion, advanced approaches include pre-aggregating the data in the high-cardinality field(s), or dropping data with invalid data (like incorrect or malformed timestamps).

In the case of logs, you would want to filter PII data, filter security data like security tokens, or sanitize URLs since often the logging system is not meant to store sensitive data. For trace data, you might like to additionally sample high-value traces or drop low-value spans from making it to the backend system.

In addition to filtering data, the telemetry pipeline can also be used to enrich the telemetry data for better usability. Often this includes adding additional metadata that is available outside the process, like region information or Kubernetes container information; resolving IPs to their hostnames to enhance usability; or augmenting log and trace data with GeoIP information.

Data Transformation

A robust telemetry pipeline may be expected to ingest a cornucopia of data types such as unstructured logs, structured logs in various formats, metrics time-series points, or events in the form of trace spans. In addition to being type-aware, the pipeline may provide APIs, either externally, or internally, in various wire formats. The functionality to transform those data types becomes a key component of a pipeline.

While it can be computationally expensive, the benefits of translating each data point into a common event format outweighs the costs associated with the compute needed to process the data. Such benefits include maximum flexibility around technology selection, minimal duplication of the same event in different formats, and the ability to further enrich the data.

Telemetry backends typically have discrete and unique APIs, and no standard pattern exists. Being able to support an external team's needs for a particular backend can be valuable and as simple as writing a plug-in in a preprocessing component to translate a common format into a format that the backend can ingest.

Slack has several real-world examples of this transformation. We transform various trace formats (e.g., Zipkin and Jaeger) into our common SpanEvent format. This common format also has the benefit of being directly writable to a data warehouse and is easily queried by common big data tools such as Presto and can support joins or aggregations. Such tracing data sets in our data warehouse support long-tail analytics and can drive powerful insights.

Ensuring Data Quality and Consistency

The telemetry data gathered from applications can potentially have data-quality issues. A common approach to ensure data quality is to drop data with a timestamp field that is too far into the past or too far into the future.

For example, misconfigured devices that report data with incorrect timestamps pollute the overall data quality of the system. Such data should be corrected by replacing the malformed timestamp with a timestamp at ingestion time or dropped. In one real-world case, mobile devices with Candy Crush installed would often report timestamps far in the future as users manually altered the system time on the device in order to gain rewards in-game. If dropping the data is not an option, the pipeline should provide an alternative location to store that data for later processing.

To use logs as an example, the pipeline can perform useful operations such as the following:

- Convert unstructured logs to structured data by extracting specific fields
- Detect and redact or filter any PII or sensitive data in the log data

- Convert IP addresses to geographic latitude/longitude fields through the use of geolocation databases such as MaxMind

- Ensure the schema of the log data, to ensure that the expected data exists and that specific fields are of specific types

- Filter low-value logs from being sent to the backend

For trace data in particular at Slack, one way we ensure data consistency is by using simple data-filtering operations like filtering low-value spans from making it to the backend, increasing the overall value of the data set. Other examples of ensuring quality include techniques like tail sampling, in which only a small subset of the reported traces are selected for storage in the backend system based on desirable attributes, such as higher reported latency.

Managing a Telemetry Pipeline: Anatomy

In this section, we cover the basic components and architecture of a functional telemetry pipeline. Simply stated, a *telemetry pipeline* is a chain of receiver, buffer, processor and exporter components, all in a series.

The following are details of these key components of a telemetry pipeline:

- A *receiver* collects data from a source.

  A receiver can collect the data directly from applications like a Prometheus scraper. Alternatively, a receiver can also ingest data from a buffer.

  A receiver can expose an HTTP API to which applications can push their data.

  A receiver can also write to a buffer to ensure data integrity during disruptions.

- A *buffer* is a store for the data, often for a short period of time.

  A buffer holds the data temporarily until it can be consumed by a backend or downstream application.

  Often a buffer is a pub-sub system like Kafka or Amazon Kinesis.

  An application can also push the data directly to a buffer. In such cases, a buffer also acts as a source of the data for a receiver.

- A *processor* often takes the data from a buffer, applies a transformation to it, and then persists the data back to a buffer.

- An *exporter* is a component that acts as a sink for the telemetry data. An exporter often takes the data from a buffer and writes that data to a telemetry backend.

In simple setups, a telemetry pipeline consists of the pattern of receiver → buffer → exporter, often for each type of telemetry backend, as shown in Figure 18-1.

Figure 18-1. A receiver, buffer, and exporter as frequently used in simple telemetry pipelines

However, a complex setup can have a chain of receiver → buffer → receiver → buffer → exporter, as shown in Figure 18-2.

Figure 18-2. An advanced example of a telemetry pipeline with a processor

A receiver or the exporter in a pipeline is often responsible for only one of the possible operations—like capacity planning, routing, or data transformation for the data. Table 18-1 shows a sample of operations that can be performed on various types of telemetry data.

Table 18-1. Roles of the receiver, processor, and exporter in a pipeline

Telemetry data type	Receiver	Exporter or processor
Trace data	• Gather trace data in different formats (e.g., Zipkin/Jaeger/AWS X-Ray, OTel) • Gather data from different services (e.g., from all Slack mobile clients)	• Ingest data into various trace backends • Perform tail sampling of the data • Drop low-value traces • Extract logs from traces • Route trace data to various backends for compliance needs • Filter data
Metrics data	Identify and scrape targets	• Relabel metrics • Downsample metrics • Aggregate metrics • Push data to multiple backends • Detect high-cardinality tags or time series • Filter high-cardinality tags or metrics
Logs data	• Gather data from different services • Endpoint for collecting logs pushed from different services	• Parse log data into semistructured or structured logs • Filter PII and sensitive data from logs • Push data to multiple backends for GDPR reasons • Route infrequently queried or audit logs to flat files, and high-value logs or frequent queries to an indexed system

In open source systems, a receiver may also be called a *source,* and an exporter is usually called a *sink.* However, this naming convention obscures the fact that these components can be chained.

Data transformations and filtering rules often differ depending on the type of the telemetry data, necessitating isolated pipelines.

Challenges When Managing a Telemetry Pipeline

Running a pipeline at scale comes with a set of challenges that are well-known to us at Slack, and we have outlined them in this section. At a smaller scale, telemetry pipelines are fairly simple to set up and run. They typically involve configuring a process such as the OpenTelemetry Collector to act as a receiver and exporter.

At a larger scale, these pipelines would be processing hundreds of streams. Keeping them up and running can be an operational challenge, as it requires ensuring the performance, correctness, reliability and availability of the pipeline. While a small amount of software engineering work is involved, a large part of the work running the pipeline reliably involves control theory.

Performance

Since applications can produce data in any format and the nature of the data they produce can change, keeping the pipeline performant can be a challenge. For example, if an application generates a lot of logs that are expensive to process in a logging pipeline, the log pipeline becomes slower and needs to be scaled up. Often slowness in one part of the pipeline may cause issues in other parts of the pipeline—like spiky loads, which, in turn, can destabilize the entire pipeline.

Correctness

Since the pipeline is made up of multiple components, determining whether the end-to-end operation of the pipeline is correct can be difficult. For example, in a complex pipeline, it can be difficult to know whether the data you are writing is transformed correctly or to ensure that the data being dropped is the only type of data being dropped. Further, since the data format of the incoming data is unknown, debugging the issues can be complex. You must, therefore, monitor for errors and data-quality issues in the pipeline.

Availability

Often the backends or various components of the pipeline can be unreliable. As long as the software components and sinks are designed to ensure resiliency and availability, you can withstand disruptions in the pipeline.

Reliability

As part of a reliable change management practice, we ensure pipeline availability when making software changes or configuration changes. It can be challenging to deploy a new version of a component and maintain pipeline end-to-end latency and saturation at acceptable levels.

Reliably managing flows requires a good understanding of the bottlenecks in the processing pipeline, or capacity planning. A saturated component can be a bottleneck that slows the entire pipeline. Once the bottleneck is identified, you should ensure that sufficient resources are allocated to the bottleneck or that the component is performing sufficiently well to keep up with the volume. In addition to capacity planning, the pipeline should have good monitoring to identify how much the rates of flows vary among components of the pipeline.

Reprocessing the data and backfilling is often one of the most complex and time-consuming parts of managing a data pipeline. For example, if you fail to filter some PII data from logs in the pipeline, you need to delete the data from your log search system and backfill the data. While most solutions work well in a normal case, they are not very equipped to deal with backfilling large amounts of historical data. In this case, you need to ensure that you have enough historical data in the buffer to reprocess the data.

Isolation

If you colocate logs or metrics from a high-volume system customer and a low-volume customer located in the same cluster, availability issues may occur if a high volume of logs causes saturation of the cluster. So, the telemetry pipeline should be set up such that these streams can be isolated from each other and possibly written to different backends.

Data Freshness

In addition to being performant, correct, and reliable, a telemetry pipeline should also operate at or near real time. Often the end-to-end latency between the production of data and it being available for consumption is in the order of seconds, or tens of seconds in the worst case. However, monitoring the pipeline for data freshness can be a challenge since you need to have a known data source that produces the data at a consistent pace.

Host metrics, such as Prometheus, can be used because they are typically scraped at a consistent interval. You can use those intervals to measure the data freshness of your logs. For logs or traces, a good, consistent data source is often not available. In those cases, it could be valuable for you to add a synthetic data source.

At Slack, we add synthetic logs to our log streams at a fixed rate of N messages per minute. This data is ingested into our sinks, and we periodically query these known logs to understand the health and freshness of the pipeline. For example, we produce 100 synthetic log messages per minute from a data source to our largest log cluster (100 GB per hour log data). Once this data is ingested, we monitor and query these logs every 10 seconds, to see whether our pipeline is ingesting the data in real time. We set our freshness SLO on the number of times we receive all the messages in a given minute in the last five minutes.

Care should be taken to ensure that the synthetic data has an unique value or is filtered out so it doesn't interfere with users querying for normal logs. We also make sure that the synthetic log is emitted from multiple areas in our infrastructure, to ensure monitoring coverage throughout our telemetry pipeline.

Use Case: Telemetry Management at Slack

Slack's telemetry management program has evolved organically to adapt to various observability use cases at Slack. To handle these use cases, the system consists of open source components and Murron, in-house software written in Go. In this section, we describe the discrete components of the pipeline and how they serve different departments within Slack.

Metrics Aggregation

Prometheus is the primary system for metrics at Slack. Our backend was first written in PHP and later in Hack. Since PHP/Hack use a process per request model, the Prometheus pull model wouldn't work because it does not have the process context and has only the host context. Instead, Slack uses a custom Prometheus library to emit metrics per request to a local daemon written in Go.

These per request metrics are collected and locally aggregated over a time window by that daemon process. The daemon process also exposes a metrics endpoint, which is scraped by our Prometheus servers, as shown in Figure 18-3. This allows us to collect metrics from our PHP/Hack application servers.

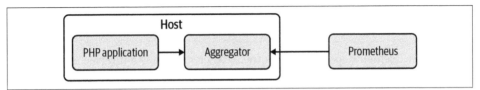

Figure 18-3. Aggregation of metrics from a per-request process application

Outside of PHP/Hack, Slack also runs applications in Go or Java that expose metric endpoints, and their metrics are able to be scraped by Prometheus directly.

Logs and Trace Events

Murron is an in-house Go application that forms the backbone of our log and trace event pipeline at Slack. Murron consists of three types of components: a receiver, a processor and an exporter. A *receiver* receives the data from a source (over HTTP, gRPC API, and in several formats like JSON, Protobuf, or custom binary formats) and sends it to a buffer like Kafka or another ingestor. A processor transforms the messages, which contain log or trace data, from one format to another. A consumer consumes the messages from Kafka and sends them to various sinks like Prometheus, Elasticsearch, or an external vendor.

The core primitive in Murron is a *stream* that is used to define the telemetry pipeline. A stream consists of a *receiver* that receives messages containing logs or trace data from the application, a *processor* to process the messages, and a *buffer* (such as a Kafka topic) for these messages. In addition, for each stream we can also define *exporters*, which consume the messages from a buffer and route them to appropriate backends after processing, if desired (see Figure 18-4).

To facilitate routing and custom processing, Murron wraps all the messages received in a custom envelope message. This envelope message contains information like the name of the stream this message belongs to, which is used to route messages within several Murron components. In addition, the envelope message contains additional metadata about the message like hostname, Kubernetes container information, and the name of the process. This metadata is used to augment the message data later in the pipeline.

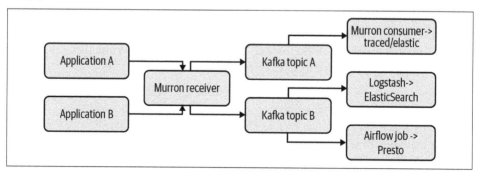

Figure 18-4. Slack telemetry pipeline with receivers, buffers, and exporters for trace data

In the OpenTelemetry specification, a trace data structure is a directed acyclic graph of linked events called *spans*. These data structures are often wrapped in a higher-level tracing API to produce traces, and the data is accessed via a Trace UI on the consumption side. This hidden structure prevents us from querying raw trace data in a way that would make the traces suitable for a wide variety of use cases.

To enable natural adoption through ease of use, we implemented a new simplified span format called a *SpanEvent* that is easier to produce and consume. A typical SpanEvent consists of the following fields: an ID, timestamp, duration, parent ID, trace ID, name, type, tags, and a special span type field. Like a trace, a causal graph is a directed acyclic graph of SpanEvents. Giving engineers the ability to easily produce and analyze traces outside of traditional instrumentation opens up a lot of new avenues, such as instrumenting CI/CD systems, as described in Chapter 11.

To support the causal graph model, we have built custom tracing libraries for languages like PHP/Hack, JavaScript, Swift, and Kotlin. In addition to those libraries, we leverage open source tracing libraries for Java and Go.

Our Hack applications are instrumented with an OpenTracing-compatible tracer (*https://opentracing.io*); we discussed OpenTracing in "Open Instrumentation Standards" on page 74. Our mobile and desktop clients trace their code and emit SpanEvents using either a high-level tracer or a low-level span-creation API. These generated SpanEvents are sent to Wallace over HTTP as JSON or Protobuf-encoded events.

Wallace, based on Murron, is a receiver and processor that operates independently from our core cloud infrastructure, so we can capture client and service errors even when Slack's core infrastructure is experiencing a full site outage. Wallace validates the span data it receives and forwards those events to another Murron receiver that writes the data to our buffer, Kafka (see Figure 18-5).

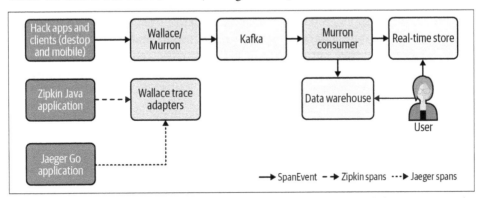

Figure 18-5. Slack's tracing infrastructure, with applications in pink (light gray in print), receivers and exporters in blue (medium gray)

Our internal Java and Go applications use the open source instrumentation libraries from Zipkin and Jaeger, respectively. To capture the spans from these applications, Wallace exposes receivers for both types of span data. These receivers, called *trace adapters*, translate the reported spans into our SpanEvent format and write them to

Wallace, which in turn forwards them to a Murron receiver that writes the data to Kafka.

The trace data written to Kafka is consumed primarily by three exporters based on Murron and Secor, which is an open source project maintained by Pinterest:

Elasticsearch exporter
A Murron exporter reads our SpanEvents from Kafka and sends them to Elasticsearch, an event store that allows us to display events on a dashboard (in our case, we primarily use Grafana) and set custom alerts on those events.

Data warehouse exporter
We use Secor, an open source project by Pinterest, to transform the data from Kafka and upload it to Amazon S3 to be ingested into our Presto data warehouse.

Honeycomb exporter
Finally, a Murron exporter consumes events from Kafka, filters out low-value spans, transforms the data into a custom event format specific to Honeycomb, and routes it to different data sets to be queried in Honeycomb.

By using those exporters, we gain almost immediate access to our trace data with an end-to-end latency on the order of seconds. We use Honeycomb and Grafana (via Elasticsearch) to visualize this data and run simple analytics, which plays an important role in making our traces useful for triage.

By comparison, our data warehouse has a typical landing time of two hours. We use Presto, which supports complex analytical queries over longer time ranges via SQL. We typically store 7 days of events in Elasticsearch, and Honeycomb supports up to 60 days of events, but our Presto backend, Hive, can store the data for up to two years. This enables our engineers to visualize long-term trends beyond the capabilities of Honeycomb and Elasticsearch.

Murron manages over 120 streams of data at a volume of several million messages per second. All of this data is buffered through over 200 Kafka topics across 20 clusters.

Open Source Alternatives

Our telemetry pipeline has organically evolved over several years and consists of a mix of open source components and in-house software. From the previous section, an astute reader would have noticed that some of our software has overlapping capabilities and that we could benefit from consolidating systems. The observability telemetry pipeline space has matured quite a bit, and several newer, viable options exist now, compared to three years ago. In this section, we will look at other open source alternatives.

In the early days of observability, no specific tools existed for setting up a telemetry pipeline. Most engineers used tools like rsyslog and wrote custom tools or used third-party vendor tools to ship data to a backend. Over time, teams recognized the gap and developed tools like Facebook's Scribe (*https://github.com/facebookarch ive/scribe*), which introduced the basic ideas of routing logs to various backends by using streams. For reliably delivering the logs when the downstream system was down, Scribe introduced ideas like local disk persistence, which would persist the logs to local disk when the downstream system couldn't keep up with the log volume or was unresponsive. Facebook's Scribe also established the ideas of chaining multiple instances together and forming a telemetry management pipeline at scale.

In later years, telemetry pipelines have evolved to more full-fledged systems that allowed for features like advanced log parsing and field manipulation, as well as advanced rate limiting or dynamic sampling capability. With the rise of modern pub/sub systems like Kinesis/Kafka, most telemetry pipelines included support to use them as a source of data and to buffer intermediate data in a pipeline. In the logging vertical, popular services like timber, Logstash (*https://www.elastic.co/log stash*)/Filebeat, Fluentd, and rsyslog are available to transport logs to receivers. For metrics use cases, projects like Prometheus Pushgateway (*https://github.com/prome theus/pushgateway*), and M3 Aggregator (*https://m3db.io/docs/how_to/m3aggregator*) were built to aggregate metrics. For trace data, tools like Refinery (*https://docs.honey comb.io/manage-data-volume/refinery*) were built to further filter, sample, and process trace data. Those tools are designed to be modular, allowing plug-ins to be developed that add support for receivers and exporters to send and receive data from and to a myriad of systems.

As more and more data is passed through these telemetry pipelines, their efficiency and reliability have become increasingly important. As a result, modern systems are being written in more efficient languages like C (Fluent Bit), Go (Cribl) and Rust (Vector (*https://vector.dev*)). If we are to process terabytes of data per second, infrastructure efficiency of the telemetry pipeline becomes very important.

Managing a Telemetry Pipeline: Build Versus Buy

For historical reasons, Slack uses a mix of open source and in-house software in its telemetry pipeline management. These days, these reasons have less meaning, as a multitude of open source alternatives exist and can be used to easily form the basis of your telemetry pipeline. These open source tools are usually modular in nature and can be easily extended to add additional functionality for your custom use cases. Given the wide availability of tools, it does not make economic sense to spend engineering resources developing in-house software to make up the basis of your telemetry management pipeline.

Open source software, naturally, is free, but the cost of maintaining and operating a telemetry pipeline should be taken into consideration. Vendors exist on the other side of the build-versus-buy equation and promise to simplify the operational burden as well as provide a strong user experience. Simplification and ease of use is an attractive proposition and may make economic sense, depending on the maturity of your organization. This balance will shift over time as your organization grows, so keep that in mind when selecting your approach. For more considerations when deciding whether to build or to buy, see Chapter 15.

Conclusion

You can get started today by using several off-the-shelf services in conjunction with one another. You may be tempted to write a new system from scratch, but we recommend adapting an open source service. Smaller pipelines can run on autopilot, but as the organization grows, managing a telemetry pipeline becomes a complex endeavor and introduces several challenges.

As you build out your telemetry management system, try to build for the current needs of the business and anticipate—but don't implement for—new needs. For example, you may want to add compliance features sometime down the road, or you may want to introduce advanced enrichment or filtering. Keeping the pipeline modular and following the producer, buffer, processor and exporter model will keep your observability function running smoothly, while providing value to your business.

PART V

Spreading Observability Culture

In Part IV, we focused on addressing challenges when practicing observability at scale. In this final section, we explore the cultural mechanisms you can use to help drive observability adoption efforts across your organization.

Observability often starts within one particular team or business unit in an organization. To spread a culture of observability, teams need support from various stakeholders across the business. This section breaks down how that support comes together to help proliferate an observability practice.

Chapter 19 presents a look at material outcomes, organizational challenges, and how to make a business case by looking at the business benefits behind adopting observability practices.

Chapter 20 looks at how teams beyond those in engineering can further their own goals with the use of observability tools. Helping adjacent teams learn how to understand and use observability data to achieve their goals will help create allies that can push your observability adoption initiatives forward.

Chapter 21 looks at industry-leading data that can help inform and measure your progress in achieving the benefits of observability laid out in earlier chapters. This model can be useful as a rough guide rather than as a rigid prescription.

Finally, in Chapter 22, we will illuminate some of the future path forward that we hope you will join us in building.

CHAPTER 19

The Business Case for Observability

Observability often starts within one particular team or business unit in an organization. To spread a culture of observability, teams need support from various stakeholders across the business.

In this chapter, we'll start breaking down how that support comes together by laying out the business case for observability. Some organizations adopt observability practices in response to overcoming dire challenges that cannot be addressed by traditional approaches. Others may need a more proactive approach to changing traditional practices. Regardless of where in your observability journey you may be, this chapter will show you how to make a business case for observability within your own company.

We start by looking at both the reactive and proactive approaches to instituting change. We'll examine nonemergency situations to identify a set of circumstances that can point to a critical need to adopt observability outside the context of catastrophic service outages. Then we'll cover the steps needed to support creation of an observability practice, evaluate various tools, and know when your organization has achieved a state of observability that is "good enough" to shift your focus to other initiatives.

The Reactive Approach to Introducing Change

Change is hard. Many organizations tend to follow the path of least resistance. Why fix the things that aren't broken (or perceived to be)? Historically, production systems have operated just fine for decades without observability. Why rock the boat now?

Simpler systems could be reasoned about by engineers intimately familiar with the finer points of their architectures. As seen in Chapter 3, it isn't until traditional approaches suddenly and drastically fall short that some organizations realize their now-critical need for observability. But introducing fundamental change into an organization in *reactive* knee-jerk ways can have unintended consequences. The rush to fix mission-critical business problems often leads to oversimplified approaches that rarely lead to useful outcomes.

Consider the case of reactive change introduced as the result of critical service outages. For example, an organization might perform a root-cause analysis to determine why an outage occurred, and the analysis might point to a singular reason. In mission-critical situations, executives are often tempted to use that reason to drive simplified remediations that demonstrate the problem has been swiftly dealt with. When the smoking gun for an outage can be pointed to as the line in the root-cause analysis that says, "We didn't have backups," that can be used to justify demoting the employee who deleted the important file, engaging consultants to introduce a new backup strategy, and the executives breathing a sigh of relief once they believe the appropriate gap has been closed.

While that approach might seem to offer a sense of security, it's ultimately false. Why was that one file able to create a cascading system failure? Why was a file that critical so easily deleted? Could the situation have been better mitigated with more immutable infrastructure? Any number of approaches in this hypothetical scenario might better treat the underlying causes rather than the most obvious symptoms. In a rush to fix problems quickly, often the oversimplified approach is the most tempting to take.

Another reactive approach in organizations originates from the inability to recognize dysfunction that no longer has to be tolerated. The most common obsolete dysfunction tolerated with traditional tooling is an undue burden on software engineering and operations teams that prevents them from focusing on delivering innovative work.

As seen in Chapter 3, teams without observability frequently waste time chasing down incidents with identical symptoms (and underlying causes). Issues often repeatedly trigger fire drills, and those drills cause stress for engineering teams and the business. Engineering teams experience alert fatigue that leads to burnout and, eventually, churn—costing the business lost expertise among staff and the time it takes to rebuild that expertise. Customers experiencing issues will abandon their transactions—costing the business revenue and customer loyalty. Being stuck in this constant firefighting and high-stress mode creates a downward spiral that undermines engineering team confidence when making changes to production, which in turn creates more fragile systems, which in turn require more time to maintain, which in turn slows the delivery of new features that provide business value.

Unfortunately, many business leaders often accept these hurdles as the normal state of operations. They introduce processes that they believe help mitigate these problems, such as change advisory boards or rules prohibiting their team from deploying code changes on a Friday. They expect on-call rotations to burn out engineers from time to time, so they allow on-call exemptions for their rockstar engineers. Many toxic cultural practices in engineering teams can be traced back to situations that start with a fundamental lack of understanding of their production systems.

Signs that your business may be hitting a breaking point without observability in its systems include—but are not limited to—some of the following scenarios:

- Customers discover and report critical bugs in production services long before they are detected and addressed internally.

- When minor incidents occur, detecting and recovering them often takes so long that they escalate into prolonged service outages.

- The backlog of investigation necessary to troubleshoot incidents and bugs continues to grow because new problems pile up faster than they can be retrospected or triaged.

- The amount of time spent on break/fix operational work exceeds the amount of time your teams spend on delivering new features.

- Customer satisfaction with your services is low because of repeated poor performance that your support teams cannot verify, replicate, or resolve.

- New features are delayed by weeks or months because engineering teams are dealing with disproportionately large amounts of unexpected work necessary to figure out how various services are all interacting with one another.

Other factors contributing to these scenarios may require additional mitigation approaches. However, teams experiencing a multitude of these symptoms more than likely need to address a systemic lack of observability in their systems. Teams operating in these ways display a fundamental lack of understanding their production systems' behavior such that it negatively impacts their ability to deliver against business goals.

The Return on Investment of Observability

At its core, observability is about enabling teams to answer previously unknowable questions, or to address unknown unknowns, as we commonly phrase it. The ability to debug application issues, in a data-driven and repeatable manner with the core analysis loop (see Chapter 8) allows teams to effectively manage systems that commonly fail in unpredictable ways. Given the ubiquity of complex distributed systems as today's de facto application architecture (heterogeneous environments comprising any mix of cloud infrastructure, on-premises systems, containers and orchestration platforms, serverless functions, various SaaS components, etc.), the ability to effectively debug unknown-unknowns can make or break your company's mission-critical digital services.

As observability tool vendors, we have learned through anecdotal feedback and industry research that companies adopting observability practices gain highly tangible business benefits. We engaged Forrester Research to quantify these benefits among our own customer base.[1] While the measures in that study are specific to our own solution, we do believe that some of the traits can be universally expected regardless of the tool (presuming it has the same observability capabilities we've described in this book).

We believe observability universally impacts the bottom line in four important ways:

Higher incremental revenue
> Observability tools help teams improve uptime and performance, leading to increased incremental revenue directly as a result of improving code quality.

Cost savings from faster incident response
> Observability significantly reduces labor costs via faster mean time to detect (MTTD) and mean time to resolve (MTTR), improved query response times, the ability to find bottlenecks quicker, reduction of time spent on call, and time saved by avoiding rollbacks.

Cost savings from avoided incidents
> Observability tools enable developers to find causes of problems before they become critical and long-lasting, which helps prevent incidents.

Cost savings from decreased employee churn
> Implementing observability results in improved job satisfaction and decrease in developer burnout, alert and on-call fatigue, and turnover.

Other quantifiable benefits may exist, depending on how tools are implemented. But the preceding benefits should be universal for businesses using tools that meet the functional requirements for observability (see Chapters 1 and 8)—and adopting the practices described in this book.

The Proactive Approach to Introducing Change

A *proactive* approach to introducing change is to recognize the symptoms in the reactive situations outlined earlier as abnormal and preventable. An early way to gain traction and make a business case for observability is to highlight the impact that can be made in reducing common metrics, like the time-to-detect (TTD) and time-to-resolve (TTR) issues within your services. While these measures are far from

---

[1] You can reference a recap of Forrester Consulting's Total Economic Impact (TEI) framework findings for Honeycomb in the blog post "What Is Honeycomb's ROI? Forrester's Study on the Benefits of Observability" (*https://hny.co/blog/forrester-tei-benefits-observability-roi-2021*) by Evelyn Chea.

perfect, they are commonly in use in many organizations and often well understood by executive stakeholders.

 Adaptive Capacity Labs has a great take on moving past shallow incident data, in a blog post written by John Allspaw (*https://oreil.ly/pZd4m*), and observability can also demonstrate wins in more nuanced ways. For the purposes of this chapter, we focus on the more flawed but more widely understood metrics of TTD and TTR.

An initial business case for introducing observability into your systems can be twofold. First, it provides your teams a way to find individual user issues that are typically hidden when using traditional monitoring tools, thereby lowering TTD (see Chapter 5). Second, automating the core analysis loop can dramatically reduce the time necessary to isolate the correct source of issues, thereby lowering TTR (see Chapter 8).

Once early gains in these areas are proven, it is easier to garner support for introducing more observability throughout your application stack and organization. Frequently, we see teams initially approach the world of observability from a reactive state—typically, seeking a better way to detect and resolve issues. Observability can immediately help in these cases. But second-order benefits should also be measured and presented when making a business case.

The upstream impact of detecting and resolving issues faster is that it reduces the amount of unexpected break/fix operational work for your teams. A qualitative improvement is often felt here by reducing the burden of triaging issues, which lowers on-call stress. This same ability to detect and resolve issues also leads to reducing the backlog of application issues, spending less time resolving bugs, and spending more time creating and delivering new features. Measuring this qualitative improvement—even just anecdotally—can help you build a business case that observability leads to happier and healthier engineering teams, which in turn creates greater employee retention and satisfaction.

A third-order benefit comes from the ability to understand the performance of individual user requests and the cause of bottlenecks: teams can quickly understand how best to optimize their services. More than half of mobile users will abandon transactions after three seconds of load time.[2] Measuring the rate of successful user transactions and correlating it with gains in service performance is both possible to

---

2 Tammy Everts, "Mobile Load Time and User Abandonment" (*https://oreil.ly/FOkr4*), Akamai Developer Blog, September 9, 2016.

measure and likely to occur in an observable application. Another obvious business use case for observability is higher customer satisfaction and retention.

If the preceding outcomes matter to your business, you have a business case for introducing observability into your organization. Rather than waiting for a series of catastrophic failures to prompt your business to address the symptoms of nonobservable systems, the proactive approach introduces observability into your sociotechnical systems with small, achievable steps that have big impacts. Let's examine how you can take those steps.

Introducing Observability as a Practice

Similar to introducing security or testability into your applications, observability is an ongoing practice that is a responsibility shared by anyone responsible for developing and running a production service. Building effective observable systems is not a one-time effort. You cannot simply take a checkbox approach to introducing technical capabilities and declare that your organization has "achieved" observability any more than you can do that with security or testability. Observability must be introduced as a *practice*.

Observability begins as a capability that can be measured as a technical attribute of a system: can your system be observed or not (see Chapter 1)? As highlighted several times throughout this book, production systems are sociotechnical. Once a system has observability as a technical attribute, the next step is measured by how well your teams and the system operate together (see Part III). Just because a system can be observed does not mean that it is being observed *effectively*.

The goal of observability is to provide engineering teams the capability to develop, operate, thoroughly debug, and report on their systems. Teams must be empowered to explore their curiosity by asking arbitrary questions about their system to better understand its behavior. They must be incentivized to interrogate their systems proactively, both by their tools and with management support. A sophisticated analytics platform is useless if the team using it feels overwhelmed by the interface or is discouraged from querying for fear of running up a large bill.

A well-functioning observability practice not only empowers engineers to ask questions that help detect and resolve issues in production, but also should encourage them to begin answering business intelligence questions in real time (see Chapter 20). If nobody is using the new feature that the engineering team has built, or if one customer is at risk of churning because they are persistently experiencing issues, that is a risk to the health of your business. Practicing observability should encourage engineers to adopt a cross-functional approach to measuring service health beyond its performance and availability.

As DevOps practices continue to gain mainstream traction, forward-thinking engineering leadership teams remove barriers between engineering and operations teams. Removing these artificial barriers empowers teams to take more ownership of the development and operation of their software. Observability helps engineers lacking on-call experience to better understand where failures are occurring and how to mitigate them, eroding the artificial wall between software development and operations. Similarly, observability erodes the artificial wall between software development, operations, and business outcomes. Observability gives software engineering teams the appropriate tools to debug and understand how their systems are being used. It helps them shed their reliance on functional handoffs, excessive manual work, runbooks, guesswork, and external views of system health measures that impact business goals.

It is beyond the scope of this chapter to outline all of the practices and traits commonly shared by high-performing engineering teams. The DORA 2019 *Accelerate State of DevOps* Report (*https://oreil.ly/2Gqjz*) describes many of the essential traits that separate elite teams from their low-performing counterparts. Similarly, teams introducing observability benefit from many of the practices described in the report.

When introducing an observability practice, engineering leaders should first ensure that they are creating a culture of psychological safety. Blameless culture fosters a psychologically safe environment that supports experimentation and rewards curious collaboration. Encouraging experimentation is necessary to evolve traditional practices. DORA's year-over-year reporting demonstrates both the benefits of blameless culture and its inextricable link with high-performing teams.

A longer-form guide to practicing blameless culture can be found in PagerDuty's Blameless Postmortem documentation (*https://postmortems.pagerduty.com*).

With a blameless culture in practice, business leaders should also ensure that a clear scope of work exists when introducing observability (for example, happening entirely within one introductory team or line of business). Baseline performance measures for TTD and TTR can be used as a benchmark to measure improvement within that scope. The infrastructure and platform work required should be identified, allocated, and budgeted in support of this effort. Only then should the technical work of instrumentation and analysis of that team's software begin.

Using the Appropriate Tools

Although observability is primarily a cultural practice, it does require engineering teams to possess the technical capability to instrument their code, store the emitted telemetry data, and analyze that data in response to their questions. A large portion of the initial technical effort to introduce observability requires setting up tooling and instrumentation.

At this point, some teams attempt to roll their own observability solutions. As seen in Chapter 15, the ROI of building a bespoke observability platform that does not align with your company's core competencies is rarely worthwhile. Most organizations find that building a bespoke solution can be prohibitively difficult, time-consuming, and expensive. Instead, a wide range of solutions are available with various trade-offs to consider, such as commercial versus open source, on-premises versus hosted, or a combination of buying and building a solution to meet your needs.

Instrumentation

The first step to consider is how your applications will emit telemetry data. Traditionally, vendor-specific agents and instrumentation libraries were your only choice, and those choices brought with them a large degree of vendor lock-in. Currently, for instrumentation of both frameworks and application code, OpenTelemetry (*http://opentelemetry.io*) is the emerging standard (see Chapter 7). It supports every open source metric and trace analytics platform, and is supported by almost every commercial vendor in the space. There is no longer a reason to lock into one specific vendor's instrumentation framework, nor to roll your own agents and libraries.

OTel allows you to configure your instrumentation to send data to the analytics tool of your choice. By using a common standard, it's possible to easily demo the capabilities of any analytics tool by simply sending your instrumentation data to multiple backends at the same time.

When considering the data that your team must analyze, it's an oversimplification to simply break observability into categories like metrics, logging, and tracing. While those can be valid categories of observability data, achieving observability requires those data types to interact in a way that gives your teams an appropriate view of their systems. While messaging that describes observability as *three pillars* is useful as a marketing headline, it misses the big picture. At this point, it is more useful to instead think about which data type or types are best suited (*https://thenewstack.io/how-the-3-pillars-of-observability-miss-the-big-picture*) to your use case, and which can be generated on demand from the others.

Data Storage and Analytics

Once you have telemetry data, you need to consider the way it's stored and analyzed. Data storage and analytics are often bundled into the same solution, but that depends on whether you decide to use open source or proprietary options.

Commercial vendors typically bundle storage and analytics. Each vendor has differentiating features for storage and analytics, and you should consider which of those best help your teams reach their observability goals. Vendors of proprietary all-in-one solutions at the time of writing include Honeycomb, Lightstep, New Relic, Splunk, Datadog, and others.

Open source solutions typically require separate approaches to data storage and analytics. These open source frontends include solutions like Grafana, Prometheus, or Jaeger. While they handle analytics, they all require a separate data store in order to scale. Popular open source data storage layers include Cassandra, Elasticsearch, M3, and InfluxDB.

 Consider how the open source software you choose is licensed and how that impacts your usage. For example, both Elasticsearch and Grafana have recently made licensing changes you should consider before using these tools.

Having so many options is great. But you must also carefully consider and be wary of the operational load incurred by running your own data storage cluster. For example, the ELK stack is popular because it fulfills needs in the log management and analytics space. But end users frequently report that their maintenance and care of their ELK cluster gobbles up systems engineering time and grows quickly in associated management and infrastructure costs. As a result, you'll find a competitive market for managed open source telemetry data storage (e.g., ELK as a service).

When considering data storage, we also caution against finding separate solutions for each category (or *pillar*) of observability data you need. Similarly, attempting to bolt modern observability functionality onto a traditional monitoring system is likely to be fraught with peril. Since observability arises from the way your engineers interact with your data to answer questions, having one cohesive solution that works seamlessly is better than maintaining three or four separate systems. Using disjointed systems for analysis places the burden of carrying context and translation between those systems on engineers and creates a poor usability and troubleshooting experience. For more details on how approaches can coexist, refer to Chapter 9.

Rolling Out Tools to Your Teams

When considering tooling options, it's important to ensure that you are investing precious engineering cycles on differentiators that are core to your business needs. Consider whether your choice of tools is providing more innovation capacity or draining that capacity into managing bespoke solutions. Does your choice of tooling require creating a larger and separate team for management? Observability's goal isn't to create bespoke work within your engineering organization; it's to save your business time and money while increasing quality.

That's not to say that certain organizations should not create observability teams. However, especially in larger organizations, a good observability team will focus on helping each product team achieve observability in its platform or partner with those teams through the initial integration process. After evaluating which platform best fits the needs of your pilot team, an observability team can help make the same solutions more accessible to your engineering teams as a whole. For more details on structuring an observability team, refer to Chapter 15.

Knowing When You Have Enough Observability

Like security and testability, more work always remains to be done with observability. Business leaders may struggle with knowing when to make investing in observability a priority and when observability is "good enough" that other concerns can take precedence. While we encourage full instrumentation coverage in your applications, we also recognize that observability exists in a landscape with competing needs. From a pragmatic perspective, it helps to know how to recognize when you have enough observability as a useful checkpoint for determining the success of a pilot project.

If the symptom of teams flying blind without observability is excessive rework, teams with sufficient observability should have predictable delivery and sufficient reliability. Let's examine how to recognize that milestone both in terms of cultural practices and key results.

Once observability practices have become a foundational practice within a team, the outside intervention required to maintain a system with excellent observability should become a minimal and routine part of ongoing work. Just as a team wouldn't think to check in new code without associated tests, so too should teams practicing observability think about associated instrumentation as part of any code-review process. Instead of merging code and shutting down their laptops at the end of the day, it should be second nature for teams practicing observability to see how their code behaves as it reaches each stage of deployment.

Instead of code behavior in production being "someone else's problem," teams with enough observability should be excited to see how real users benefit from the features they are delivering. Every code review should consider whether the telemetry bundled with the change is appropriate to understand the impact this change will have in production. Observability should also not just be limited to engineers; bundled telemetry should empower product managers and customer success representatives to answer their own questions about production (see Chapter 20). Two useful measures indicating that enough observability is present are a marked improvement in self-serve fulfillment for one-off data requests about production behavior and a reduction in product management guesswork.

As teams reap the benefits of observability, their confidence level for understanding and operating in production should rise. The proportion of unresolved "mystery" incidents should decrease, and time to detect and resolve incidents will decrease across the organization. However, a frequent mistake for measuring success at this point is over-indexing on shallow metrics such as the overall number of incidents detected. Finding more incidents and comfortably digging into near misses is a positive step as your teams gain an increased understanding of the way production behaves. That often means previously undetected problems are now being more fully understood. You'll know you've reached an equilibrium when your engineering teams live within its modern observability tooling to understand problems and when disjointed legacy tooling is no longer a primary troubleshooting method.

Whenever your teams encounter a new problem that poses questions your data cannot answer, they will find it easier to take the time to fill in that telemetry gap rather than attempting to guess at what might be wrong. For example, if a mystery trace span is taking too long for inexplicable reasons, they will add subspans to capture smaller units of work within it, or add attributes to understand what is triggering the slow behavior. Observability always requires some care and feeding as integrations are added or the surface area of your code changes. But even so, the right choice of observability platform will still drastically reduce your overall operational burdens and TCO.

Conclusion

The need for observability is recognized within teams for a variety of reasons. Whether that need arises reactively in response to a critical outage, or proactively by realizing how its absence is stifling innovation on your teams, it's critical to create a business case in support of your observability initiative.

Similar to security and testability, observability must be approached as an ongoing practice. Teams practicing observability must make a habit of ensuring that any changes to code are bundled with proper instrumentation, just as they're bundled with tests. Code reviews should ensure that the instrumentation for new code achieves proper observability standards, just as they ensure it also meets security standards. Observability requires ongoing care and maintenance, but you'll know that observability has been achieved well enough by looking for the cultural behaviors and key results outlined in this chapter.

In the next chapter, we'll look at how engineering teams can create alliances with other internal teams to help accelerate the adoption of observability culture.

CHAPTER 20

Observability's Stakeholders and Allies

Most of this book has focused on introducing the practice of observability to software engineering teams. But when it comes to organization-wide adoption, engineering teams cannot, and should not, go forward alone. Once you've instrumented rich wide events, your telemetry data set contains a treasure trove of information about your services' behavior in the marketplace.

Observability's knack for providing fast answers to any arbitrary question means it can also fill knowledge gaps for various nonengineering stakeholders across your organization. A successful tactic for spreading a culture of observability is to build allies in engineering-adjacent teams by helping them address those gaps. In this chapter, you'll learn about engineering-adjacent use cases for observability, which teams are likely adoption allies, and how helping them can help you build momentum toward making observability a core part of organizational practices.

Recognizing Nonengineering Observability Needs

Engineering teams have a constellation of tools, practices, habits, goals, aspirations, responsibilities, and requirements that combine in ways that deliver value to their customers. Some engineering teams may focus more on software development, while others may be more operationally focused. While different engineering teams have different specializations, creating an excellent customer experience for people using your company's software is never "someone else's job." That's a shared responsibility, and it's everyone's job.

Observability can be thought of similarly. As you've seen in this book, observability is a lens that quickly shows you the discrepancies between how you *think* your software should behave, or how you *declare* that your software should behave (in code, documentation, knowledge bases, blog posts, etc.), and how it *actually* behaves in the hands of real users. With observability, you can understand, at any given point in time, your customers' experience of using your software in the real world. It's everyone's job to understand and improve that experience.

The need for observability is recognized by engineering teams for a variety of reasons. Functional gaps may exist for quite some time before they're recognized, and a catalytic event may spur the need for change—often, a critical outage. Or perhaps the need is recognized more proactively, such as realizing that the constant firefighting that comes with chasing elusive bugs is stifling a development team's ability to innovate. In either case, a supporting business case exists that drives an observability adoption initiative.

Similarly, when it comes to observability adoption for nonengineering teams, you must ask yourself which business cases it can support. Which business cases exist for understanding, at any given point in time, your customers' experience using your software in the real world? Who in your organization needs to understand and improve customer experience?

Let's be clear: not every team will specialize in observability. Even among engineering teams that do specialize in it, some will do far more coding and instrumentation than others. But almost everyone in your company has a stake in being able to query your observability data to analyze details about the current state of production.

Because observability allows you to arbitrarily slice and dice data across various dimensions, you can use it to understand the behaviors of individual users, groups of users, or the entire system. Those views can be compared, contrasted, or further mined to answer any combination of questions that are extremely relevant to nonengineering business units in your organization.

Some business use cases that are supported by observability might include:

- Understanding the adoption of new features. Which customers are using your newly shipped features? Does that match the list of customers who expressed interest in it? In what ways do usage patterns of active feature users differ from those who tried it but later abandoned the experience?

- Finding successful product usage trends for new customers. Does the sales team understand which combination of features seems to resonate with prospects who go on to become customers? Do you understand the product usage commonalities in users that failed to activate your product? Do those point to friction that needs to be eroded somehow?

- Accurately relaying service availability information to both customers and internal support teams via up-to-date service status pages. Can you provide templated queries so that support teams can self-serve when users report outages?

- Understanding both short-term and long-term reliability trends. Is reliability improving for users of your software? Does the shape of that reliability graph match other sources of data, like customer complaints? Are you experiencing fewer outages or more? Are those outages recovering more slowly?

- Resolving issues proactively. Are you able to find and resolve customer-impacting issues before they are reported by a critical mass of customers via support tickets? Are you proactively resolving issues, or are you relying on customers to find them for you?

- Shipping features to customers more quickly and reliably. Are deployments to production being closely watched to spot performance anomalies and fix them? Can you decouple deployments from releases so that shipping new features is less likely to cause widespread outages?

In your company, understanding and improving customer experience should be everyone's job. You can recognize a need for observability for nonengineering teams by asking yourself who cares about your application's availability, the new features being shipped to customers, usage trends within your products, and customer experience of the digital services you offer.

The best way to further your organization-wide observability adoption initiative is to reach out to adjacent teams that could benefit from this knowledge. With observability, you can enable everyone in your organization, regardless of their technical ability, to work with that data comfortably and to feel comfortable talking about it in ways that enable them to make informed decisions about building better customer experiences.

In other words, democratize your observability data. Let everyone see what's happening and how your software behaves in the hands of real users. Just as with any other team that is onboarded, you may have to provide initial guidance and tutoring to show them how to get answers to their questions. But soon you'll discover that each adjacent team will bring its own unique set of perspectives and questions to the table.

Work with stakeholders on adjacent teams to ensure that their questions can be answered. If their questions can't be answered today, could they be answered tomorrow by adding new custom instrumentation? Iterating on instrumentation with adjacent stakeholders will also help engineering teams get a better understanding of questions relevant to other parts of the business. This level of collaboration presents the kind of learning opportunities that help erode communication silos.

Similar to security and testability, observability must be approached as an ongoing practice. Teams practicing observability must make a habit of ensuring that any changes to code are bundled with proper instrumentation, just as they're bundled with tests. Code reviews should ensure that the instrumentation for new code achieves proper observability standards, just as they ensure it also meets security standards. These reviews should also ensure that the needs of nonengineering business units are being addressed when instrumentation to support business functions is added to their codebase.

Observability requires ongoing care and maintenance, but you'll know that you've achieved an adequate level of observability by looking for the cultural behaviors and key results outlined in this chapter.

Creating Observability Allies in Practice

Now that you've learned how to recognize knowledge gaps where observability can help solve business problems, the next step is working with various stakeholders to show them how that's done. Your observability adoption efforts will most likely start within engineering before spreading to adjacent teams (e.g., support) by the nature of shared responsibilities and workflows. With a relatively small bit of work, once your adoption effort is well underway, you can reach out to other stakeholders—whether in finance, sales, marketing, product development, customer success, the executive team, or others—to show them what's possible to understand about customer use of your applications in the real world.

By showing them how to use observability data to further their own business objectives, you can convert passive stakeholders into allies with an active interest in your adoption project. Allies will help actively bolster and prioritize needs for your project, rather than passively observing or just staying informed of your latest developments.

No universal approach to how that's done exists; it depends on the unique challenges of your particular business. But in this section, we'll look at a few examples of creating organizational allies who support your adoption initiatives by applying observability principles to their daily work.

Customer Support Teams

Most of this book has been about engineering practices used to debug production applications. Even when following a DevOps/SRE model, many sufficiently large organizations will have at least one separate team that handles frontline customer support issues including general troubleshooting, maintenance, and providing assistance with technical questions.

Customer support teams usually need to know about system issues before engineering/operations teams are ready to share information. When an issue first occurs, your customers notice. Generally, they'll refresh their browser or retry their transactions long before calling support. During this buffer, auto-remediations come in handy. Ideally, issues are experienced as small blips by your customers. But when persistent issues occur, the engineer on call must be paged and mobilized to respond. In the meantime, it's possible some customers are noticing more than just a blip.

With traditional monitoring, several minutes may pass before an issue is detected, the on-call engineer responds and triages an issue, an incident is declared, and a dashboard that the support team sees gets updated to reflect that a known issue is occurring within your applications. In the meantime, the support team may be hearing about customer issues manifesting in several ways and blindly piling up trouble tickets that must later be sifted through and manually resolved.

Instead, with observability, support teams have a few options. The easiest and simplest is to glance at your SLO dashboards to see if any customer-impacting issues have been detected (see Chapter 12). While this may be more granular than traditional monitoring and provide useful feedback sooner, it's far from perfect. Modern systems are modular, resilient, and self-healing, which means that outages are rarely binary: they look less like your entire site being up or down, and more like your "shopping cart checkout breaking 50% of the time for Android users in Europe" or "only customers with our new ACL feature enabled see a partial failure."

Enabling your support team members to debug issues reported by customers with observability can help them take a more proactive approach. How do transactions for this specific customer with customer ID 5678901 look right now? Have they been using the shopping cart feature on an Android device in Europe? Do they have access control lists (ACLs) enabled? The support team can quickly confirm or deny that support requests coming in are related to known issues and triage appropriately. Or, given a sufficient level of savvy and training with your observability tooling, the team can help identify new issues that may not be automatically detected—such as using an SLI with insufficient parameters.

Customer Success and Product Teams

In product-led organizations, it's increasingly common to find customer success teams. Whereas support is a reactive approach to assisting customers with issues, *customer success teams* take a more proactive approach to helping customers avoid problems by using your product effectively. This team often provides assistance with things like onboarding, planning, training, assisting with upgrades, and more.

Both customer support and customer success teams hear the most direct customer feedback in their day-to-day work. They know which parts of your applications people complain about the most. But are those loudest squeaky wheels actually the parts of the customer journey that matter for overall success?

For example, you may have recently released a new feature that isn't seeing much uptake from customers. Why? Are users using this feature as a live demo and just kicking the proverbial tires? Or are they using it as part of your product's workflow? When and how is that feature called, with which parameters? And in which sequence of events?

The type of event data captured by an observability solution is useful to understand product usage, which is immensely useful to product teams. Both product and customer success teams have a vested interest in understanding how your company's software behaves when operated by real customers. Being able to arbitrarily slice and dice your observability data across any relevant dimensions to find interesting patterns means that its usefulness extends well beyond just supporting availability and resiliency concerns in production.

Further, when certain product features are deprecated and a sunset date is set, success teams with observability can see which users are still actively using features that will soon be retired. They can also gauge if new features are being adopted and proactively help customers who may be impacted by product retirement timelines, but who have prioritized dealing with other issues during monthly syncs.

Success teams can also learn which traits are likely to signal activation with new product features by analyzing current usage patterns. Just as you can find performance outliers in your data, you can use observability to find adoption outliers in your performance data. Arbitrarily slicing and dicing your data across any dimension means you can do things like comparing users who made a particular request, more than a particular number of times, against users who did not. What separates those users?

For example, you could discover that a main difference for users who adopt your new analytics feature is that they are also 10 times more likely to create custom reports. If your goal is to boost adoption of the analytics feature, the success team can respond by creating training material that shows customers why and how they would use analytics that include in-depth walk-throughs of creating custom reports. They can also measure the efficacy of that training before and after workshops to gauge whether it's having the desired effect.

Sales and Executive Teams

Sales teams are also helpful allies in your observability adoption efforts. Depending on how your company is structured, engineering and sales teams may not frequently interact in their daily work. But sales teams are one of the most powerful allies you can have in driving observability adoption. Sales teams have a vested interest in understanding and supporting product features that sell.

Anecdotally, the sales team will pass along reactions received during a pitch or a demo to build a collective understanding of what's resonating in your product. Qualitative understandings are useful to spot trends and form hypotheses about how to further sales goals. But the types of quantitative analyses this team can pull from your observability data are useful to inform and validate sales execution strategy.

For example, which customers are using which features and how often? Which features are most heavily used and therefore need the highest availability targets? Which features are your strategic customers most reliant upon, when, and in which parts of their workflows? Which features are used most often in sales demos and should therefore always be available? Which features are prospects most interested in, have a wow-factor, and should always be performing fastest?

These types of questions, and more, can be answered with your observability data. The answers to these questions are helpful for sales, but they're also core to key business decisions about where to make strategic investments.

Executive stakeholders want to definitively understand how to make the biggest business impacts, and observability data can help. What is the most important thing your digital business needs to do this year? For example, which engineering investments will drive impacts with sales?

A traditional top-down control-and-command approach to express strategic business goals for engineering may be something vague—for example, get as close to 100% availability as possible—yet it often doesn't connect the dots on how or why that's done. Instead, by using observability data to connect those dots, goals can be expressed in technical terms that drill down through user experience, architecture, product features, and the teams that use them. Defining goals clearly with a common cross-cutting language is what actually creates organizational alignment among teams. Where exactly are you making investments? Who will that impact? Is an appropriate level of engineering investment being made to deliver on your availability and reliability targets?

Using Observability Versus Business Intelligence Tools

Some of you may have read the earlier sections and asked yourself whether a business intelligence (BI) tool could accomplish the same job. Indeed, the types of understanding of various moving parts of your company that we're describing are a bit of a quasi-BI use case. Why would you not just use a BI tool for that?

It can be hard to generalize about BI tools, as they consist of online analytical processing (OLAP), mobile BI, real-time BI, operational BI, location intelligence, data visualization and chart mapping, tools for building dashboards, billing systems, ad hoc analysis and querying, enterprise reporting, and more. You name the data, and a tool somewhere is optimized to analyze it. It's also hard to generalize characteristics of the data warehouses that power these tools, but we can at least say those are nonvolatile and time-variant, and contain raw data, metadata, and summary data.

But whereas BI tools are all very generalized, observability tools are hyper-specialized for a particular use case: understanding the intersection of code, infrastructure, users, and time. Let's take a look at some of the trade-offs made by observability tooling.

Query Execution Time

Observability tools need to be fast, with queries ranging from subsecond to low seconds. A key tenet of observability is explorability, since you don't always know what you're looking for. You spend less time running the same queries over and over, and more time following a trail of breadcrumbs. During an investigative flow, disruptions when you have to sit and wait for a minute or longer for results can mean you lose your entire train of thought.

In comparison, BI tools are often optimized to run reports, or to craft complex queries that will be used again and again. It's OK if these take longer to run, because this data isn't being used to react in real time, but rather to feed into other tools or systems. You typically make decisions about steering the business over time measured in weeks, months, or years, not minutes or seconds. If you're making strategic business decisions every few seconds, something has gone terribly wrong.

Accuracy

For observability workloads, if you have to choose, it's better to return results that are fast as opposed to perfect (as long as they are very close to correct). For iterative investigations, you would almost always rather get a result that scans 99.5% of the events in one second than a result that scans 100% in one minute. This is a real and common trade-off that must be made in massively parallelized distributed systems across imperfect and flaky networks (see Chapter 16).

Also (as covered in Chapter 17), some form of dynamic sampling is often employed to achieve observability at scale. Both of these approaches trade a slight bit of accuracy for massive gains in performance. When it comes to BI tools and business data warehouses, both sampling and a "close to right" approach are typically verboten. When it comes to billing, for example, you will always want the accurate result no matter how long it takes.

Recency

The questions you answer with observability tools have a strong recency bias, and the most important data is often the freshest. A delay of more than a few seconds between when something happened in production and when you can query for those results is unacceptable, especially when you're dealing with an incident.

As data fades into months past, you tend to care about historical events more in terms of aggregates and trends, rather than granular individual requests. And when you do care about specific requests, taking a bit longer to find them is acceptable. But when data is fresh, you need query results to be raw, rich, and up-to-the-second current.

BI tools typically exist on the other end of that spectrum. It's generally fine for it to take longer to process data in a BI tool. Often you can increase performance by caching more recent results, or by preprocessing, indexing, or aggregating older data. But generally, with BI tools, you want to retain the full fidelity of the data (practically) forever. With an observability tool, you would almost never search for something that happened five years ago, or even two years ago. Modern BI data warehouses are designed to store data forever and grow infinitely.

Structure

Observability data is built from arbitrarily wide and structured data blobs: one event per request per service (or per polling interval in long-running batch processes). For observability needs (to answer any question about what's happening at any time), you need to append as many event details as possible, to provide as much context as needed, so investigators can spy something that might be relevant in the future. Often those details quickly change and evolve as teams learn what data may be helpful. Defining a data schema up front would defeat that purpose.

Therefore, with observability workloads, schemas must be inferred after the fact or changed on the fly (just start sending a new dimension or stop sending it at any time). Indexes are similarly unhelpful (see Chapter 16).

In comparison, BI tools often collect and process large amounts of unstructured data into structured, queryable form. BI data warehouses would be an ungovernable mess without structures and predefined schemas. You need consistent schemas in order to perform any kind of useful analysis over time. And BI workloads tend to ask similar questions in repeatable ways to power things like dashboards. BI data can be optimized with indexes, compound indexes, summaries, etc.

Because BI data warehouses are designed to grow forever, it is important that they have predefined schemas and grow at a predictable rate. Observability data is designed for rapid feedback loops and flexibility: it is typically most important under times of duress, when predictability is far less important than immediacy.

Time Windows

Observability and BI tools both have the concept of a session, or trace. But observability tends to be limited to a time span measured in seconds, or minutes at most. BI tools can handle long-term journeys, or traces that can take days or weeks to complete. That type of trace longevity is not a use case typically supported by observability tools. With observability tools, longer-running processes (like import/export jobs or queues) are typically handled with a polling process, and not with a single trace.

Ephemerality

Summarizing many of these points, debugging data is inherently more ephemeral than business data. You might need to retrieve a specific transaction record or billing record from two years ago with total precision, for example. In contrast, you are unlikely to need to know if the latency between service A and service B was high for a particular user request two years ago.

You may, however, want to know if the latency between service A and service B has increased over the last year or two, or if the 95% percentile latency has gone up over that time. That type of question is common, and it is actually best served not by either BI tools/data warehouses or by observability tools. Aggregate historical performance data is best served by our good old pal monitoring (see Chapter 9).

Using Observability and BI Tools Together in Practice

BI tools come in many forms, often designed to analyze various business metrics that originate from financial, customer relationship management (CRM), enterprise resource planning (ERP), marketing funnel, or supply chain systems. Those metrics are crafted into dashboards and reports by many engineers. But, especially for tech-driven companies where application service experience is critical, there is often a need to drill further into details that BI systems are designed to provide.

The data granularity for BI tools is arbitrarily large, often reporting metrics per month or per week. Your BI tool can help you understand which feature was most used in the month of February. Your observability tool can provide much more granularity, down to the individual request level. Similar to the way observability and monitoring come together, business intelligence and observability come together by ensuring that you always have micro-level data available that can be used to build macro-level views of the world.

BI tools often lock you into being able to see only an overall super-big-picture representation of your business world by relying on aggregate metrics. Those views are helpful when visualizing overall business trends, but they're not as useful when trying to answer questions about product usage or user behavior (detailed earlier in this chapter).

Sharing observability tools across departments is a great way to promote a single-domain language. Observability captures data at a level of abstraction—services and APIs—that can be comprehended by everyone from operations engineers to executives. With that sharing, engineers are encouraged to use business language to describe their domain models, and business people are exposed to the broad (and real) diversity of use cases present in their user base (beyond the few abstract composite user personas they typically see).

Conclusion

With observability, you can understand customers' experience of using your software in the real world. Because multiple teams in your business have a vested interest in understanding the customer experience and improving or capitalizing on it, you can use observability to help various teams within your organization better achieve their goals.

Beyond engineering teams, adjacent technical teams like product, support, and customer success can become powerful allies to boost your organization-wide observability adoption initiatives. Less technical teams, like sales and executives, can also become allies with a bit of additional support on your part. The teams outlined in this chapter as examples are by no means definitive. Hopefully, you can use this chapter as a primer to think about the types of business teams that can be better informed and can better achieve desired results by using the observability data you're capturing. Helping additional business teams achieve their goals will create stakeholders and allies who can, in turn, help prioritize your observability adoption efforts.

In the next chapter, we'll look at how you can gauge your organization's overall progress on the observability adoption maturity curve.

CHAPTER 21

An Observability Maturity Model

Spreading a culture of observability is best achieved by having a plan that measures progress and prioritizes target areas of investment. In this chapter, we go beyond the benefits of observability and its tangible technical steps by introducing the Observability Maturity Model as a way to benchmark and measure progress. You will learn about the key capabilities an organization can measure and prioritize as a way of driving observability adoption.

A Note About Maturity Models

In the early 1990s, the Software Engineering Institute at Carnegie Mellon University popularized the Capability Maturity Model (*https://oreil.ly/zc9DP*) as a way to evaluate the ability of various vendors to deliver effectively against software development projects. The model defines progressive stages of maturity and a classification system used to assign scores based on how well a particular vendor's process matches each stage. Those scores are then used to influence purchasing decisions, engagement models, and other activities.

Since then, maturity models have become somewhat of a darling for the software marketing industry. Going well beyond scoping purchasing decisions, maturity models are now used as a generic way to model organizational practices. To their credit, maturity models can be helpful for an organization to profile its capabilities against its peers or to target a set of desired practices. However, maturity models are not without their limitations.

When it comes to measuring organizational practices, the performance level of a software engineering team has no upper bound. Practices, as opposed to procedures, are an evolving and continuously improving state of the art. They're never done and perfect, as reaching the highest level of a maturity model seems to imply. Further, that end state is a static snapshot of an ideal future reflecting only what was known when the model was created, often with the biases of its authors baked into its many assumptions. Objectives shift, priorities change, better approaches are discovered, and—more to the point—each approach is unique to individual organizations and cannot be universally scored.

When looking at a maturity model, it's important to always remember that no one-size-fits-all model applies to every organization. Maturity models can, however, be useful as starting points against which you can critically and methodically weigh your own needs and desired outcomes to create an approach that's right for you. Maturity models can help you identify and quantify tangible and measurable objectives that are useful in driving long-term initiatives. It is critical that you create hypotheses to test the assumptions of any maturity model within your own organization and evaluate which paths are and aren't viable given your particular constraints. Those hypotheses, and the maturity model itself, should be continuously improved over time as more data becomes available.

Why Observability Needs a Maturity Model

When it comes to developing and operating software, practices that drive engineering teams toward a highly productive state have rarely been formalized and documented. Instead, they are often passed along informally from senior engineers to junior engineers based on the peculiar history of individual company cultures. That institutional knowledge sharing has given rise to certain identifiable strains of engineering philosophy or collections of habits with monikers that tag their origin (e.g., "the Etsy way," "the Google way," etc.). Those philosophies are familiar to others with the same heritage and have become heretical to those without.

Collectively, we authors have over six decades of experience watching engineering teams fail and succeed, and fail all over again. We've seen organizations of all shapes, sizes, and locations succeed in forming high-performing teams, given they adopt the right culture and focus on essential techniques. Software engineering success is not limited to those fortunate enough to live in Silicon Valley or those who have worked at FAANG companies (Facebook, Amazon, Apple, Netflix, and Google). It shouldn't matter where teams are located, or what companies their employees have worked at previously.

As mentioned throughout this book, production software systems present sociotechnical challenges. While tooling for observability can address the technical challenges in software systems, we need to consider other factors beyond the technical. The Observability Maturity Model considers the context of engineering organizations, their constraints, and their goals. Technical and social features of observability contribute to each of the identified team characteristics and capabilities in the model.

To make a maturity model broadly applicable, it must be agnostic to an organization's pedigree or the tools it uses. Instead of mentioning any specific software solutions or technical implementation details, it must instead focus on the costliness and benefits of the journey in human terms: "How will you know if you are weak in this area?" "How will you know if you're doing well in this area and should prioritize improvements elsewhere?"

Based on our experiences watching teams adopt observability, we'd seen common qualitative trends like their increased confidence interacting with production and ability to spend more time working on new product features. To quantify those perceptions, we surveyed a spectrum of teams in various phases of observability adoption and teams that hadn't yet started or were not adopting observability. We found that teams that adopt observability were three times as likely to feel confident in their ability to ensure software quality in production, compared to teams that had not adopted observability.[1] Additionally, those teams that hadn't adopted observability spent over half their time toiling away on work that did not result in releasing new product features.

Those patterns are emergent properties of today's modern and complex sociotechnical systems. Analyzing capabilities like ensuring software quality in production and time spent innovating on features exposes both the pathologies of group behavior and their solutions. Adopting a practice of observability can help teams find solutions to problems that can't be solved by individuals "just writing better code," or, "just doing a better job." Creating a maturity model for observability ties together the various capabilities outlined throughout this book and can serve as a starting point for teams to model their own outcome-oriented goals that guide adoption.

About the Observability Maturity Model

We originally developed the *Observability Maturity Model* (*OMM*) based on the following goals for an engineering organization:[2]

Sustainable systems and quality of life for engineers
> This goal may seem aspirational to some, but the reality is that engineer quality of life and the sustainability of systems are closely entwined. Systems that are observable are easier to own and maintain, improving the quality of life for an engineer who owns those systems. Engineers spending more than half of their time working on things that don't deliver customer value (toil) report higher

---

1 Honeycomb, "Observability Maturity Report," 2020 edition (*https://hny.co/wp-content/uploads/2020/04/observability-maturity-report-4-2-2020-1-1-1.pdf*) and 2021 edition (*https://hny.co/wp-content/uploads/2021/06/Observability_Maturity_Report.pdf*).

2 Charity Majors and Liz Fong-Jones, "Framework for an Observability Maturity Model" (*https://hny.co/wp-content/uploads/2019/06/Framework-for-an-Observability-Maturity-Model.pdf*), Honeycomb, June 2019.

rates of burnout, apathy, and lower engineering team morale. Observable systems reduce toil and that, in turn, creates higher rates of employee retention and reduces the time and money teams need to spend on finding and training new engineers.

Delivering against business needs by increasing customer satisfaction
Observability enables engineering teams to better understand customers' interactions with the services they develop. That understanding allows engineers to home in on customer needs and deliver the performance, stability, and functionality that will delight their customers. Ultimately, observability is about operating your business successfully.

The framework described here is a starting point. With it, organizations have the structure and tools to begin asking themselves questions, and the context to interpret and describe their own situation—both where they are now and what they should aim for.

The quality of your observability practice depends on technical and social factors. Observability is not a property of the computer system alone or the people alone. Too often, discussions of observability are focused only on the technicalities of instrumentation, storage, and querying, and not on what they can enable a team to do. The OMM approaches improving software delivery and operations as a sociotechnical problem.

If team members feel unsafe applying their tooling to solve problems, they won't be able to achieve results. Tooling quality depends on factors such as the ease of adding instrumentation, the granularity of data ingested, and whether it can answer any arbitrary questions that humans pose. The same tooling need not be used to address each capability, nor does strength of tooling in addressing one capability necessarily translate to an aptitude in addressing all other suggested capabilities.

Capabilities Referenced in the OMM

The capabilities detailed in this section are directly impacted by the quality of your observability practice. The OMM list is not exhaustive but is intended to represent the breadth of potential business needs. The capabilities listed and their associated business outcomes overlap with many of the principles necessary to create production excellence.

 For more on production excellence, we recommend the 2019 InfoQ blog post "Sustainable Operations in Complex Systems with Production Excellence" (*https://oreil.ly/fWiPD*) by Liz Fong-Jones.

There is no singular and correct order or prescriptive way of doing these things. Instead, every organization faces an array of potential journeys. At each step, focus on what you're hoping to achieve. Make sure you will get appropriate business impact from making progress in that area right now, as opposed to doing it later.

It's also important to understand that building up these capabilities is a pursuit that is never "done." There's always room for continuous improvement. Pragmatically speaking, however, once organizational muscle memory exists such that these capabilities are second nature, and they are systematically supported as part of your culture, that's a good indication of having reached the upper levels of maturity. For example, prior to CI systems, code was often checked in without much thought paid to bundling in tests. Now, engineers in any modern organization practicing CI/CD would never think of checking in code without bundled tests. Similarly, observability practices must become second nature for development teams.

Respond to System Failure with Resilience

Resilience is the adaptive capacity of a team, together with the system it supports, that enables it to restore service and minimize impact to users. Resilience refers not only to the capabilities of an isolated operations team or to the robustness and fault tolerance in its software. Resilience must also measure both the technical outcomes and social outcomes of your emergency response process in order to measure its maturity.

For more on resilience engineering, we recommend John Allspaw's 2019 talk "Amplifying Sources of Resilience" (*https://oreil.ly/gDN3S*), delivered at QCon London.

Measuring technical outcomes can, at first approximation, take the form of examining the amount of time it takes to restore service and the number of people who become involved when the system experiences a failure. For example, the DORA 2018 *Accelerate State of DevOps* Report (*https://oreil.ly/H0Pn5*) defines elite performers as those whose MTTR is less than one hour, and low performers as those with a MTTR that is between one week and one month.

Emergency response is a necessary part of running a scalable, reliable service. But emergency response may have different meanings to different teams. One team might consider a satisfactory emergency response to mean "power cycle the box," while another might interpret that to mean "understand exactly how the auto-remediation that restores redundancy in data striped across multiple disks broke, and mitigate future risk." There are three distinct areas to measure: the amount of time it takes to detect issues, to initially mitigate those issues, and to fully understand what happened and address those risks.

But the more important dimension that team managers need to focus on is the people operating that service. Is the on-call rotation sustainable for your team so that staff remain attentive, engaged, and retained? Does a systematic plan exist for educating and involving everyone responsible for production in an orderly and safe manner, or is every response an all-hands-on-deck emergency, no matter the experience level? If your service requires many people to be on call or context switching to handle break/fix scenarios, that's time and energy they are not spending generating business value by delivering new features. Over time, team morale will inevitably suffer if a majority of engineering time is devoted to toil, including break/fix work.

If your team is doing well

- System uptime meets your business goals and is improving.
- On-call response to alerts is efficient, and alerts are not ignored.
- On-call duty is not excessively stressful, and engineers are not hesitant to take additional shifts as needed.
- Engineers can handle incident workload without working extra hours or feeling unduly stressed.

If your team is doing poorly

- The organization is spending a lot of additional time and money staffing on-call rotations.
- Incidents are frequent and prolonged.
- Those on call suffer from alert fatigue or aren't alerted about real failures.
- Incident responders cannot easily diagnose issues.
- Some team members are disproportionately pulled into emergencies.

How observability is related

Alerts are relevant, focused, and actionable (thereby reducing alert fatigue). A clear relationship exists between the error budget and customer needs. When incident investigators respond, context-rich events make it possible to effectively troubleshoot incidents when they occur. The ability to drill into high-cardinality data and quickly aggregate results on the fly supports pinpointing error sources and faster incident resolution. Preparing incident responders with the tools they need to effectively debug complex systems reduces the stress and drudgery of being on call. Democratization of troubleshooting techniques by easily sharing past investigation paths helps distribute incident resolution skills across a team, so anyone can effectively respond to incidents as they occur.

Deliver High-Quality Code

High-quality code is measured by more than how well it is understood and maintained, or how often bugs are discovered in a sterile lab environment (e.g., a CI test suite). While code readability and traditional validation techniques are useful, they do nothing to validate how that code actually behaves during the chaotic conditions inherent to running in production systems. The code must be adaptable to changing business needs, rather than brittle and fixed in features. Thus, code quality must be measured by validating its operation and extensibility as it matters to your customers and your business.

If your team is doing well

- Code is stable, fewer bugs are discovered in production, and fewer outages occur.
- After code is deployed to production, your team focuses on customer solutions rather than support.
- Engineers find it intuitive to debug problems at any stage, from writing code in development to troubleshooting incidents in production at full release scale.
- Isolated issues that occur can typically be fixed without triggering cascading failures.

If your team is doing poorly

- Customer support costs are high.
- A high percentage of engineering time is spent fixing bugs instead of working on new features.
- Team members are often reluctant to deploy new features because of perceived risk.
- It takes a long time to identify an issue, construct a way to reproduce the failure case, and repair it.
- Developers have low confidence in their code's reliability after it has shipped.

How observability is related

Well-monitored and tracked code makes it easy to see when and how a process is failing, and easy to identify and fix vulnerable spots. High-quality observability allows using the same tooling to debug code on one machine as on 10,000. A high level of relevant, context-rich telemetry means engineers can watch code in action during deployments, be alerted rapidly, and repair issues before they become visible to users. When bugs do appear, validating that they have been fixed is easy.

Manage Complexity and Technical Debt

Technical debt is not necessarily a bad thing. Engineering organizations are constantly faced with choices between short-term gain and longer-term outcomes. Sometimes the short-term win is the right decision if a specific plan exists to address the debt, or to otherwise mitigate the negative aspects of the choice. With that in mind, code with high technical debt prioritizes quick solutions over more architecturally stable options. When unmanaged, these choices lead to longer-term costs, as maintenance becomes expensive and future revisions become dependent on costs.

If your team is doing well

- Engineers spend the majority of their time making forward progress on core business goals.
- Bug fixing and other reactive work takes up a minority of the team's time.
- Engineers spend very little time disoriented or trying to find where in the codebase they need to plumb through changes.

If your team is doing poorly

- Engineering time is wasted rebuilding things when their scaling limits are reached or edge cases are hit.
- Teams are distracted by fixing the wrong thing or picking the wrong way to fix something.
- Engineers frequently experience uncontrollable ripple effects from a localized change.
- People are afraid to make changes to the code, aka the "haunted graveyard" effect.[3]

How observability is related

Observability enables teams to understand the end-to-end performance of their systems and debug failures and slowness without wasting time. Troubleshooters can find the right breadcrumbs when exploring an unknown part of their system. Tracing behavior becomes easily possible. Engineers can identify the right part of the system to optimize rather than taking random guesses of where to look, and they can change code when attempting to find performance bottlenecks.

---

3 Betsy B. Beyer et al., "Invent More, Toil Less" (*https://oreil.ly/4bfLc*), *;login:* 41, no. 3 (Fall 2016).

Release on a Predictable Cadence

The value of software development reaches users only after new features and optimizations are released. The process begins when a developer commits a change set to the repository, includes testing and validation and delivery, and ends when the release is deemed sufficiently stable and mature to move on. Many people think of continuous integration and deployment as the nirvana end-stage of releasing. But CI/CD tools and processes are just the basic building blocks needed to develop a robust release cycle. Every business needs a predictable, stable, frequent *release cadence* to meet customer demands and remain competitive in their market.[4]

If your team is doing well

- The release cadence matches business needs and customer expectations.
- Code gets into production shortly after being written. Engineers can trigger deployment of their own code after it's been peer reviewed, satisfies controls, and is checked in.
- Code paths can be enabled or disabled instantly, without needing a deployment.
- Deployments and rollbacks are fast.

If your team is doing poorly

- Releases are infrequent and require lots of human intervention.
- Lots of changes are shipped at once.
- Releases have to happen in a particular order.
- The sales team has to gate promises on a particular release train.
- Teams avoid deploying on certain days or times of year. They are hesitant because poorly managed release cycles have frequently interfered with quality of life during nonbusiness hours.

How observability is related

Observability is how you understand the build pipeline as well as production. It shows you any performance degradation in tests or errors during the build-and-release process. Instrumentation is how you know whether the build is good, whether the feature you added is doing what you expected it to, and whether anything else looks weird; instrumentation lets you gather the context you need to reproduce any error.

---

4 Darragh Curran, "Shipping Is Your Company's Heartbeat" (*https://oreil.ly/3PFX8*), Intercom, last modified August 18, 2021.

Observability and instrumentation are also how you gain confidence in your release. If it's properly instrumented, you should be able to break down by old and new build ID and examine them side by side. You can validate consistent and smooth production performance between deployments, or you can see whether your new code is having its intended impact and whether anything else looks suspicious. You can also drill down into specific events—for example, to see which dimensions or values a spike of errors all have in common.

Understand User Behavior

Product managers, product engineers, and systems engineers all need to understand the impact that their software has on users. It's how we reach product-market fit as well as how we feel purpose and impact as engineers. When users have a bad experience with a product, it's important to understand what they were trying to do as well as the outcome.

If your team is doing well

- Instrumentation is easy to add and augment.
- Developers have easy access to key performance indicators (KPIs) for customer outcomes and system utilization/cost, and can visualize them side by side.
- Feature flagging or similar makes it possible to iterate rapidly with a small subset of users before fully launching.
- Product managers can get a useful view of customer feedback and behavior.
- Product-market fit is easier to achieve.

If your team is doing poorly

- Product managers don't have enough data to make good decisions about what to build next.
- Developers feel that their work doesn't have impact.
- Product features grow to excessive scope, are designed by committee, or don't receive customer feedback until late in the cycle.
- Product-market fit is not achieved.

How observability is related

Effective product management requires access to relevant data. Observability is about generating the necessary data, encouraging teams to ask open-ended questions, and enabling them to iterate. With the level of visibility offered by event-driven data analysis and the predictable cadence of releases both enabled by observability, product managers can investigate and iterate on feature direction with a true understanding of how well their changes are meeting business goals.

Using the OMM for Your Organization

The OMM can be a useful tool for reviewing your organization's capabilities when it comes to utilizing observability effectively. The model provides a starting point for measuring where your team capabilities are lacking and where they excel. When creating a plan for your organization to adopt and spread a culture of observability, it is useful to prioritize capabilities that most directly impact the bottom line for your business and improve your performance.

It's important to remember that creating a mature observability practice is not a linear progression and that these capabilities do not exist in a vacuum. Observability is entwined in each capability, and improvements in one capability can sometimes contribute to results in others. The way that process unfolds is unique to the needs of each organization, and where to start depends on your current areas of expertise.

Wardley mapping is a technique that can help you figure out how these capabilities relate in priority and interdependency with respect to your current organizational abilities. Understanding which capabilities are most critical to your business can help prioritize and unblock the steps necessary to further your observability adoption journey.

As you review and prioritize each capability, you should identify clear owners responsible for driving this change within your teams. Review those initiatives with those owners and ensure that you develop clear outcome-oriented measures relevant to the needs of your particular organization. It's difficult to make progress unless you have clear ownership, accountability, and sponsorship in terms of financing and time. Without executive sponsorship, a team may be able to make small incremental improvements within its own silo. However, it is impossible to reach a mature high-performing state if the entire organization is unable to demonstrate these capabilities and instead relies on a few key individuals, no matter how advanced and talented those individuals may be.

Conclusion

The Observability Maturity Model provides a starting point against which your organization can measure its desired outcomes and create its own customized adoption path. The key capabilities driving high-performing teams that have matured their observability practice are measured along these axes:

- How they respond to system failure with resilience
- How easily they can deliver high-quality code

- How well they manage complexity and technical debt
- How predictable their software release cadence is
- How well they can understand user behavior

The OMM is a synthesis of qualitative trends we've noticed across organizations adopting observability paired with quantitative analysis from surveying software engineering professionals. The conclusions represented in this chapter reflect research studies conducted in 2020 and 2021. It's important to remember that maturity models are static snapshots of an ideal future generalized well enough to be applicable across an entire industry. The maturity model itself will evolve as observability adoption continues to spread.

Similarly, observability practices will also evolve, and the path toward maturity will be unique to your particular organization. However, this chapter provides the basis for your organization to create its own pragmatic approach. In the next chapter, we'll conclude with a few additional tips on where to go from here.

CHAPTER 22

Where to Go from Here

In this book, we've looked at observability for software systems from many angles. We've covered what observability is and how that concept operates when adapted for software systems—from its functional requirements, to functional outcomes, to sociotechnical practices that must change to support its adoption.

To review, this is how we defined *observability* at the start of this book:

> Observability for software systems is a measure of how well you can understand and explain any state your system can get into, no matter how novel or bizarre. You must be able to comparatively debug that bizarre or novel state across all dimensions of system state data, and combinations of dimensions, in an ad hoc iterative investigation, without being required to define or predict those debugging needs in advance. If you can understand any bizarre or novel state without needing to ship new code, you have observability.

Now that we've covered the many concepts and practices intertwined with observability in this book, we can tighten that definition a bit:

> If you can understand any state of your software system, no matter how novel or bizarre, by arbitrarily slicing and dicing high-cardinality and high-dimensionality telemetry data into any view you need, and use the core analysis loop to comparatively debug and quickly isolate the correct source of issues, without being required to define or predict those debugging needs in advance, then you have observability.

Observability, Then Versus Now

We started writing this book more than three years ago. You might ask why on earth it has taken so long to get here.

First off, the state of observability has been a moving target. When we started writing this book, conversing with anyone about the topic required us to stop and first define "observability." Nobody really understood what we meant whenever we talked about the cardinality of data or its dimensionality. We would frequently and passionately need to argue that the so-called *three pillars* view of observability was only about the data types, and that it completely ignores the analysis and practices needed to gain new insights.

As Cindy Sridharan states in the Foreword, the rise in prominence of the term "observability" has also led (inevitably and unfortunately) to it being used interchangeably with an adjacent concept: monitoring. We would frequently need to explain that "observability" is not a synonym for "monitoring," or "telemetry," or even "visibility."

Back then, OpenTelemetry was in its infancy, and that was yet another thing to explain: how it was different from (or inherited from) OpenTracing and OpenCensus? Why would you use a new open standard that required a bit more setup work instead of your vendor's more mature agent that worked right away? Why should anyone care?

Now, many people we speak to don't need those explanations. There's more agreement on how observability is different from monitoring. More people understand the basic concepts and that data misses the point without analysis. They also understand the benefits and the so-called promised land of observability, because they hear about the results from many of their peers. What many of the people we speak to today are looking for is more sophisticated analyses and low-level, specific guidance on how to get from where they are today to a place where they're successfully practicing observability.

Second, this book initially started with a much shorter list of chapters. It had more basic material and a smaller scope. As we started to better understand which concerns were common and which had successful emergent patterns, we added more depth and detail. As we encountered more and more organizations using observability at massive scale, we were able to learn comparatively and incorporate those lessons by inviting direct participation in this book (we're looking at you, Slack!).

Third, this book has been a collaborative effort with several reviewers, including those who work for our competitors. We've revised our takes, incorporated broader viewpoints, and revisited concepts throughout the authoring process to ensure that we're reflecting an inclusive state of the art in the world of observability. Although we (the authors of this book) all work for Honeycomb, our goal has always been to write an objective and inclusive book detailing how observability works in practice, regardless of specific tool choices. We thank our reviewers for keeping us honest and helping us develop a stronger narrative.

Based on your feedback, we added more content around the sociotechnical challenges in adopting observability. Like any technological shift that also requires changing associated practices, you can't just buy a tool and achieve observability. Adopting observability practices means changing the way you think about understanding your software's behavior and, in turn, changing the relationship you have with your customers. Observability lets you empathize and align with your customers by letting you understand exactly how the changes you make impact their experience, day after day. Illustrating the way that plays out in practice across multiple teams within an organization and sifting out useful advice for beginners has taken time as repeatable patterns have emerged (and as they continue to evolve).

So, where should you go from here? First, we'll recommend additional resources to fill in essential topics that are outside the scope of this book. Then, we'll make some predictions about what to expect in the world of observability.

Additional Resources

The following are some resources we recommend:

Site Reliability Engineering by Betsy Beyer et al. (O'Reilly)
We've referenced this book a few times within our own. Also known as "the Google SRE book," this book details how Google implemented DevOps practices within its SRE teams. This book details several concepts and practices that are adjacent to using observability practices when managing production systems. It focuses on practices that make production software systems more scalable, reliable, and efficient. The book introduces SRE practices and details how they are different from conventional industry approaches. It explores both the theory and practice of building and operating large-scale distributed systems. It also covers management practices that can help guide your own SRE adoption initiatives. Many of the techniques described in this book are most valuable when managing distributed systems. If you haven't started down the path of using SRE principles within your own organization, this book will help you establish practices that will be complemented by the information you've learned in our book.

Implementing Service Level Objectives by Alex Hidalgo (O'Reilly)
This book provides an in-depth exploration of SLOs, which our book only briefly touches on (see Chapter 12 and Chapter 13). Hidalgo is a site reliability engineer, an expert at all things related to SLOs, and a friend to Honeycomb. His book outlines many more concepts, philosophies, and definitions relevant to the SLO world to introduce fundamentals you need in order to take further steps. He covers the implementation of SLOs in great detail with mathematical and statistical models, which are helpful to further understand why observability data is so uniquely suited to SLOs (the basis of Chapter 13). His book also covers cultural practices that must shift as a result of adopting SLOs and that further illustrate some of the concepts introduced in our book.

Cloud Native Observability with OpenTelemetry by Alex Boten (Packt Publishing)

This book explores OTel with more depth and detail than we covered in this book. Boten's book details core components of OTel (APIs, libraries, tools) as well as its base concepts and signal types. If you are interested in using pipelines to manage telemetry data, this book shows you how that's done using the OpenTelemetry Collector. While we touched on the OpenTelemetry Collector, this book covers it in much greater detail. If you would like to dive deeper into OTel core concepts to discover more of what's possible, we recommend picking up a copy.

Distributed Tracing in Practice by Austin Parker et al. (O'Reilly)

This book offers an in-depth guide to approaching application instrumentation for tracing, collecting the data that your instrumentation produces, and mining it for operational insights. While specific to tracing, this book covers instrumentation best practices and choosing span characteristics that lead to valuable traces. It is written by our friends at Lightstep, and it presents additional views on where distributed tracing is headed that are both informative and useful.

Honeycomb's blog (https://hny.co/blog)

Here, you can find more information from us regarding the latest in the moving target of emergent observability practices. This blog is occasionally specific to Honeycomb's own observability tools. But, more often, it explores general observability concepts, advice (see "Ask Miss o11y," our observability advice column), and write-ups from Honeycomb's engineering team that often illustrate how observability shapes our own evolving practices.

Additionally, the footnotes and notes throughout this book lead to many more interesting sources of relevant information from sources and authors that we respect and look to when shaping our own views and opinions.

Predictions for Where Observability Is Going

It's a bold move to commit predictions to print in publications and an even bolder move to circle back and see how well they aged. But, given our position in the center of the observability ecosystem, we feel relatively well equipped to make a few informed predictions about where this industry is headed in the coming years. These predictions are being generated in March 2022.

Three years from now, we think that OTel and observability will be successfully intertwined and may seem inseparable. We already see a lot of overlap among groups of people interested in developing and adopting OTel and people who are interested in further developing the category of tooling that fits the definition of observability as outlined in this book. The momentum and rise of OTel as the de facto solution for application instrumentation has been greatly helped by the fact that support for trace data is its most mature format. Metrics, log data, and profiling are in earlier stages of development, but we expect to see those reach the same level of maturity quickly, opening the door for even wider adoption in a variety of settings. We also believe that the ability to trivially switch between different backend solutions with just a few configuration changes will become much easier than it is today (which is already fairly simple).[1] We predict that more how-to articles detailing how to switch from one vendor to another will proliferate and become hot commodities.

Most of this book focused on examples of debugging backend applications and infrastructure. However, we predict that observability will creep into more frontend applications as well. Today's state of the art with understanding and testing browser applications involves either real user monitoring (RUM) or synthetic monitoring.

As the name indicates, RUM involves measuring and recording the experience of real application users from the browser. The focus of RUM is to determine the actual service-level quality delivered to users, to detect application errors or slowdowns, and to determine whether changes to your code have the intended effect on user experience. RUM works by collecting and recording web traffic without impacting code performance. In most cases, JavaScript snippets are injected into the page or native code within the application to provide feedback from the browser or client. To make this large volume of data manageable, RUM tools often use sampling or aggregation for consolidation. That consolidation often means that you can understand overall performance as a whole, but you can't break it down to the level of understanding performance for any one given user in detail.

However, despite those limitations, RUM does have the advantage of measuring real user experiences. This means RUM tools can catch a broad range of unexpected real-world issues in application behavior. RUM can help you see anything from a regression that presents itself in only a new version of a niche mobile browser your development team has never heard of, to network delays for certain IP addresses in a specific country or region halfway across the globe. RUM can be helpful in identifying and troubleshooting last-mile issues. RUM differs from synthetic monitoring in that it relies on actual people clicking a page in order to take measurements.

Synthetic monitoring is a different approach that relies on automated tests going over a given set of test steps in order to take measurements. These tools take detailed application performance and experience measurements in a controlled environment. Behavioral scripts (or paths) are created to simulate the actions that customers might take with your applications. The performance of those paths are then continuously monitored at specified intervals. Somewhat like unit tests in your code, these paths are typically ones that a developer owns and runs themselves. These paths—or simulations of typical user behavior when using your frontend application—must

---

1 Vera Reynolds, for example, provides the tutorial "OpenTelemetry (OTel) Is Key to Avoiding Vendor Lock-in" (*https://oreil.ly/416OA*) on sending trace data to Honeycomb and New Relic by using OTel.

be developed and maintained, which takes effort and time. Commonly, only heavily used paths or business-critical processes are monitored for performance. Because synthetic tests must be scripted in advance, it's simply not feasible to measure performance for every permutation of a navigational path that a user might take.

However, while synthetic monitoring tools don't show you performance for real user experiences, they do have some advantages. They allow proactive testing for a wide array of known conditions you may care about (e.g., specific device types or browser versions). Because they typically create somewhat reproducible results, they can be included in automated regression test suites. That allows them to be run before code is deployed to real users, allowing them to catch performance issues before they can possibly create impacts to real users.

RUM and synthetic monitoring serve specific and different use cases. The use case for observability is to measure real user experiences in production—similar to RUM, but with a much higher degree of fidelity that allows you to debug individual customer experiences. As seen in Chapter 14, many teams use observability data in their CI/CD build pipelines (or in test suites). That means you can run end-to-end test scripts that exercise user paths in your system and monitor their performance by simply tagging originating test requests as such within your telemetry. We predict that within a few years, you won't have to choose between RUM or synthetic monitoring for frontend applications. Instead, you'll simply use observability for both use cases.

We also predict that within three years, OTel's automatic instrumentation will have caught up and be comparable to the non-OTel auto-instrumentation packages offered in a variety of vendor-specific libraries and agents. Today, using OTel is still a choice for most teams because (depending on your language of choice) the automatic instrumentation included with OTel may not be up to par with the instrumentation offered by a specific vendor's proprietary offerings. The open source nature of OTel, paired with its incredibly vibrant developer ecosystem, means that this will eventually no longer be the case. Automatic instrumentation with OTel will be at least as rich as alternative instrumentation that brings with it the trap of vendor lock-in. In time, using OTel will become a no-brainer and the de facto starting point for any application observability initiative (this is already starting to happen today).

You shouldn't interpret that to mean that automatic instrumentation will become the only thing needed to generate useful telemetry for an observability tool. Custom instrumentation (see Chapter 7) will continue to be absolutely essential to debug the issues most relevant to the code driving your business logic. We predict that just as having code without comments is unthinkable, so too will having code without custom instrumentation. As engineers, we will all get accustomed to thinking in terms of instrumentation needed as we write new code.

In three years, build pipelines will be immensely faster, feedback loops will be shorter, and more teams will be automatically deploying changes to production at the final stage of their CI/CD pipelines (and they'll really start practicing the *D* part of the *CI/CD* acronym). Continuous deployment can be a tricky affair, but the practice of decoupling feature releases from feature deployments will make it attainable for most organizations. Feature flags will continue to see more adoption, and deployment patterns like progressive delivery will become more common.

The space that we will personally be watching closely is that of developer workflows. As an industry, we need more ways to connect observability to the act of writing and shipping code, as early as possible (see Chapter 11). As an industry, we need to continue to collapse the space between input (writing code) and output (running code). Few developers have the tooling today to get fast feedback on how the behavior of their code changes after each deployment. Developers need to closely understand how changes to their code impact users in production with each new iteration. Incredibly few developers have the ability to actually do that. But, for those developers who do, the difference in experience is transformational.

Anecdotally, we hear stories from these developers about how that experience is so foundationally necessary that they can't imagine working without that ability ever again. Quantitatively, we're starting to see tangible benefits materialize: the ability to move faster, waste less time, make fewer errors, and catch those few errors more swiftly when they do occur (see Chapter 19). In short, learning how to use observability helps them become better software engineers. We believe the industry needs fundamentally better developer workflows in production, and we predict observability will be the path for many to get there.

Can observability lower the bar to achieve that type of transformational experience for more developers? Will those dopamine hits of feeling like a freaking wizard every time you solve a previously unsolvable problem in production be enough to keep the surge of observability adoption going? Can we, as an industry, make observability more accessible to every engineering team?

Time will tell. Watch this space. And let us know how you're progressing. You can always drop us a line on Twitter: *@mipsytipsy*, *@lizthegrey*, and *@gmiranda23* (respectively).

Charity, Liz, and George

Index

burn alerts
  context aware, 148-151
  predictive, 142-154
    baseline window, 151-152
    lookahead window, 144-151
    proportional extrapolation, 148
    response, 152-154
    short term, 147-148
    trajectory calculation, 142
business intelligence (BI) (see BI (business intelligence))

C

Capability Maturity Model, 267
cardinality, 13-14
  events and, 58
  telemetry data, 27
CD (continuous deployment), 157
change
  proactive approach, 246-248
  reactive approach, 243-245
Checkpoint, 159
Chen, Frank, 157
CI (Continuous Integration), Slack, 161-164
CI/CD (Continuous Integration/Continuous Delivery), 157-159, 180, 271
cloud computing, system versus software, 98
cloud native computing, 43-45
CNCF (Cloud Native Computing Foundation), 44
code, infrastructure as, 32
collectors, OpenTelemetry, 76
column-based storage, 190-193
commercial software
  benefits, 181-182
  hidden costs, 179-180
    nonfinancial, 180-181
  risks, 182
community groups, 108
compliance, telemetry pipelines, 227
constant-probability sampling, 209
context propagation, OpenTelemetry and, 76
context, tooling and, 164-166
context-aware burn alerts, 148-151
continuous deployment (CD), 157
Continuous Integration (CI), Slack, 161-164
Continuous Integration/Continuous Delivery (CI/CD), 157-159, 180, 271
core analysis loop, debugging and, 86-88

brute-force, automating, 88-91
correctness, telemetry pipelines, 233
CPU load average, 23
CPU metrics, 101
CPU utilization, 20
  debugging and, 45
  deviations, 128
CRM (customer relationship management), 264
customer success teams, 259-260
customer support teams, 258-259

D

Dapper paper, 62
dashboards
  metrics and, 20
  troubleshooting and, 21
  troubleshooting behaviors, 21
data augmentation, telemetry pipelines, 229
data buffering, telemetry pipelines, 228
data filters, telemetry pipelines, 229
data freshness, telemetry pipelines, 234
data storage
  column based, 190-193
  functional requirements, 185-193
  iterative analysis approach, 189
  row-based, 190-193
  tools, 250-251
  TSDB (time-series databases), 187-189
data transformation, telemetry pipelines, 230
data, pre-aggregated, 186
databases
  round-robin, 96
  time-series, 187-189
debugging
  artificial intelligence and, 91
  core analysis loop, 86-88
    brute-force, automating, 88-91
  customer support team, 259
  events, properties, 57-58
  first principles and, 85-91
  known conditions, 84-85
  metrics versus observability, 11-13
  microservices and, 120-121
  monitoring data and, 19-26
  novel problems, 58
  observability and, advantages, 26-27
  problem location, 119
  structured events and, 52-53

tracers, OpenTelemetry and, 76
traces
    distributed (see distributed traces)
    events
        stitching in, 70-71
        wide events, 74
    interdependencies, 62
    querying for, 199
    sampling decisions, 211-212
    services, 64
        names, 65
    system, manual example, 65-68
    trace ID, 64
        generating, 66
    waterfall method and, 63
tracing, 61
    components, 63-65
    distributed, 46, 62
traffic, sampling and, 210
trends, metrics, 20
troubleshooting
    behaviors, dashboards, and, 21

by intuition, 23
    correlation and, 23
    drilling down and, 24
    tool hopping, 24
dashboards and, 21
TTD (time-to-detect), 246
TTR (time-to-resolve), 246

U
unstructured logs, 55-56
user experience, alerts and, 131
UUID (universal unique identifier), 13

W
Wallace, 237
waterfall technique, traces and, 63
wide events, 74, 79
    core analysis loop and, 90
workload isolation, telemetry pipelines, 227
wrappers, 77

About the Authors

Charity Majors is the cofounder and CTO at Honeycomb, and the coauthor of *Database Reliability Engineering*. Before that, she worked as a systems engineer and engineering manager for companies like Parse, Facebook, and Linden Lab.

Liz Fong-Jones is a developer advocate and site reliability engineer (SRE) with more than 17 years of experience. She is an advocate at Honeycomb for the SRE and observability communities.

George Miranda is a former systems engineer turned product marketer and GTM leader at Honeycomb. Previously, he spent more than 15 years building large-scale distributed systems in the finance and video game industries.

Colophon

The animal on the cover of *Observability Engineering* is a maned wolf (*Chrysocyon brachyurus*). Maned wolves are the largest canids in South America and can be found in Argentina, Brazil, Paraguay, Bolivia, and parts of Peru. Their habitat includes the Cerrado biome, which is made up of wet and dry forests, grasslands, savannas, marshes, and wetlands. Despite the name, maned wolves are not actually wolves but a separate species entirely.

Maned wolves have narrow bodies, large ears, and long black legs that allow them to see above tall grasses as they run. They stand nearly 3 feet tall at the shoulder and weigh around 50 pounds. Much of their bodies are covered in a mix of black and long, golden-red hairs that stand straight up when danger is near. Unlike gray wolves and most other canid species that form packs, the maned wolf is solitary and often hunts alone. They are omnivorous and crepuscular, venturing out during dusk and dawn to prey on small mammals, rabbits, birds, and insects, and to scavenge for fruit and vegetables like lobeira, a small berry whose name means "fruit of the wolf."

Maned wolves live in monogamous pairs sharing a territory of 10 miles during the breeding season, which lasts from April to June in the wild. In captivity, maned wolves give birth to litters of one to five pups. Both parents have been known to groom, feed, and defend their young in captivity, but they are rarely seen with their pups in the wild. Pups develop quickly; they are usually considered fully grown and ready to leave their parents' territory after one year. The maned wolf is classified as "near threatened" by the IUCN, mostly due to loss of habitat. Many of the animals on O'Reilly covers are endangered; all of them are important to the world.

The cover illustration is by Karen Montgomery, based on a black and white engraving from *Braukhaus Lexicon*. The cover fonts are Gilroy Semibold and Guardian Sans. The text font is Adobe Minion Pro; the heading font is Adobe Myriad Condensed; and the code font is Dalton Maag's Ubuntu Mono.